TOP
YOUNG EUROPEAN
ARCHITECTS

Author
May Cambert

Coordination
Mª Jesús Vives, Architect

Texts
Celia Lozano Irigoyen, Raquel Casals Roca, Architects

Traslation
Mark Holloway

Design and layout
Joan Márquez

Production
Cristobal Ferrer

Editorial Director
Alejandro Asensio

Copyright © 2005 Atrium Group

Published by:
Atrium Group de ediciones y publicaciones, S.L.
C/ Ganduxer, 112

08022 BARCELONA
Tel: +34 93 254 00 99
Fax: +34 93 211 81 39
e-mail: atrium@atriumgroup.org
www.atriumbooks.com

ISBN:84-96099-50-4
Dép. Legal: B-22.198/2.005
Imprenta: Ferré Olsina
Printed in Spain

TOP
YOUNG EUROPEAN
ARCHITECTS

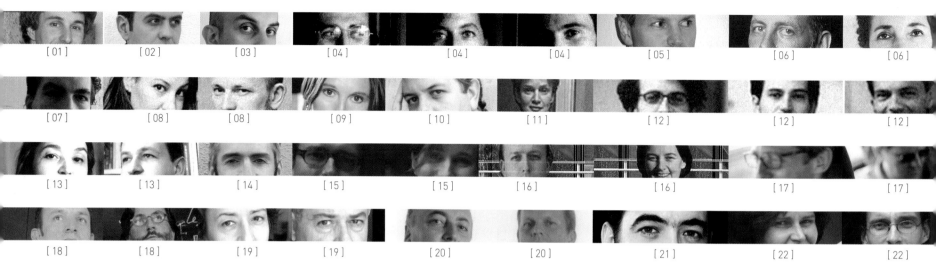

[01] [02] [03] [04] [04] [04] [05] [06] [06]

[07] [08] [08] [09] [10] [11] [12] [12] [12]

[13] [13] [14] [15] [15] [16] [16] [17] [17]

[18] [18] [19] [19] [20] [20] [21] [22] [22]

ARCHITECTS

PROJECTS

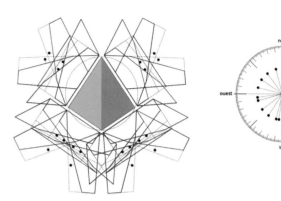

Architecture and the world

This publication is intended to document present trends in the international architectural panorama by means of a compilation of works carried out by some twenty odd young European figures who propose, with their designs, new ways of facing up to contemporary realities.

We are before a group of professionals who have overcome the panic experienced by the previous generation of reconstructivist architects caused by living in a world that is becoming more

and more globalized. They are experts who have known how to adapt to the demands of a rapidly changing society that is becoming more insistent on complete and fully investigated results.

Their reflections are concerned with environments associated with the ways we have started to inhabit places and relate to one another that have substituted traditional perceptions and are organized by more ambiguous, complex, more diversified and fragmented realities.

The architecture that comes out of these proposals is recognized as being more sensitive with its surroundings given that it intends to recover its particularities and its virtues.

The architecture created is not formalist, but simply functional. One that does away with limits so as to adapt itself to the complex environments of the urban landscapes with the intention of respectfully organizing it through a richer, more abstract or figurative interpretation.

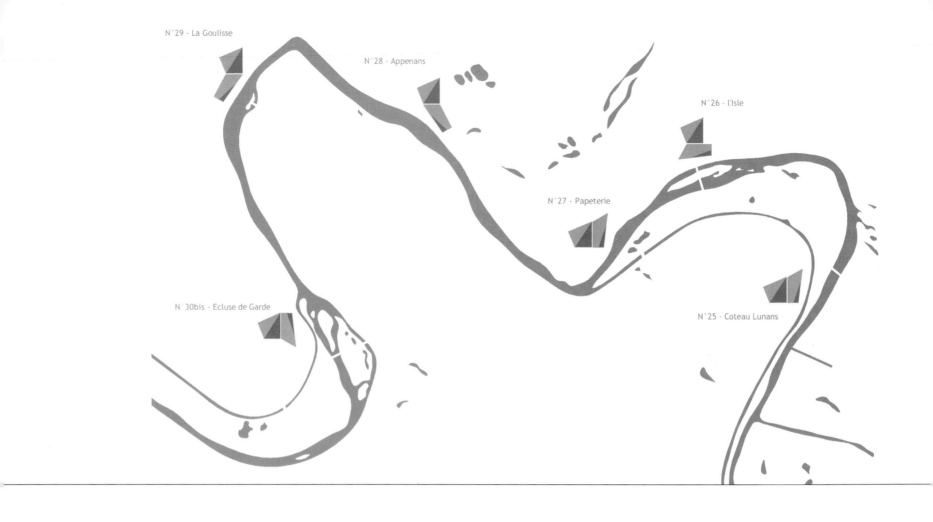

N°29 - La Goulisse

N°28 - Appenans

N°26 - l'Isle

N°27 - Papeterie

N°30bis - Ecluse de Garde

N°25 - Coteau Lunans

The project
and its context

The architect is no longer a creator, a mere artist, but a professional who analyzes the city, who interprets it as a large living mechanism, changing, altered and highly influenced by the speed of the develop of communications. In conclusion, it is a reflection of our lives.

The requirements that should fulfill any new project have to adapt perfectly to its function, complement, extend and solve any void with a constant dialog between its flows and interventions with the existing environment, between the user and the landsca-

pe, between the individual and the global. The investigation is centered on achieving the technical precision of the mechanism, as if it were a question of a living organism that requires a synchronized organization of its vital functions and that is subjected to, as anyone of us, to constant change and that tries to achieve a balance among its parts.

This way of understanding Architecture is reaffirmed by the multidisciplinary work carried out alongside specialized collaborators in a diversity of areas: a team of compromised investigators with the desire of controlling and modeling reality until it is formalized in an architectural object.

They are brilliant promises that have been popularized worldwide by their labor, who carry out academic practice in exhibitions and faculties and who develop their work in a multidiscipline nucleus in collaboration with other professionals.

They wager, in this way, on a more competent way of understanding the work of architecture with a viewpoint closer to that of a company.

Digital technology

The new multimedia technologies have revolutionized all aspects of work and also the reality of Architecture. The times of the paralex and pens, of the perspectives and hand-sketched elevations belong to the past. Not a single team work without computer CAD supports, without their own website or data transference facilities. Architectural offices have become centers of spatial and formal investigation. Some recent and pioneering architectural practices have taken over, have extended the limits of architectural projects and propose work on free forms brought to reality thanks to animation and spatial prototype software. Little by little, the first constructed examples have come into existence. Essentially, the experimental proposals from the future promises in the architectural field are materializing and being shown in exhibitions worldwide. However, even in the architectural magazines, the initial renders are preferred as they are more suggestive than the final constructed forms.

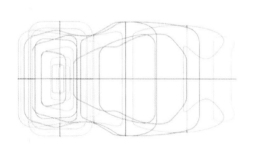 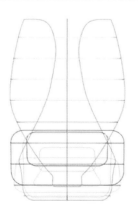 

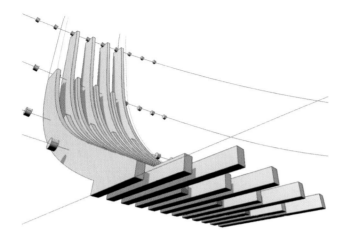

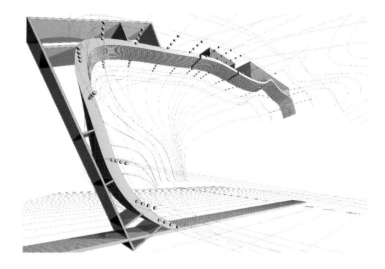

In this way, the cyberarchitects have been born. They convert their designs into reality and show, on the other hand, the pragmatism of real construction. Only constructed architecture limits time, the alternatives and the possibilities that are implicated in every detail.

Rigid spaces are confronted by the new proposals of the studies in which the designs are a result of a volume in animated 3D that even include videos which define, photogram for photogram, all of the movements and evolution. A long number of digital impressions substitute the usual photos of the scale models which allow for everything from the overall design to the smallest of details to be shown. It is the making of the complete building and it allows details, reproduced at real scale 1:1, to be shown. The photomontages with visual application of the real materials convince the clients and the scale models that are basic to the work acquire an increasing definition as they become closer to reality.

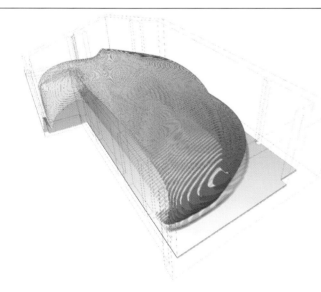

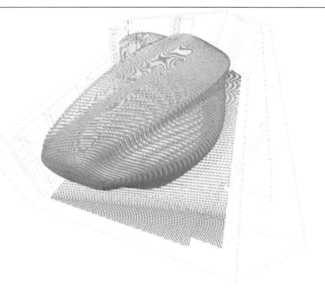

Form versus function

M uch of the work shown in this book is the product of a computerized methodology: computerized architectonic models that actively participate in its spatial conception; meticulous projects, precision, even parametrized with a balanced care between the abstraction of the three dimensional scale model, the process of production and the physical final materialization. The geometry opens, it transforms, now it is not a question

of identifying exclusively with the function, but to give way to objects that are elaborated by means of laws of internal configuration that are abstract and independent. The formal and technological limits are challenged and this leaves a door open to other ways of evolution and emphasizes the preoccupation for the use of new materials or the invention of alternative construction solutions. A new symbolic significance is sought for the projects that break away from tradi-tional elements. New metaphoric images should help with the cre-ation of different public spaces. The tools of geometry are substi-tuted by figurative language. In this way, boats run aground, artificial forests or references to natural or geologic organisms (tapestries, cobwebs, swarms, mineral structures...) they become transformed into basic elements in order to capture the users' attention, to initi-ate a suggestive dialog.

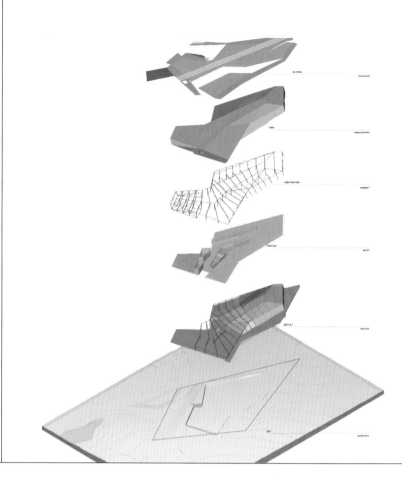

Tendencies of sustainable development

The continuous studies of contemporary and future Architecture emphasize, above all, the problems derived from the theme: "future and sustainability".

The new prototypes include all sorts of criteria for ecoeficiency in the building: separation and recycling systems from gray waters, the use of renewable alternative energies, the use of solar energy, insulation for openings, construction techniques with new materials and, above all, a great sensitivity when it comes to the treatment of wastes and an respectful integration in its immediate

surroundings, in dialog with the landscape. The new designs wager for compactness of form and density of construction in order to avoid creating an infrastructure that appears disperse in the landscape in an unnecessary way. The final form of the building responds in a precise way to the fulfillment of its function without opting for uncalled unjustified compositions. This is why building no longer materialize as mere empty sculptures.

The chosen materials are submitted to an exhaustive study as of early decision making. Preferably, recycled materials are chosen, or those that assure pre-industrial systems of low environmental incident in their manufacture. Materials that are made up of elements easily adaptable to the uses of a specific program in constant evolution that help create flexible spaces and components that can be unassembled, substituted and are of easy handling. In this way, ephemeral architecture, changeable, in which it is important to resolve the management of wastes generated from the building itself without compromising the environment and awaking conflicts with that already in existence.

The users and the users' perception of Architecture

When Le Corbusier referred to Architecture, he spoke of it as an architectonic impression or turmoil: games, wisdom, relationships, dualities, volumes, lights, which cause an "architectonic sensation".

The users' experience of moving through and living an architectural work is what generates true Architecture. In this way -

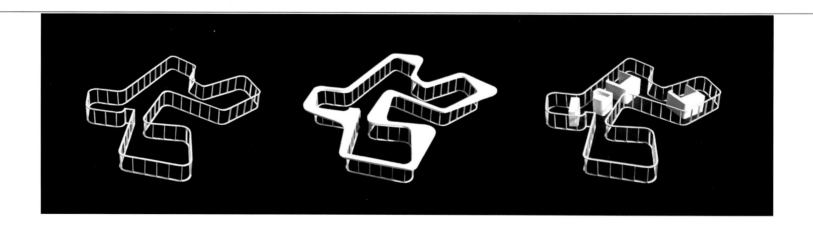

experiencing, moving around the world, living, all of this together-- is how Architecture is learnt. The rest is the trade, drawing, construction, town planning...

Architecture should once again become an experience. It is primarily the user's positive perception of a new proposal that makes it acceptable. The architects count on the sensory impact that the building is to have, respectful in forms, a determined landscape, with a particular backdrop or of a prototype study of the elements in which the place is an undetermined universal context.

This new Architecture should be efficient and attractive as well as awaking sympathy for its development and generating an atmosphere that transmits improvements in its overall resolution.

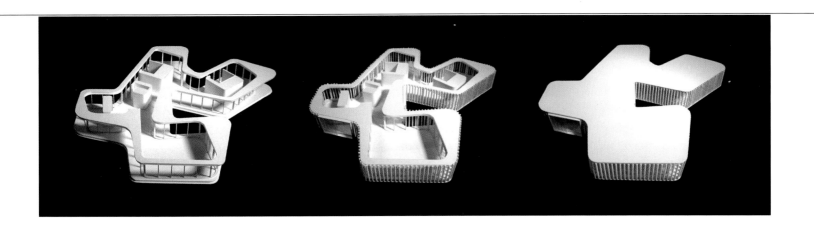

MICHA DE HAAS | HAIFA

architectenbureau |

Micha Josef de Haas began his architectural studies in the Bezalel Academy of Arts & Design in Jerusalem and graduated in the Technical University of Delft, in Holland. His work experience began with his joining the team of architects Kertesz and Groag, between 1989-1990. Later, in 1994, he collaborated with Minuten 2, in Bergen (Holland) and with Roy Gelders & Partners Architectuur, in Amsterdam (Holland) during the same year.

In 1996 he formed his own architectural studio. In 2003 he received a mention for his architectural talent, winning the European prize for architecture and technology, and since then he has collaborated as assistant professor in the Faculty of Architecture of Amsterdam.

aluminium

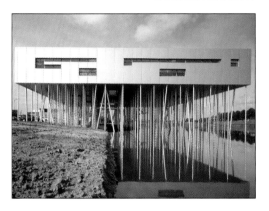

notions

Micha de Haas offers an architecture of great conceptual complexity. Among his most prominent projects are the Bergen-Belsen commemorative center which received a prize in 2003, the Bilgard project in Leeuwarden (1999) and the Dutch Aluminium Center which gained him a world reputation in 1997.

A profound language of meanings is the base which provides the project with its final language. His designs creates metaphors, subordinating materials to the role of transmitters of these. Well acquainted with hi-tech options, he also does not hesitate to put in practice experimental techniques if it facilitates the transmission of that language. The final objective is to give emphasis to the meaning of the program.

His bold proposals usually reflect a decided penchant for modernity, eschewing the elitism of justifications with little understanding, and opting for a direct and modern language. The projects of Micha de Haas are also seriously thought out from the point of view of the environment; he observes all measures to achieve integration into the landscape, using recyclable materials easy to disassemble and meeting the aims of efficient energy-use.

The projects involve a purified working of the building to make the user's task of comprehension easy, as the end-receiver of everything that the project wants to communicate. By means of spaces, forms and materials, the aim is to make that perception clear for everyone.

aluminium

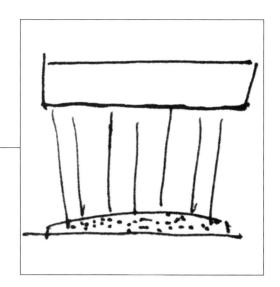

TECHNICAL DATA

Location Houten (Utrecht), Holland.

Architects Micha de Haas.

Client Stichting Aluminium Centrum, Houten.

Consulting firms Structural engineering: TNO-Bouw, Rijswijk.
D3BN structural engineers, den Haag
Installations. Huygen instalatie adviseur, Rotterdam.
Instalatiebedrijf Andriessen, Houten
Building physics and sustainability: DGMR, Arnhem.
Building supervision: Bouwteam General Contractors, Delft.

Date of project 1997.

Completion of work 2001.

Building surface 3570 m².

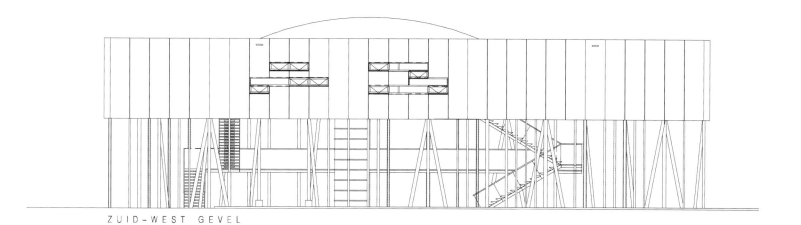

ZUID-WEST GEVEL

Elevations of the Aluminium Center.

A box supported on a forest of slim columns.

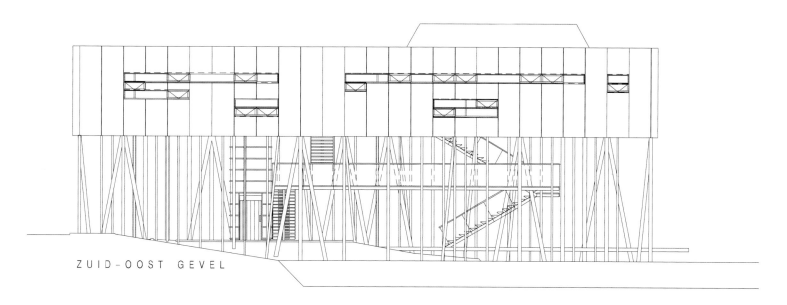

ZUID-OOST GEVEL

On a site close to Utrecht stands this building which houses the Dutch aluminum headquarters.

The building, comprising a perfect prism with a square base, 100 m per side, stands over a lake, supported on a forest of very slim cylindrical aluminum pillars. The result is a striking combination of aesthetics and technology, built as a case-study of the enormous versatility offered by the material to which it pays homage: aluminum.

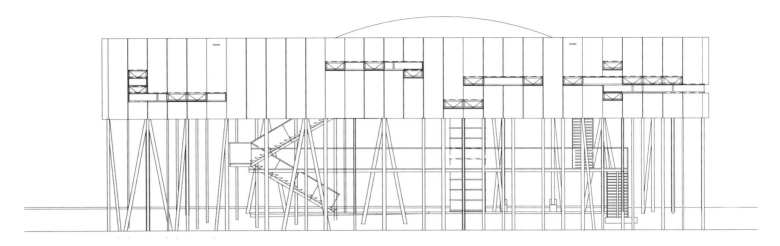

South elevation.

Elevation of access from the shore.

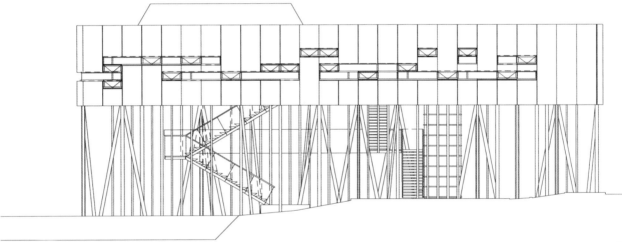

The access staircase introduces the visitor in scenic style.

The building aims at integrating the concept of the Dutch landscape, formalizing an aluminum box, glittering, light and simple, supported by a grove of light columns, which like thin elm trunks hold it up in the air achieving an effect of weightlessness. Just as in a natural environment, some columns appear slightly bent, leaning ... doubtless by the effect of the wind which blows freely between the building and the lake.

The stability of the building, apparently simple, is a synthesis of complicated calculations with advanced programs of structures in 3-D.

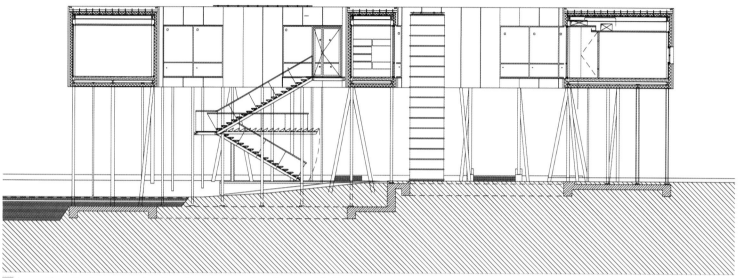

In section, the inner courts allow for a large entry of natural light.

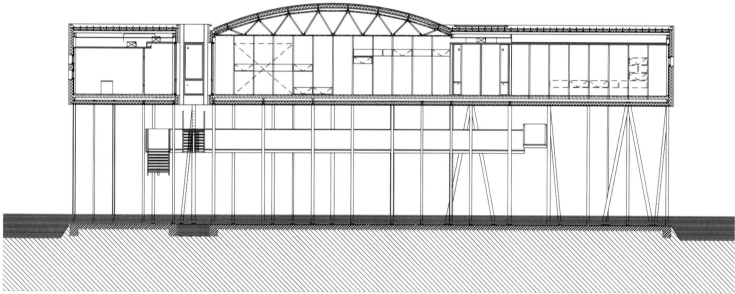

Cross section through the lake.

The new Aluminium Center is an icon, an emblem of the material, which is used integrally in the formal treatment of each element, resulting in the first public building made of aluminum.

The pillars, the girders, the staircases, the roofs, the carpentry network, the finishes ... everything is aluminum, even the gravel used for the foundations is bauxite, the raw material from which aluminum is obtained. The silver prism rises defying gravity, and its elegant reflection is etched on the surface of the lake on which

it stands. The slim columns, pins holding up the prism, are arranged in groups, excessively in formal terms.

In the first models the project had an obsession with achieving an ideal support, with a minimum diameter; this led to an exaggerated support formed by 1200 columns, with only 50 cm between their centers. The project finally built was simplified with 368 light columns 6 meters in height and with a diameter varying between 90 mm and 210 mm.

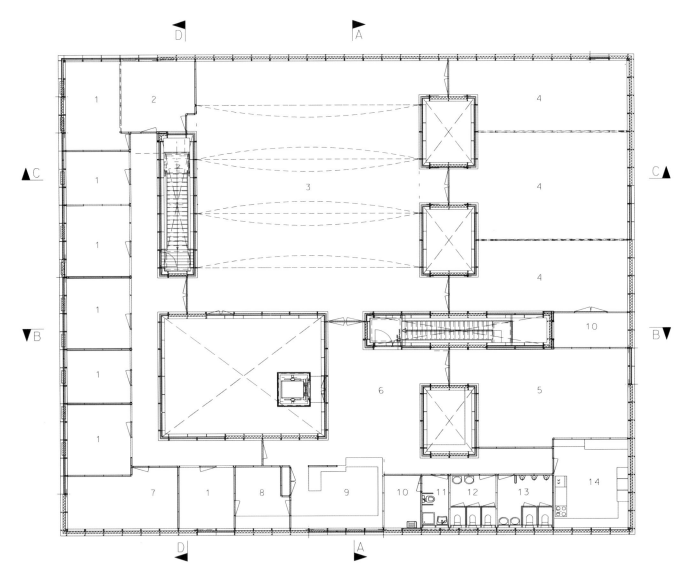

First floor as central lobby.

Functionally, the interior of the first floor demonstrates, with simple distribution and orthogonal shapes, that the building is to be used as an exhibition fair of innovative elements directed principally at businesses in the aluminum sector.

It also incorporates a public space for exhibiting the great creative and employment potential of aluminum, including a large and extendable catalog of manufactured elements.

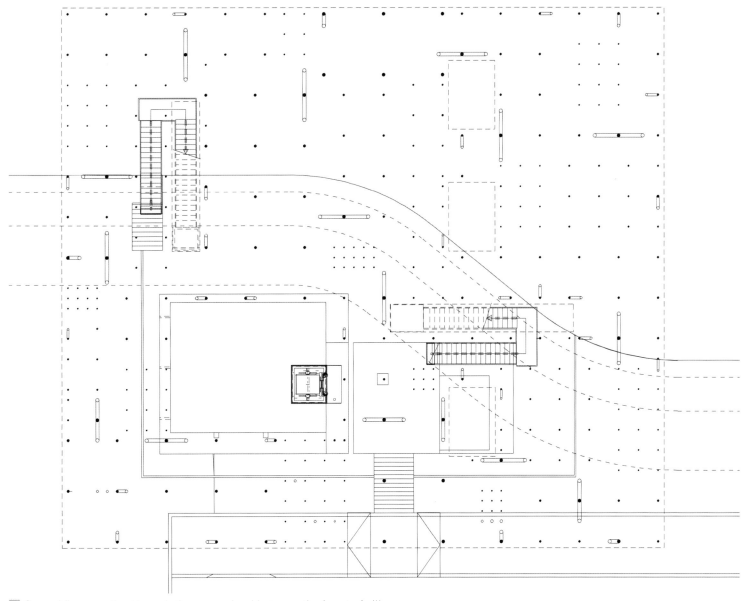

Ground floor, section through the access level between the forest of pillars.

Demonstrating its versatility and beauty, aluminum provides the answer for the structural support.

By contrast, the access level remains free from division. The forest of aluminum dominates the scene, diffusing the landscape next to the lake.

The slim supports mingle among their geometry the access staircases which rise from ground-level like slim aluminum gangways, to graft themselves into the pure shape of the prism which houses the functional layout. Among the multitude of columns, not all act as structural supports, some incorporate drainage mechanisms and the wiring channels needed to serve the service and plant requirements.

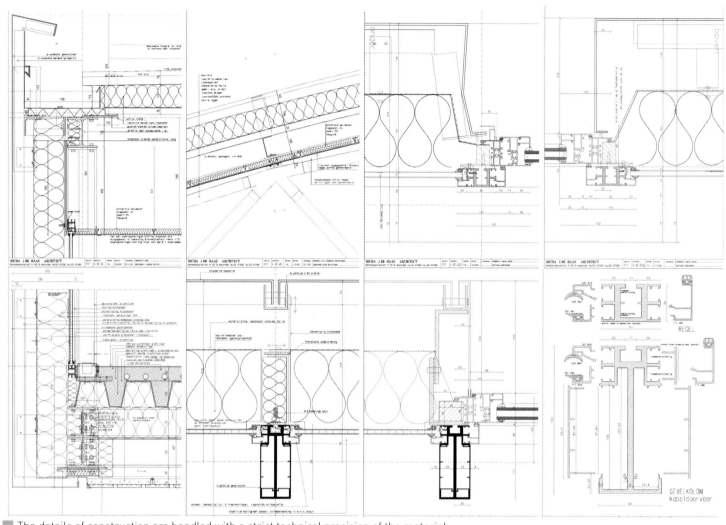

■ The details of construction are handled with a strict technical precision of the material.

■ The cover is supported by three-dimensional triangular trusses.

All the angles of the building, the finishes, the corners are handled by means of a very full range of constructive details, with the aim of a perfect control of construction. The manufacture of the majority of elements is based on an industrial process designed for a conceptually new building; the design incorporates distinctive details of aerospace technology which are used for the first time in a building for public use.

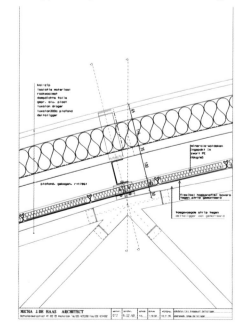

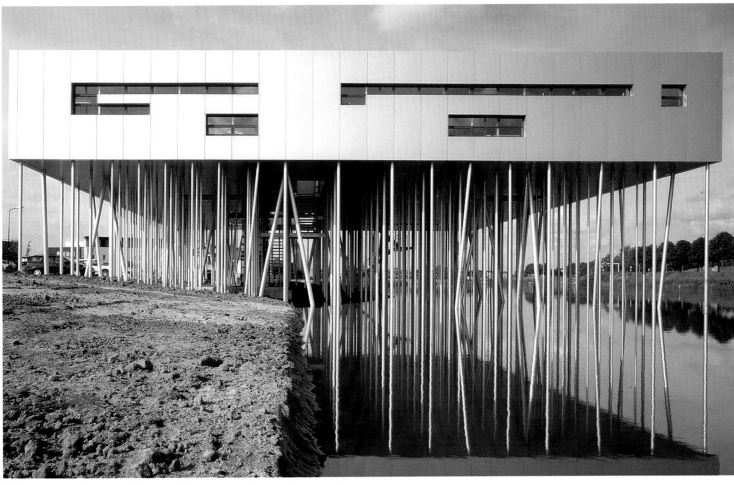

The simple prism sits like a cushion stuck on light knitting-needles.

All the angles are resolved technically.

Three-dimensional trusses are built, with a tubular structure which permit a space 14 meters wide to be covered, forming the exhibition hall. The aluminum bars which compose them are joined together by fusion at the top, applying the aerospace technology already mentioned, and avoiding riveted and soldered joins.

All the elements arrive mechanized and are assembled on-site, bringing out the special characteristic of aluminum as an eco-sustainable material. The building is a Meccano structure of 100% dismountable modular elements, recyclable and easily interchangeable among themselves.

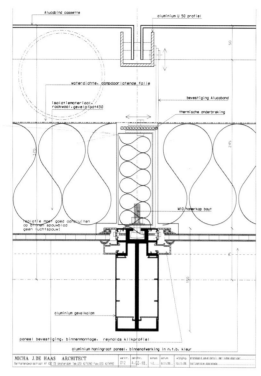

■ Detail of join of the Alucobond wall.

■ Detail of Alucobond join - opening in the façade.

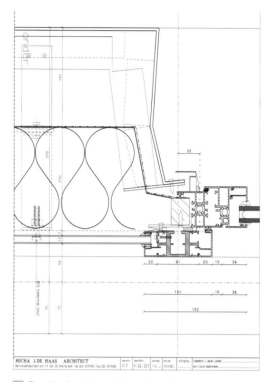

■ Detail of a ridge without profiling of a support

■ Detail of join of two glass modules.

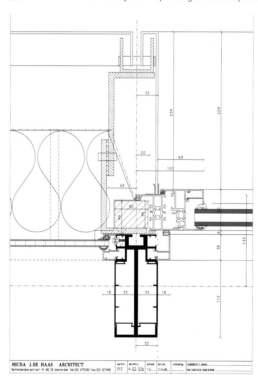

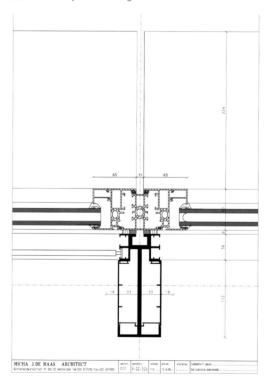

The façade is treated by means of modular panels of Alucobond, the openings of the windows are integrated into the modeling of the wall in a slightly recessed second plane, with a slim carpentry of aluminum and transparent glass. This arrangement reinforces the effect of compactness of the aluminum prism, a solid volume of silver metal raised on piles.

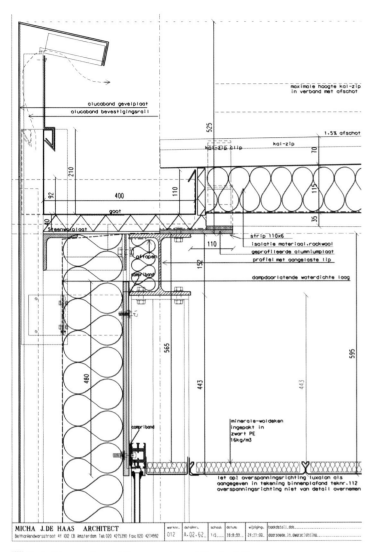

Detail in section of the covering of the building.

The fluid relation between interior and exterior, landscape and building.

In the inner court, the circulation unit rises skyward.

On the ground floor, the access staircases come together in the inner court with a nucleus of elevators enclosed in glass rising airily towards the sky. The courtyard sees the mingling of the slim supports, the perception of the inner space, the landscape, the reflection on the lake, the weightlessness of the materials and the stark formalization stripped of superfluous adornments ... creating a feeling of calm, of warmth, which is emphasized in the visual framing of the sky above.

▨ Board and conference rooms.

▨ Waiting rooms.

The interiors are dominated by a minimalist aesthetic, opting for open spaces which visually enlarge their area by absorbing a maximum volume of natural light thanks to the arrangement of inner courts.

Aluminum gives a light and ephemeral effect, though technically strong and functional.

Inner lobby. The lightness is accentuated by the details.

The building lit up at night sums up the technical precision of its precise formalization, in an element charged with an elegant aesthetic. Suggestive, apparently light, simple, the building colonizes the place, conveying to us a host of unfamiliar sensations. A new environment has been created, of poetic atmosphere, creating a pleasing dialog between the observer, the building and the landscape.

"notions of absence"

(bergen-belsen memorial)

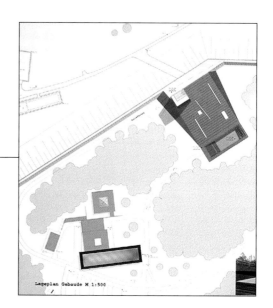

The project for the Bergen-Belsen Memorial is a commemorative place set in the old location where during the second world war a prison-camp was built, within the magnificent Dutch forest.

The work is marked by strong symbolic connotations of an emotional character, with the object of adding a moving witness to our historical memory.

The main building is buried in the site, marking the traces on the ground of the perimeter of the old camp. It is important to emphasize the vastness of the wood, so that the visitor perceives the landscape, steeps himself in its almost unaltered atmos-phere, to take in the magnitude of the disaster. The roof, freeing a large open space, lies level with the ground like an enormous cold, inhospitable public square which evokes our memory to-wards the absent, our recollection of all those who lost their lives

here, giving us an awareness of what took place. The square paved in dark slate, in sign of mourning, indicates the access through a courtyard located in a lower level of the exhibition hall excavated in the earth.

The building is a great mausoleum, austere and monumental, above which rises a tower which stands out on the plain symbolically like a bulwark. The tower, clad in the same dark slate, includes an impressive lantern which floods with light the inner space of the exhibition, a space of reflection for the visitor before the evidence of what occurred. The light, orientating us physically and emotionally, leads us through the enclosure with a single visual open to the sky.

The functional premises are concentrated in the basement.

The roof of the building is integrated into the landscape.

The project is a work of landscape, in which the priority is creating awareness of what occurred. A procession of articulated symbols explain to us as we move along the history of the place. A ring forming a skirting of steel rises above the old perimeter of the camp. On it are written the names of the more than 70,000 victims, each in a tiny space of 5 cm, thus bringing out the sense of the insignificant existence of the human being in the face of annihilation. The marks on the ground show the paths the prisoners followed and the borders which many never recrossed. The empty space in the wood created by the tomb-building, the square of the absent, will be used from time to time as a commemorative place in official ceremonies.

YANNIS AESOPOS
ARCHITECT

Yannis Aesopos (Athens, 1966) graduated in the National Technical University of Athens (1989) and gained his Master's degree in Architecture in the Harvard Graduate School of Design (1991). After working with Bernard Tschumi, he set up his studio in Athens in 1995.

He is assistant professor in the Department of Architecture of Patras University, and a collaborator in Athens University. His projects have been published in international reviews such as

poly/mono-katoikia

Blueprint, Bauwelt and Archis, and recently in The Phaidon Atlas of Contemporary World Architecture (2004).

He has also co-edited the books 'Landscapes of Modernisation: Greek Architecture 1960s and 1990s' (Athens, 1999) and 'The Contemporary (Greek) City/ Metapolis 2001' (Athens, 2001), which address the process of urbanization of present-day Greek cities as the product of post-war modernization.

Works	presented in the following exhibitions:
2000	7th Venice Biennale of Architecture.
2002	New Trends of Architecture in Europe and Japan 2002" (Tokyo).
2003	RIBA Gallery (London).

poly/mono-
katoikia

TECHNICAL DATA

Location Parnithos 10, Nea Filothei, Athens, Greece.

Architect Yannis Aesopos.

Client ARIS SA.

Structural Engineers Georgios Christou (reinforced concrete structure), Mary Constantakopoulou (steel structure).
Alekos Aesopos, Vassilis Douridas, Sotiris Yannoukaris.

Dates Construction 2000-2003.

Total Floor Area 623 m².

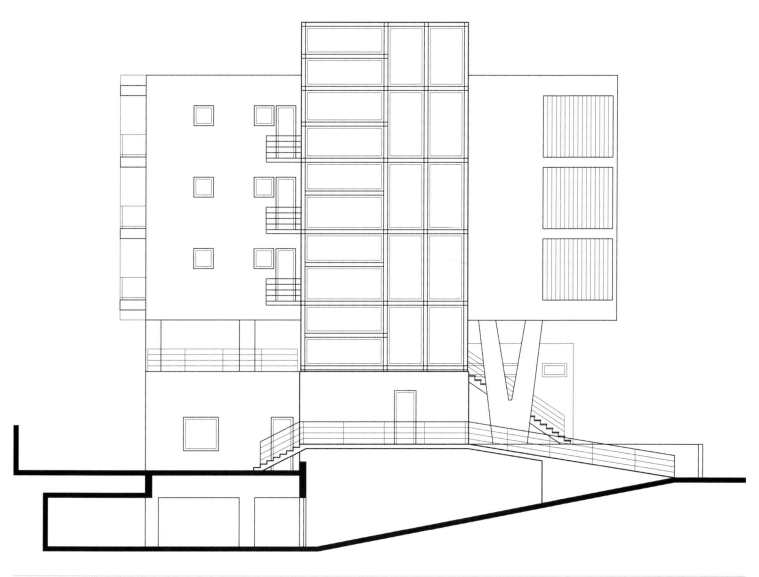

West elevation.

The building is located in a residential suburb of Athens where single-family houses (monokatoikias) co-exist randomly with apartment blocks (polykatoikias).

The "polykatoikias" are the Greek version of the Dom-ino system of Le Corbusier: elemental and economical constructions permitting a great flexibility of use: dwellings, offices, shops, lab-

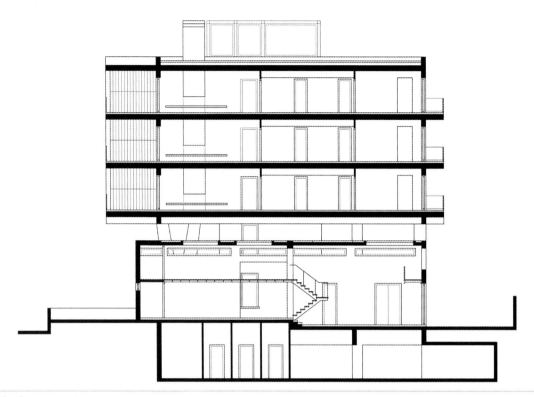

Longitudinal section1.

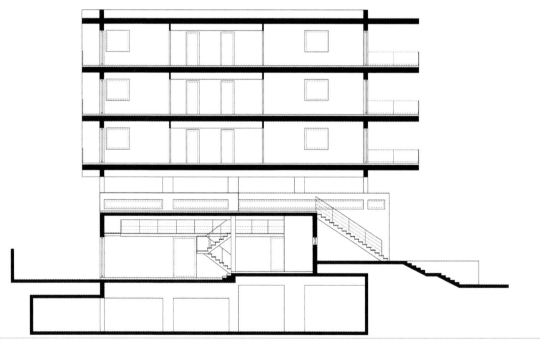

Longitudinal section2.

oratories, restaurants, supermarkets, car-repair workshops... The project aims at integrating these two types into a single hybrid construction combining a two-story suburban "monokatoikia" within the structural framework of a "polykatoikia". The "monokatoikia", situated on the ground floor, forms a monolithic gray volume closed to the street and open to the surrounding garden.

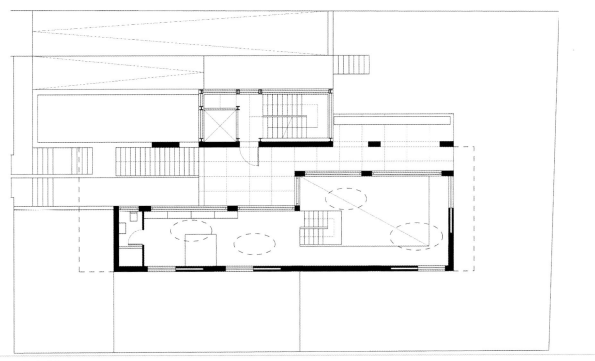

Plan of loft- monokatoikia.

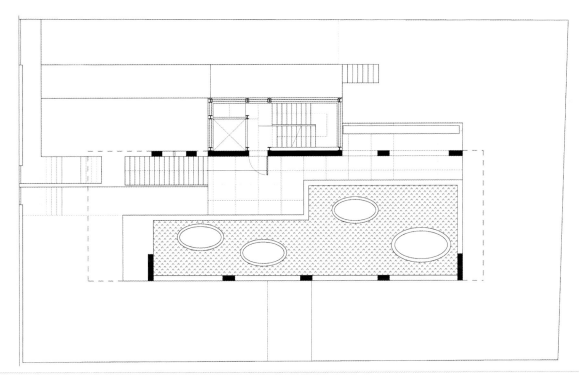

Middle level - entrances.

It comprises a two-level space which includes a loft used as a bedroom, a kitchen, a dining-room and a work space. The "polykatoikia" by contrast is a white volume standing on piles and comprising three floors of identical apartments with large balconies. Between the two an empty space is created, an intermediate place reached by a long staircase, which gives access to the

■ Typical ground-plan - polykatoikia.

■ Ground floor- monokatoikia.

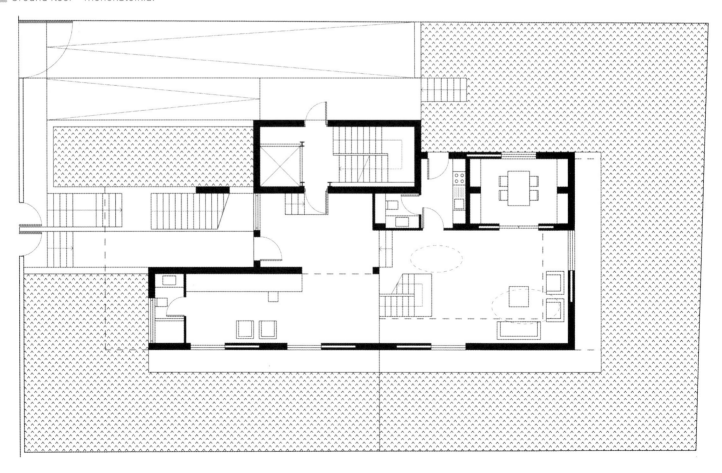

South-east view of the complex.

South-west view of the complex.

dwellings. This access is provided by a free-standing vertical communication unit, built of glass and steel, and allowing a glimpse of the activities within the building.

Access to the middle level and entrance to the monokatoikia.

Vertical communication unit.

The two types of building thus offer antithetical material conditions: the "monokatoikia" relates with the surroundings, the plants and the ground, while the high-rising "polykatoikia" relates with the air, the sky and the views.

Interior of the one-family dwelling.

Interior of the one-family dwelling.

Middle space.

mediateca

DIGITAL
ALL STUDIO

Ammar Eloueni is the name of the Lebanese architect that directs this architectural studio that was set up in 1997 and that is now based in both Paris and Chicago. An enthusiast of the new technologies and fascinated by the possibilities of virtual architecture, he develops his designs in an architectural laboratory that creates virtual environments with animation software and the most advanced research and development techniques available. A theoretic of an avant-garde architecture, he brings his ideas together in experimental projects of a diverse nature.

In his work, we find structures in abstract forms that represent an unconventional way of understanding architecture, forms that are perceived as different because of the changing way in which the light falls over them.

Critical with the traditional way of understanding architecture, his ideas of space and the relationship of this with the user is subjected to a preliminary investigation and posterior comprehen-

osaka

miyake

sion of the dynamics of the city itself and its complexities. Virtual architecture is not in opposition to traditional architecture; virtual space is an extension of real space and technology should be applied to the design of buildings to convert them into interactive spaces with mobile elements that are adaptable to the necessities of their users.

Ammar Eloueini has developed an academic practice in the University of Illinois in Chicago (UIC) since 1999. The same year, he received a mention of honor from the French Ministry of Culture and decided to develop his work between America and Europe.

In 2001, he received the prestigious Nouveaux Albums des Jeunes Architectes prize from the French Institute of Architecture which made him stand out as a great promise in the field of architecture before he was 35 years old. In 2002, he received a new prize for his project for the Station of Osaka.

Since then, he has developed projects that mix the digital with the real. He exercises as a collaborator with various specialized magazines, he participates in symposiums, conferences and exhibitions. His activity is not limited to the field of architecture. His labor as creator of the scenery for "California" by John Jasperse or the sculptural architecture of his project Nubik, an experimental space that shows avant-garde work located in Kansas City, also stand out.

His path has casually crossed with that of the famous designer Issey Miyake who he closely collaborated with in the development of the project for a new space-boutique that received a third prize in the Miami Biennale in 2003 in the category of project non-constructed.

His last exhibition, Skin Tight, is the backdrop over which the collections of ten international avant-garde fashion designers was shown.

virtual_library
of_proximity

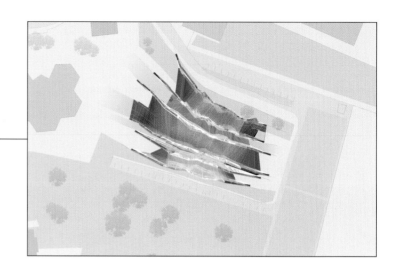

TECHNICAL DATA
Location Vingeanne, Champagne-Ardenne, France.
Architects Ammar Eloueini.
Client French Ministry of Culture.
Collaborators Hill Corcoran, Grez Denisiuk, Prince Ambooken, Masha Safina, Karla Sierralta, Louis Shell, Climent Blanchet, Zane Karpova.
Consultant companies Engineering. Jim Dalton.
Project date 2003.

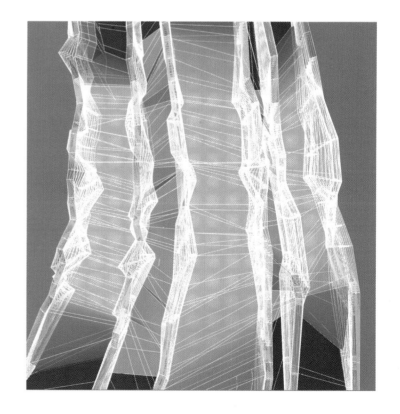

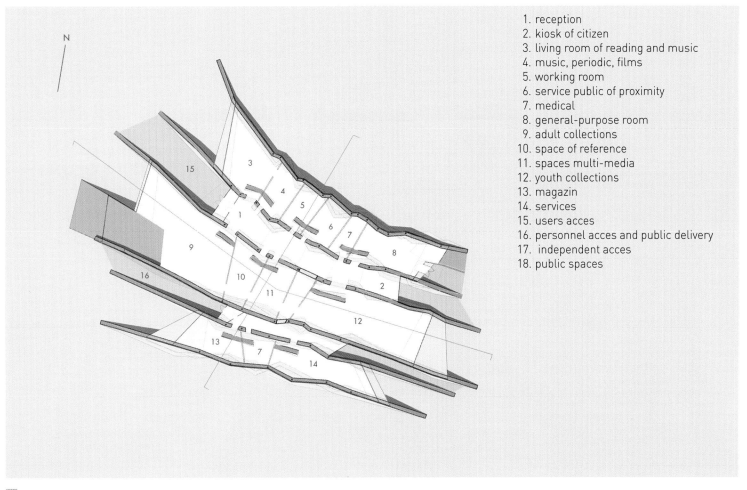

1. reception
2. kiosk of citizen
3. living room of reading and music
4. music, periodic, films
5. working room
6. service public of proximity
7. medical
8. general-purpose room
9. adult collections
10. space of reference
11. spaces multi-media
12. youth collections
13. magazin
14. services
15. users acces
16. personnel acces and public delivery
17. independent acces
18. public spaces

▨ Pan.

▨ The large amount of light obtained through the roof is essential.

This project revives the eternal debate in architecture of the box verses design... The building is not a delimited container, but a series of different flows. Its enclosures seem to emerge form the ground itself in a natural way, they are scales that are stacked in layers and that extend into the spaces marking continuous and irregular lines.

![] Three principal wings are communicated by the transit areas.

![] The enclosure is made up of thin laminas of wood.

As we slowly approach, the divisions slowly lead us from the exterior to the interior in a progressive sequence. Suddenly, the stacking of the laminas provokes a change in perception and come together in a sequence of spaces delimited by dividers treated with the identical formal language as that of the exterior enclosing.

The design pays special attention to its integration in the surroundings. There is a clear desire for it to go unnoticed. The building sinks into the ground in order to emphasize the idea of natural growth, of juxtaposition. The idea proportions complete flexibility thanks to its longitudinal formalization. It is its fluidity, its evolution that generates the project.

West view. The design has the clear intention of integrating itself into the surroundings.

The interior of the building is a fluid and flexible space.

The program is developed in three principal wings separated by transit areas that are joined one with the other like a bellows. The supporting elements are thin metal shafts with an exaggerated curved shape which in the way of small trunks sustain the small wooden stepped boards that make up the neutral continual enclosure.

The architecture is a structure of an abstract form. It depends on the routes it provides and time. The building pulls us inside. It directs us around its inclined irregular walls.

It is fundamental for the building to provide abundant quantities of light to its spaces as due to the way this falls on the irregu-

The spaces are separated by divisions that mark the directions in which to circulate.

A simple constructive system.

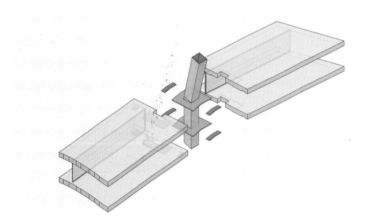

The strips are held in place by a structural steel support.

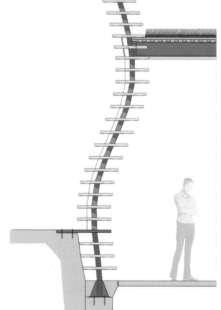

lar surfaces and the constant movement of the user, we perceived a suggestive flexible space in constant change.

The light that is generously filtered in through the openings left between the laminas by the supporting structure helps us orientate ourselves in the interior of a number of undifferentiated

The building gently slopes in order to provide access to the roof-lookout point.

The public space progressively devours the interior space.

spaces. We are in a dynamic almost geological space which has been entirely generated by three dimensional virtual analysis.

The walls of the building are constructed in 5x60 cm wooden boards hung horizontally and supported by steel tubes firmly anchored in the ground. The gaps between the horizontal boards are completed with glass panels fixed vertically to ensure the stability of the enclosure.

The areas of the program of the building are stepped. The building is sunken 90 cm into the ground in order to allow for an easy access onto the roof that fulfills the function of lookout point open onto a public green zone.

osaka

TECHNICAL DATA
Location Osaka and Keihanshin region. Japan.
Architect Amman Eloueni.
Client City of Osaka.
Collaborators Colin Franzen, Zane Karpova.
Project date 2002-2003.

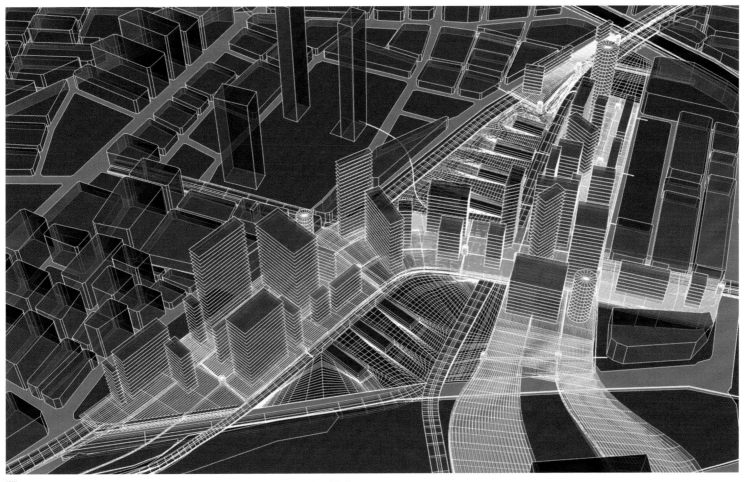

The ordination of the sector was marked by certain overall guidelines.

The project takes on a territorial analysis.

The objective of the project is the reorganization of an urban area of Osaka. The project is centered in the search for a strategy, not for a composition. The first step was to act over an area of six hectares which are later to be extended to 24.

The conceptual development of the project allows for flexibility in the final result and marks some guidelines that will not be altered by future possible economic or infrastructural changes that compromise the original design.

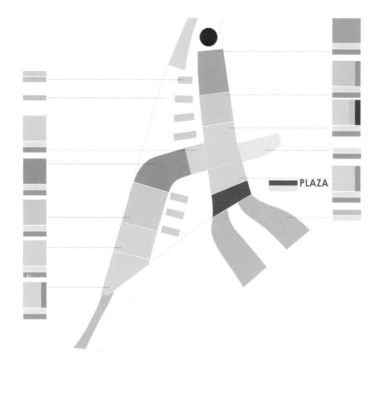

PLAZA

SPORTS
GREEN SPACE

BUSINESS
GOVERNMENTAL
RESIDENTIAL
EDUCATIONAL
RECREATION
CULTURAL
COMMERCIAL
PARKING

The infrastructure is made up by creating areas of different use.

The virtual work brings us closer to its materialization.

A meticulous study of the surrounding areas on a territorial level was undertaken. The principal idea was to create a network of lines of circulation that connect the different areas. These areas are subdivided into routes defined by the zoning of uses which are interrelated by means of a general network and are subdivided into: parking areas, retail spaces, public spaces, leisure areas and private buildings. Vehicles and trains are principally situated in the extremes so that pedestrians can enjoy the remainder of the space.

The residential buildings are arranged strategically so that the users are connected to the retail area while being able to enjoy the green zone.

The project is flexible and allows for changes without compromising the design.

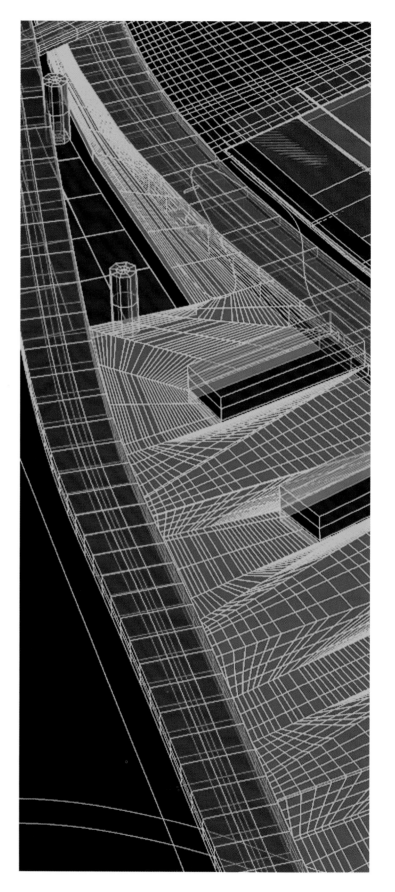

The buildings were conceived as elements to link the retail area with the park.

The project allows changes to be incorporated without the overall concept being affected.

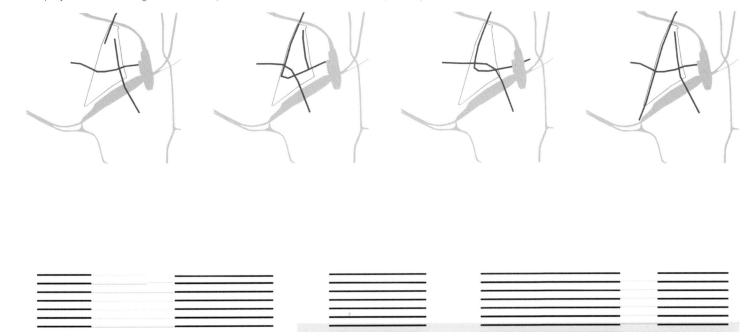

Cities are changing very quickly. They are dynamic elements and so as to understand their necessities, it is indispensable to use potent instruments that are able to isolate correctly the characteristics of a place and of a moment. It is necessary to find a suitable solution to the interrelations of the living organism that is the city.

Traditional architecture, conceptually static does not manage to find the right solution.

miyake

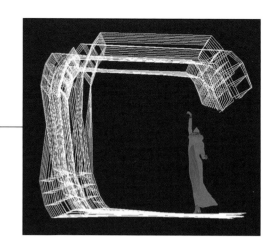

TECHNICAL DATA
Location France.
Architects Amman Eloueni & Celine Parmentier.
Client Issey Miyake Europe.
Project date 2001-2003.

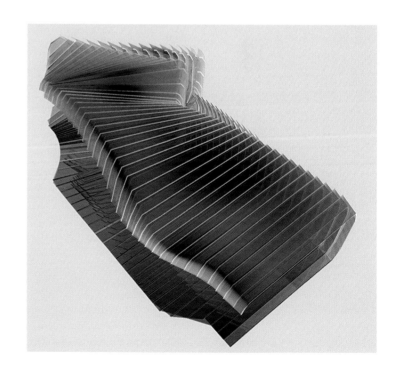

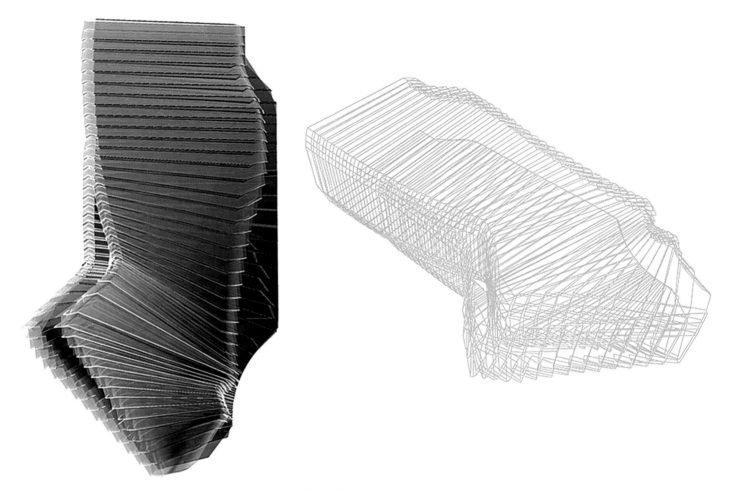

▦ The project is based on the superposition of strips that advance in an irregular arrangement.

▦ Virtual images of the enclosing.

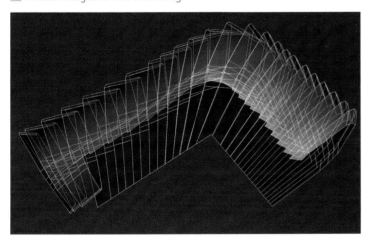
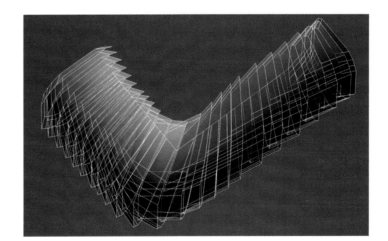

Fate would have it that the famous designer Issey Miyake happened to open a new store alongside the Parisian gallery where Eloueni was developmenting one of his projects. Impressed, Issey Miyake proposed that he should collaborate in the development of a project for premises for retail or the display of the designer's collections. Since then, Miyake has become popular for his innovation in the use of new textiles, and Eloueni deepens into the use of materials known with the term of non-con-

The flexibility allows the area to be adapted to the designer's diversity of aspects.

Rendering the structure of the skin.

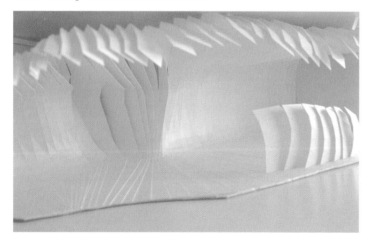

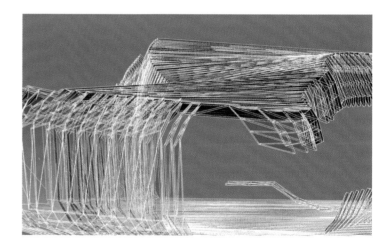

ventional. The project investigates by means of virtual generation an abstract space made up by the juxtaposition of strips of differing widths and textures that are juxtapositioned along an irregular structure and which allow light to enter through the joints that are left around the edges. The result is that of a continual space formed by the repeated placing of cut outs that are bent from the ceiling to the floor in a clear reference to the process of fabrication and design of the Japanese designer's clothes.

The interior space formed by superimposed fragments of differing thicknesses.

Virtual example of the different textures.

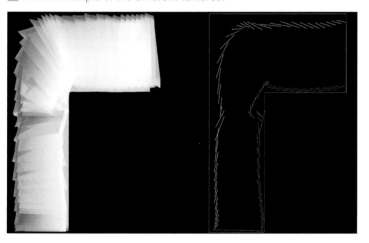

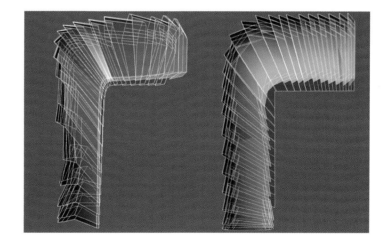

The strips that can be made in various different materials enclose a space while maintaining the virtue of adapting to the necessities of use. The flexibility of this use leads to an element initially conceived as part of the enclosure becoming an element that exhibits clothes or makes up the furnishing of the store. The proposal has been accepted as a prototype for three new stores in France. In each case, the stores are to be developed in one unique material, translucent or opaque.

IaN+

The objective of IaN+'s work is to merge architectural theory and practice in order to redefine the concept of territory as a space that relates the landscape to the user. They belong to a generation of architects that understand the city as a complex mechanism of relationships and exchanges and as a result, for them, the formal resolution of a project is the interpretation of the site as a subsystem of the large machinery that makes up the city.

The development of their projects is carried out with a great consciousness of the impact they are to have on their surroundings, an aspect that is treated with great care. The dynamics of the territory, the permanent encounter between subject and object and the possible integration in the new landscape are studied.

All of their work has been strongly influenced by the theories of the Living Systems developed in 1978 by James Grier Miller. The

tomishiro_museum

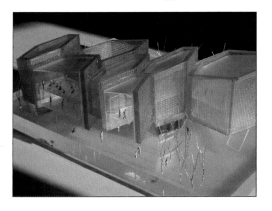

parking_rome

buildings are elements that integrate flows, they are membranes that connect with the landscape. This approach is translated into a language of anthropomorphic forms of geometric enclosures based on the study of nature and that also allows a concept of architecture far removed from symbolism to be generated.

A fragment of nature which creates a new landscape and in which the landscape exercises an enormous influence over the type of building to be designed which is always conceived as a perimeter, a boarder between in and out. The traditional idea of architecture as a object and container is rejected. The building is to be a permeable membrane, a living system.

IaN+ publish articles and participate in debates in order to make their way of understanding architecture known. Their designs have been selected to participate in exhibitions all around

Prizes	Prizewinning designs
2005	Art-Musem of glass, Tittot, Taipei.
2004	Tallin Modul - Tallin. Estonia.
2003	The Daugava Enbankment - Riga Latvia.
2003	Central European Bank.
2001	Parking lot - Rome, Italy.
1999	Trevi Flash Art Museum - Perugia.

the world and this is not only for their organizational qualities. The studies of vulnerable and fragile forms in their projects have given them an important place in the present panorama of contemporary architecture.

tomishiro_museum

FICHA TÉCNICA
Location Azuma (Japan).
Architects Carmelo Baglivo, Luca Galofaro.
Client New Tomhiro Museum of Shi-ga Azuma.
Collaborators Stefania Manna, engineering. Marco Galofaro, scale models.
Project date 2001.

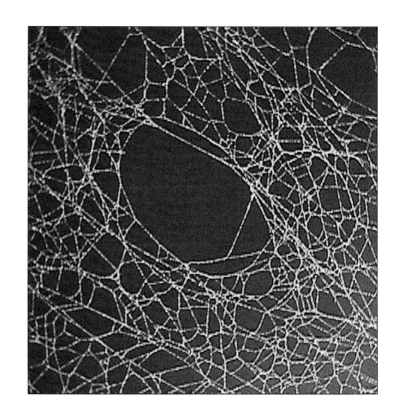

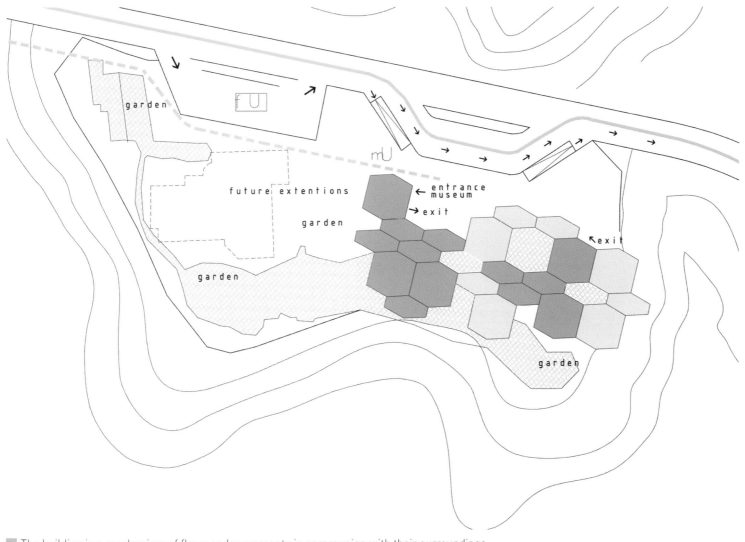

The building is a mechanism of flows and movements in communion with their surroundings.

Cross section. The complex frees the ground floor so as not to block the way to nature.

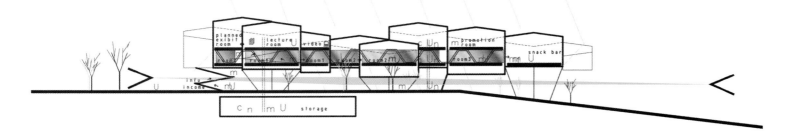

The museum situated in the delicate landscape of the valleys of Azuma is dedicated to the work of the Japanese painter Tomihiro Hoshino. From his work, the concept and quality of the ethereal, fragile and transparent are taken in order to create a space dedicated to the enjoyment of art displayed in an idyllic environment. The building is to be understood as a natural system and not as an building container, a fragile membrane that interweaves relationships with required uses and extends in space in an undetermined way.

Its constant communion with the landscape is basic for the design and for this reason the green is mixed with the light formalization of the museum.

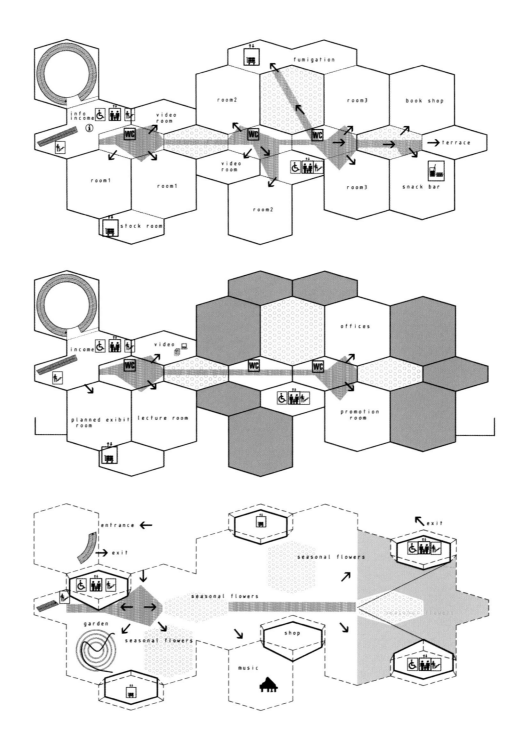

The project synthesizes three concepts: the functionality of the museum, nature and the artist's work.

As far as the floor plan is concerned, the museum responds to a grouping of light hexagonal forms that are structurally autonomous and of diverse dimensions. The requirements of the functional program are understood as something changeable and extendable with the passing of time. For this reason, the grouping can be easily varied. The building is a large mechanism, a hive of alveolar cells in which uses and flows are developed, the different rooms of the museum.

Visual communication with the exterior is complete; the enclosures are made up of a light skin of glass blocks that completely

The building is formalized as a collection of irregular hexagonal cells.

The glass enclosing achieves complete visual and functional permeability.

dematerialize and that create holes so that nature enters visually and forms part of the exhibitions. The ephemeral, the changeable, the vulnerable... impregnate the idea and the formalization of the complex.

The ground floor of the building is free from the program so that the visitor enters into contact with the landscape of Azuma, inspiration of Hoshino's work, before going into the exhibition.

Once inside, the spaces are bidimensional and perception of the surroundings is not lost. The flow of visitors advances over clear guidelines that link large art exhibitions spaces or leisure areas with smaller cells in which more enclosed activities such as videos, photographs, experimental work and small objects are located.

The necessary technical areas disappear from our view and are situated on an underground floor. They are "these roots" that are invisible, those that assure the required regulation of humidity and temperature in the uncluttered exhibition rooms and also to assure the stability of the lightweight complex in case of fire, earthquakes and electrical incidents as well as to accommodate the air conditioning system.

The hollows in the façade transport the landscape into the interior. Scenery and use blend together into one identity. The lightness is able to give meaning to the passing of time and to the changing of the seasons, an infinite cycle, a living mechanism in constant evolution.

parking_rome

TECHNICAL DATA

Location Rome, Italy.
Architects Carmelo Baglivo & Galofaro Luca,
Laura Negrini.
Collaborators Stefania Manna, engineering
Marco Galofaro, scale models
Andrea Klinge, Sebastiane Winance.
Project date 2002.

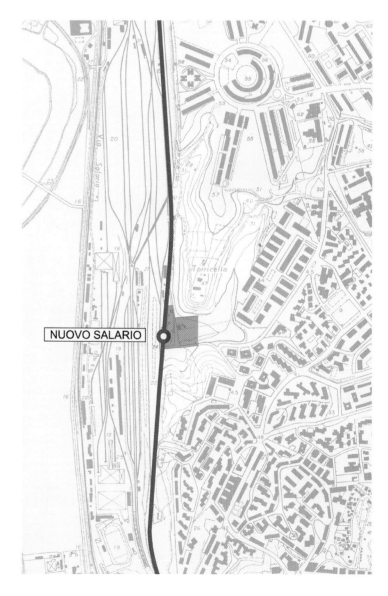

NUOVO SALARIO

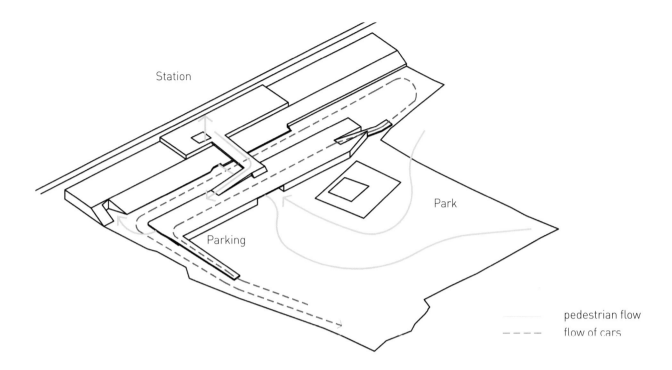

Station

Park

Parking

——————— pedestrian flow
- - - - - - flow of cars

▓ The diverse thoroughfares have been made independent to avoid inferences.
▓ The permeability is the principal character of the structural façade.

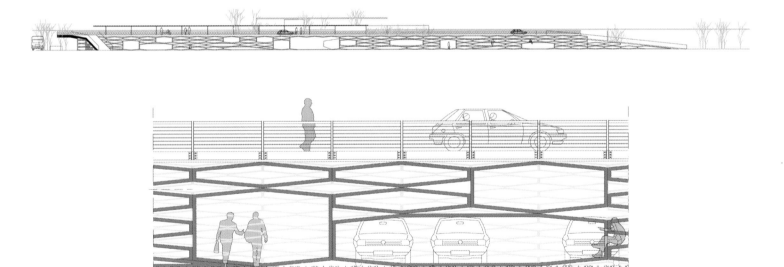

▓ Elevation.

The site for this project runs alongside a large green area situated between two natural hills in a location that responds to the condition of urban sprawl next to a consolidated area.

The program responds to the necessity of creating a parking lot that can be accessed from the city to the existing train station. The design has been intended to be extremely respectful with the surroundings and extends its program so as to create a mechanism that relates activities with exchanges.

The creation of a determined building is not the intention, but that of a territorial infrastructure that organizes the system of flows. As a result, the parking lot occupies the area and extends considerably beyond the station making the best of this great

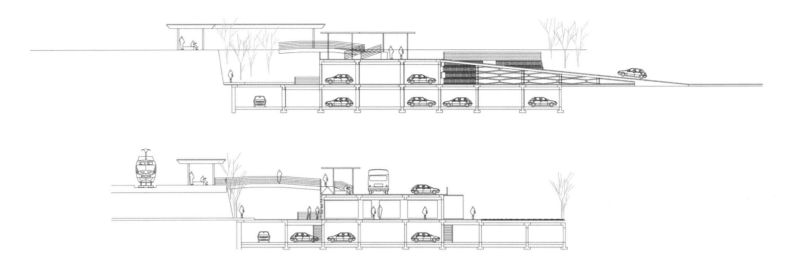

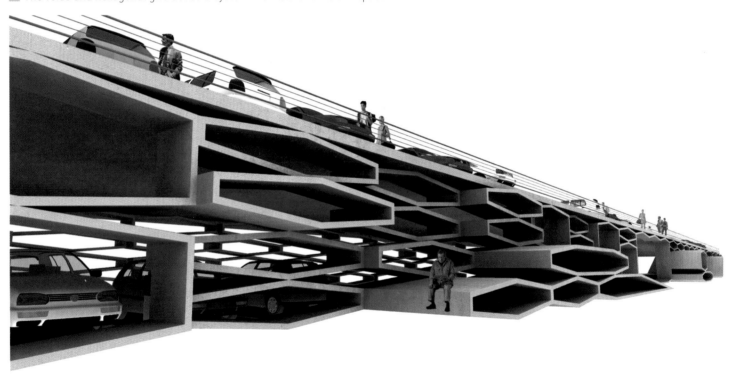

■ The building becomes an infrastructure and intercepts the urban flows.

■ The voids and hexagonal grid act as a system that relates different spaces.

opportunity to integrate the urban weave that had become isolated.

The design, competition prizewinner, for the siting of a parking lot close to the station that should structure traffic between the station, the parking lot, the green zone and the residential zone, chooses to impose an identity its own onto the project and emphasis the complexity of the context.

The space occupied by the building acts as mediator between the natural surroundings and the artificial surroundings in which it is situated in such a way that it manages to create a dynamic language.

The building organizes the territory according to the limitations imposed by the station and from the point of view of how its function is understood within the extension of the program.

The parking lot creates a strong contrast in the relationship between what is natural and what is artificial.

The road network, like a fine lamina, is raised so as to become the roof of the building.

Exciting places that show us new ways of life.

The functionality is assured by the capacity of the mechanism to unravel or fold over its skin to gather up the flows and activities of the city in one unique element.

The flows are intercepted which provokes changes in speed of different natures for cars, trains and pedestrians. Finally, the different levels are organized in such a way so as to avoid interferences.

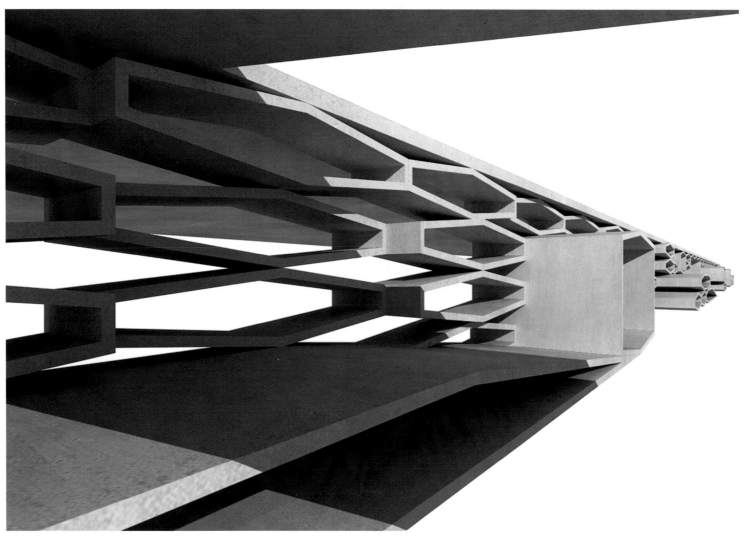

A membrane in space organizes the flows and activities between the city and the station.

The building colonizes the territory.

It is a dynamic mechanism, an adaptable diaphragm that allows the classification of uses by layers that are completely permeable one with another in a visual and functional way.

The permeability is the principal characteristic of the façade that at the same time is the structure of the building. The collection of cells that create an irregular continual panel allow for total visual connection interior - exterior. The collection of pieces can be understood as living, changing mechanism that can be easily added to or substituted.

The pieces are displaced horizontally one respect another. As a result, some of them duplicate their functions as being partly the structure for the façade and partly integrated into the exterior space.

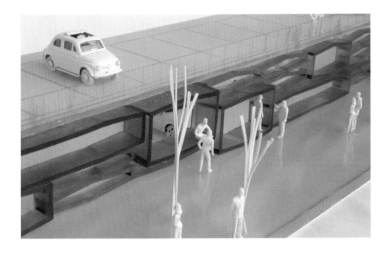 

A three dimensional façade of hexagonal cells that not only provides a solution for the play of sun, shade and necessary ventilation, but which can also be used as the urban furniture of the park.

It is an ephemeral structure that settles itself over the terrain which it maintains open and untouchable. It generates a field of relationships, a dynamic space with a radius of action that includes all of the surrounding areas.

dECOi
ARCHITECTS

Set up by Mark Goulthorpe as an investigation group centered above all on the cultural effects of technology, dECOi opened its studio in Paris in 1991. It bases itself on a speculative practice within the fields of architecture and design with the object of developing a creative podium that extends the frontiers of conventional practice and that frees the profession from its traditional formulation.

Its work embraces an extensive experimental field that includes design, architectural projects and theoretical practice. With offices in London, Paris and Kuala Lumpur, dECOi counts on the collaboration of a pluridisciplinary team made up of architects, mathematicians and investigators.

The prestige obtained from the development of new technological practices has enabled the studio to collaborate with engi-

bankside_paramorph

miran_gallerie

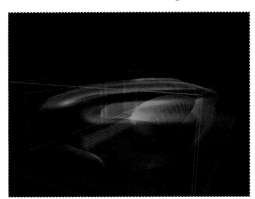

neers such as Ove Arup (London) and Rice Francis Ritchie (Paris). The studio is presently working on designs for a number of different projects in collaboration with Foster & Partners (London).

The studio has received prizes from the Royal Academy of London, the French Ministry of Culture and the Architectural League of New York and has represented France in the Venice Biennale and at the United Nations.

The practice has also received invitations to exhibit its work in the Venice Biennale (2000 and 2002) as well as in the FRAC Center in Orleans.

Mark Goulthorpe's career has been strengthened by numerous publications, conferences and by frequent collaborations such as visiting lecturer at the AA in London, at the École Speciale in Paris and currently at the MIT in Boston.

Prize	winning entry's
2001	The best design in the International FEIDAD Competition for Digital Design.
1999	Birmingham Hippodrome Interactive Art Competition.
1995	NARA/TOTO World Architecture Triennial of Tokyo.
1991	Europan.

bankside_paramorph

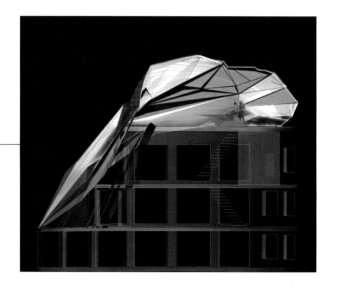

TECHNICAL DATA
Location London.
Architect Mark Goulthorpe.
Collaborators Matteo Grimaldi, Julian Lomessy, Maruan Halabi, Stelios Dritsas, Raphael Crespin.
Project date 2002.
Engineering Arup & Partners.
Consultants Axel Kilian, Erik Demaine & Marty (MIT), Robert Aish (Bentley Systems).

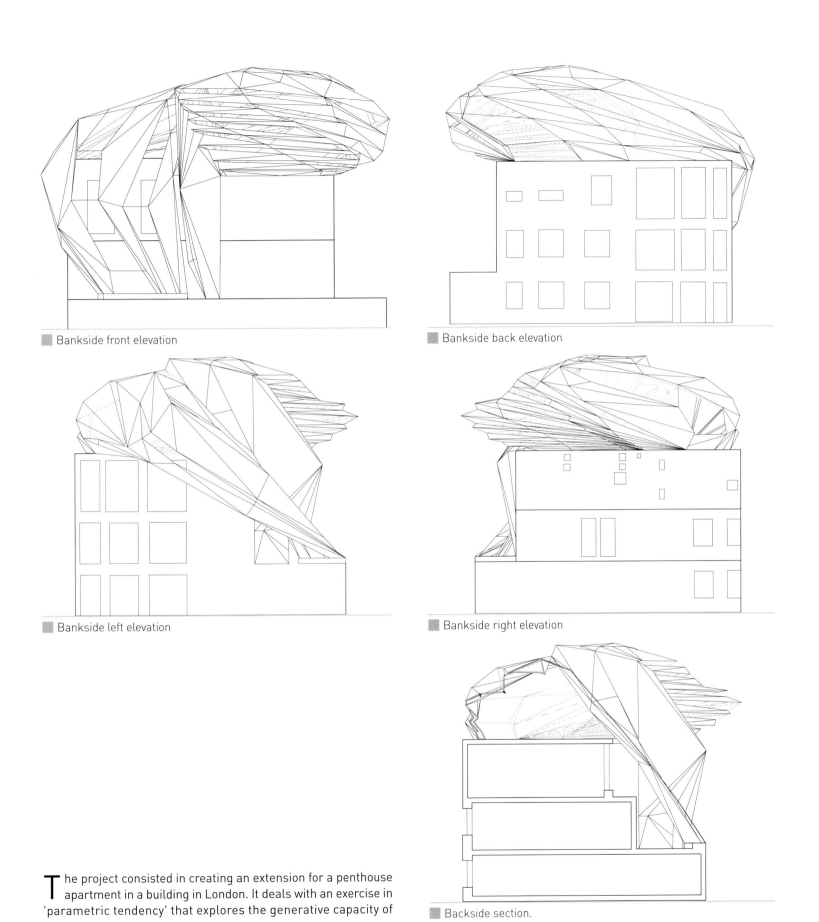

Bankside front elevation

Bankside back elevation

Bankside left elevation

Bankside right elevation

Backside section.

The project consisted in creating an extension for a penthouse apartment in a building in London. It deals with an exercise in 'parametric tendency' that explores the generative capacity of

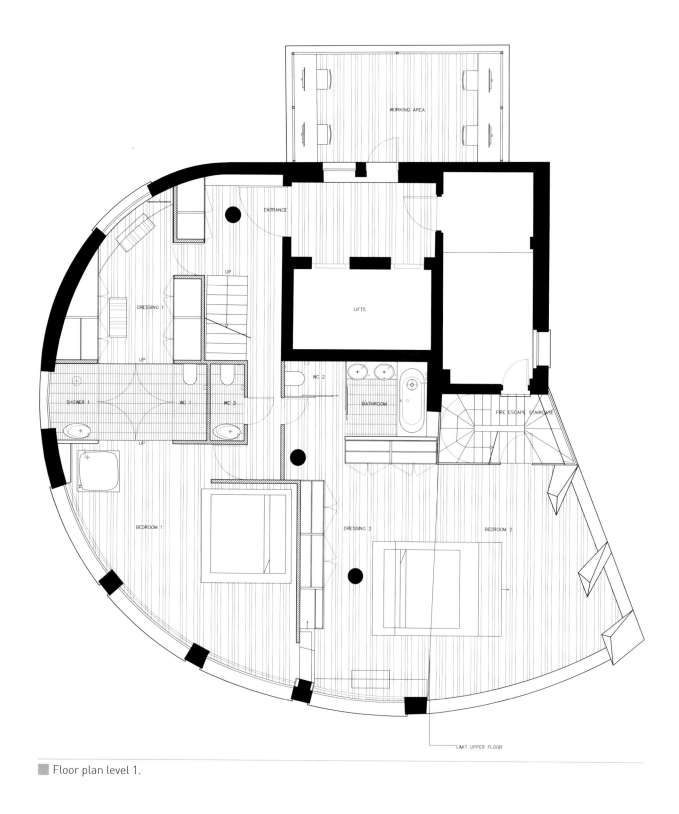

WORKING AREA

ENTRANCE

UP

DRESSING 1

UP

LIFTS

UP

SHOWER 1

WC 2

WC 1

WC 3

BATHROOM

FIRE ESCAPE STAIRCASE

UP

BEDROOM 1

DRESSING 2

BEDROOM 2

LIMIT UPPER FLOOR

Floor plan level 1.

modeling offered by digital technology. Conceived as a three-dimensional spiral that follows on from the geometry of the existing building, the project proposes a solution in which the enclosure itself simultaneously acts as structure and roof while ensuring, in this way, stability, watertight integrity and insulation. This form, fabricated by means of precise cuts over resin-

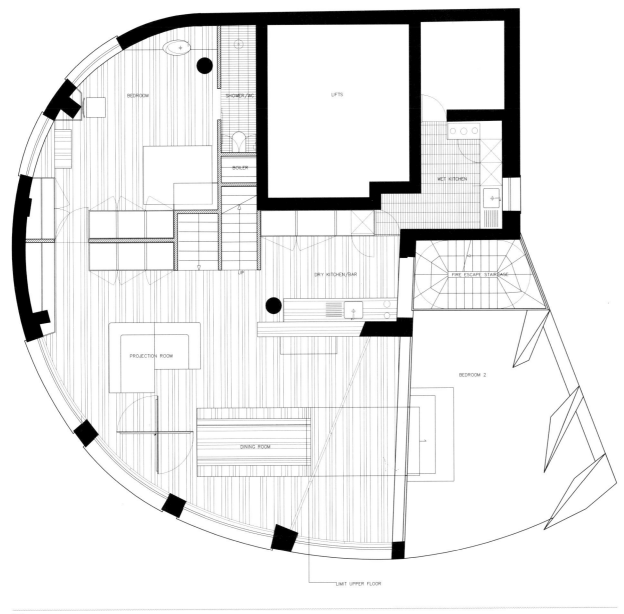

BEDROOM

SHOWER/WC

LIFTS

BOILER

WET KITCHEN

DRY KITCHEN/BAR

FIRE ESCAPE STAIRCASE

UP

PROJECTION ROOM

BEDROOM 2

DINING ROOM

LIMIT UPPER FLOOR

Floor plan level 2.

filled perforated aluminum panels, has been made up of light triangular supports assembled in the workshop and screwed into place in situ. The design is not an undetermined random form, but a paramorphic body which can be modified with no alteration of its fundamental characteristics.

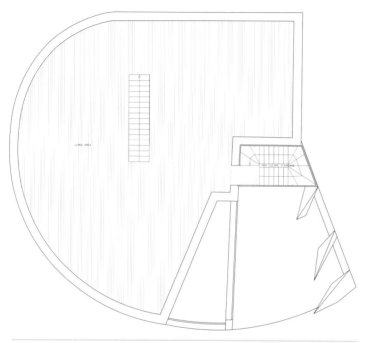

Roof floor plan.

In this way, the formulization of the volume in space depends directly on the parameters used: spatial qualities, views, thermal conditions, structure, weight, assembling speed and so on.

Paramorphic evolution.

Bankside Foster. Integration in existing building.

Bankside front below. Three-dimensional spiral.

This transformational capacity allows for an architectural model that is precise and economically competitive to be created which reduces the logic of traditional rigid fabrication to a unique procedure of interpolation of data.

miran_gallery

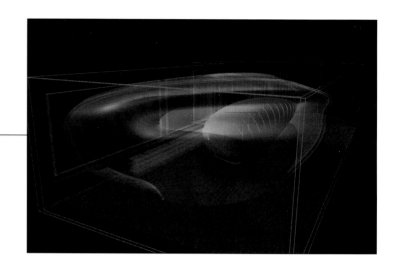

TECHNICAL DATA
Location Paris.
Architects dECOi.
Design Mark Goulthorpe, Raphael Crespin,
Rosalie Kim, Maruan Halabi
Project date 2003.
Collaborator Dr Alex Scott.
3D model MIT SMArchs.

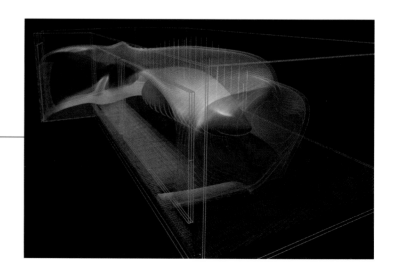

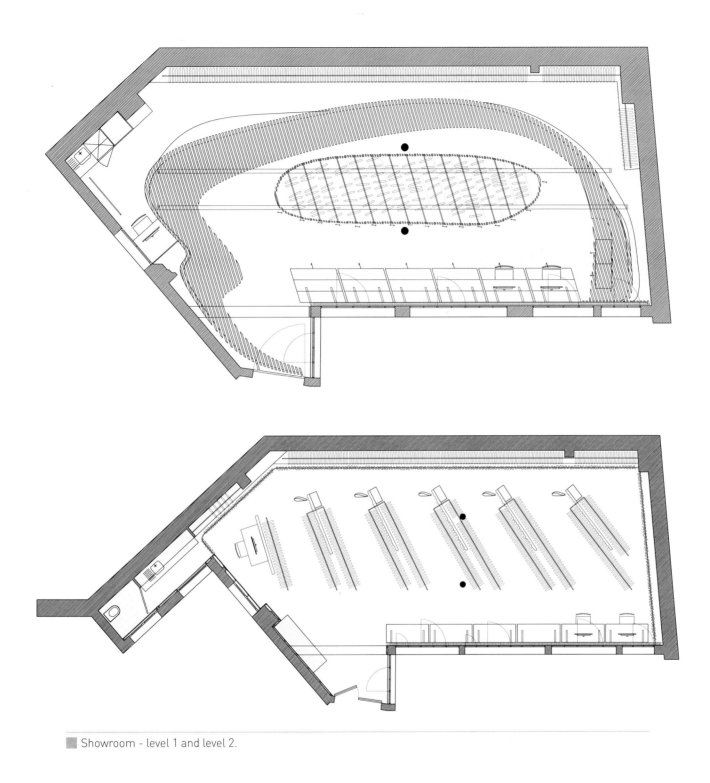

Showroom - level 1 and level 2.

The Miran Gallery forms part of the interior refurbishing of a Parisian workshop converted into a showroom for a fashion firm. The design has been conceived as a curved framework that has been pulled out, stretched and bent until it has filled the space of the gallery. Hung in the interior, there is a long curved object on which clothes are exhibited.

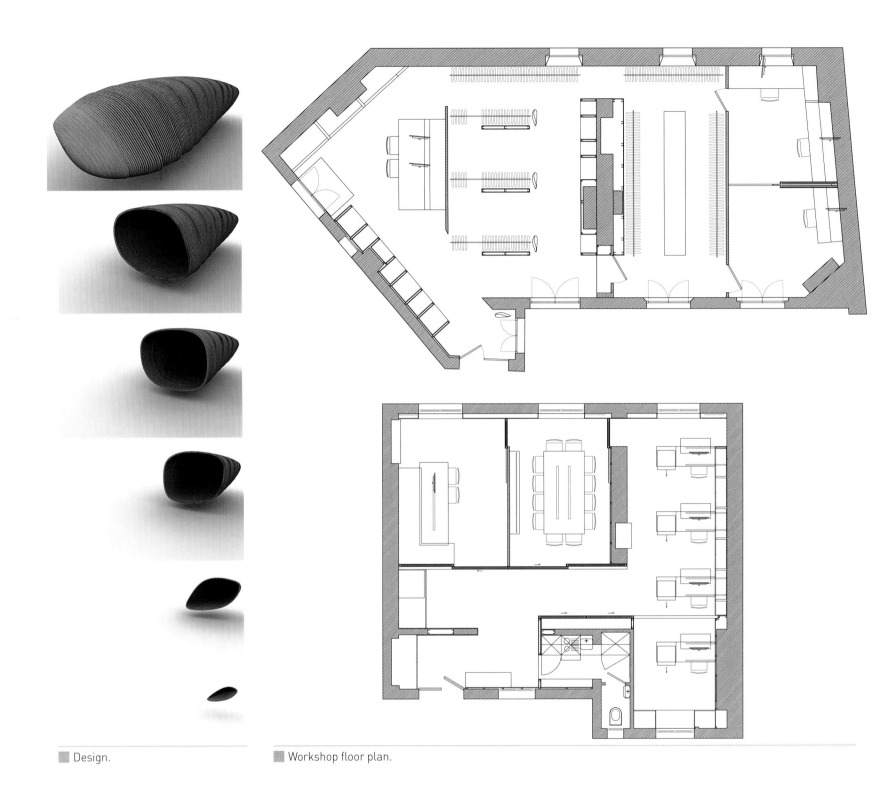

Design.

Workshop floor plan.

All of the walls, ceiling and floor make up a unique continual surface finished, for the most part, in plywood molded in machines governed by numerical parameters. The apparent complexity of the space is, in reality, a product of the process by which it was created and its considerably economic fabrication. This reduction in costs leads to the offer of a large range of formal pos-

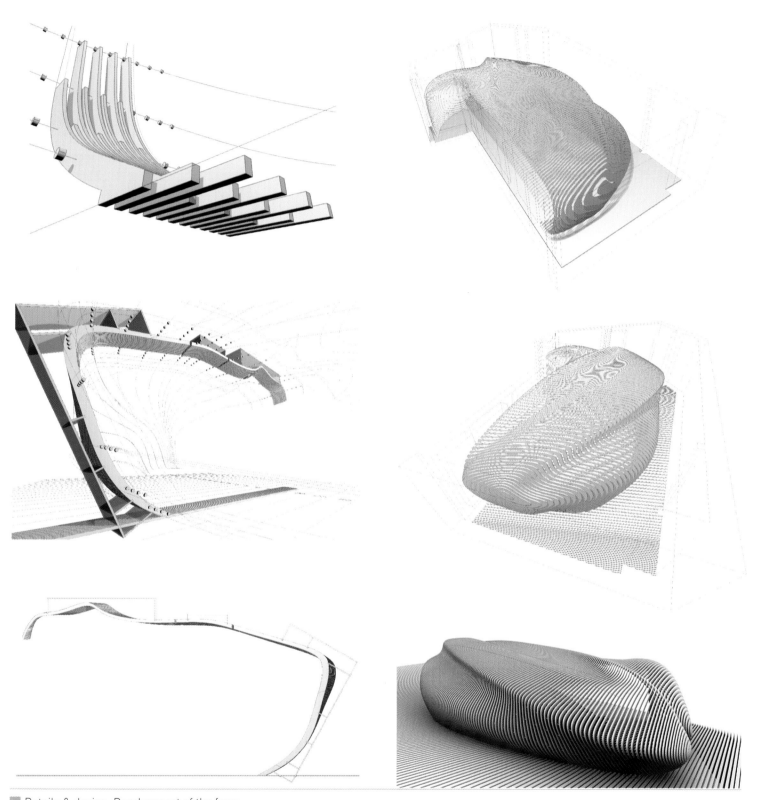

Details & design. Development of the form.

sibilities. This contrasts the traditional system of construction with a precise calibrated procedure which, by means of a computerized architectural model, permits an active working method-

ology. The resulting object/surface constitutes a direct expression of the means of production, the machines used and the costs of the material.

UN STUDIO
ARCHITECTS

Un Studio (United Net) was founded in 1998. Under the direction of Ben van Berkel, architect, and Carolina Bos, a graduate in the History of Art, it aims at being a studio in which specialists in architecture, urban development and infrastructure work together in a collaborative network.

Un Studio has the special characteristic, not commonly found, that one of its directors approaches architecture from an exclusively theoretical point of view, making in the initial phase of a project an exhaustive analysis of all its parameters, and seeking the cooperation of a full team necessary for the optimum development of the design.

Un Studio is planned as a research workshop, an experimental center for new materials, techniques and methods of production

offices_"la_defense"

living_tomorrow_pavilion

to make the work more effective. A professional, efficient space incorporating the most advanced technology.

The joint work of specialists in different disciplines is essential and, as has been demonstrated, effective from the point of view of the quality of the end product obtained.

An architectural project is no more than a product, and an architectural studio is a business. The analyses that are carried out start from a business target in which the quality control of the end product, and its profitability assimilated to its optimum exploitation, are the priority for the favorable development of the architectural business which produces a specific service.

It is an architecture which rejects any language of abstract content and finds its justification in the purest material language.

A profoundly modern conception, which helps us to understand the end product in terms of its function in the service of a steadily more globalized and competitive world.

This workshop is responsible for a long list of prize-winning projects in different fields, owing to the great capacity and quality of work contributed by its multi-disciplinary team of professionals. Notable among the most recent ones are: the Research Laboratory in Groningen, Holland (2003); the Theater Lelystad, in Holland (2003); the Mercedes Benz Museum, in Stuttgart, Germany (2002); the "La Defense" office building, in Almere (Holland, 2000); second prize in the IFCCA competition (Urban Research Manhattan, in New York, 1999); The Music theater in Graz, in Austria (1998) and the Prins Clausbridge, in Utrecht (Holland, 1998).

Offices
"La Defense"

TECHNICAL DATA

Location "La Defense", Almere Business center. Holland.

Architect Ben van Berkel.

Client Eurocommerce, Deventer.

Collaborators Martin Kuitert, Marco Hemmerling, Aad Krom, Henri SNEM, Gianni Cito, Tanja Koch, Katrin Meyer, Stella Vesselinova, Igor Kebel, Olaf Gisper, Marco van Helden, Yuri Werner, Marc Prins.

Date of project 1999.

Final de obra 2004.

Completion of work 23.000 m² Offices / 15.000 m². Parking.

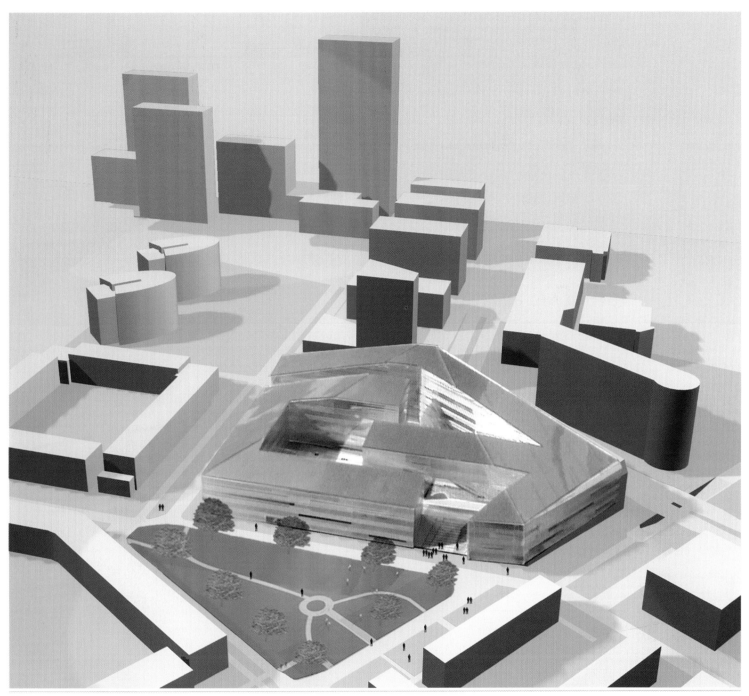

Virtual model of the location of the office complex in the urban context.

An enormous office complex stands forcibly on a large defined urban site in the important business center of Almere, in Holland. This macro-building has to unify the offices of important business groups, and therefore the objective is to address in a precise form the complicated logistics of internal functioning, of workplaces, parking areas, circulation areas, visitor access and a great flexibility towards the adaptability of the continuous changes of the businesses it includes.

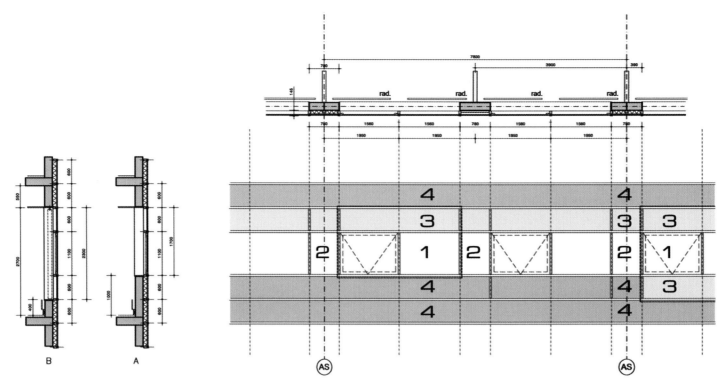

The façades are defined as a strict modular framework of aluminum carpentry and panes of glass.

General sections of the offices. Relation between the built volumes and the internal courts.

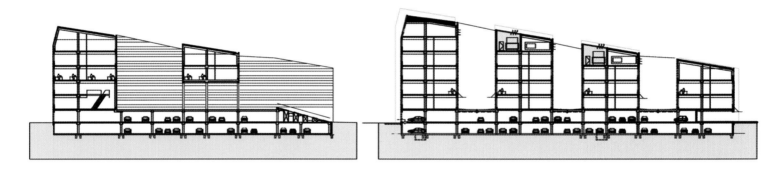

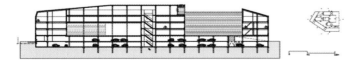

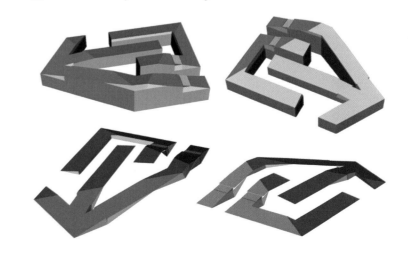

Volumetric study of the solar degree of direction of each facade.

The external formalization needs to offer a homogeneous and comprehensive image of a business complex, a powerful corporate image.

The treatment of the façades is consequently crucial to the project. The flexibility of internal distribution is projected into regular façades defined by a repetitive framework of modules. A correct formal solution, the product of careful study, and spectacularly surprising in the choice of materials in the finish.

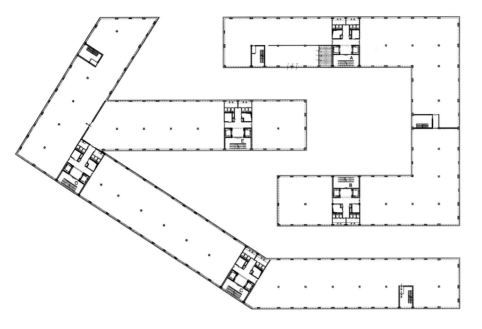

10

First floor. Diaphanous distributions interrupted by necessary communication nuclei.

Second floor. The macro-building begins to be graded, freeing the southern orientation.

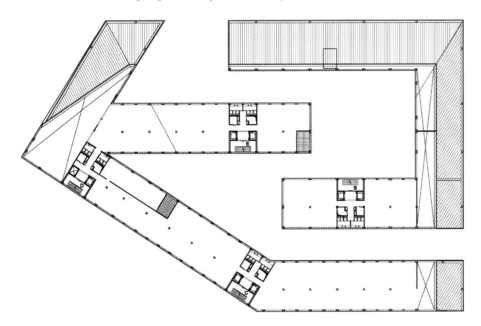

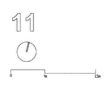

11

Virtual simulation of the play of sunlight according to day and hour.

The building presents itself as a glittering complex, its surfaces reflecting the immediate environment. The use of a curious system of panels of colored reflecting glass, in an iridescent range which varies according to the angle at which the light falls on it. The surface offers a striking assembly of reflections and colors which change continuously from the range of yellow tones to blue, from reds to greens passing through purple. In the volumetric definition, the analysis of the angle at which the sunlight falls, according to the season and the time of day, is one of the bases de-

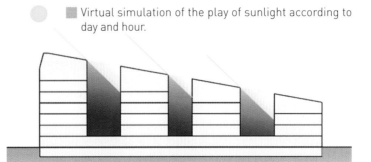

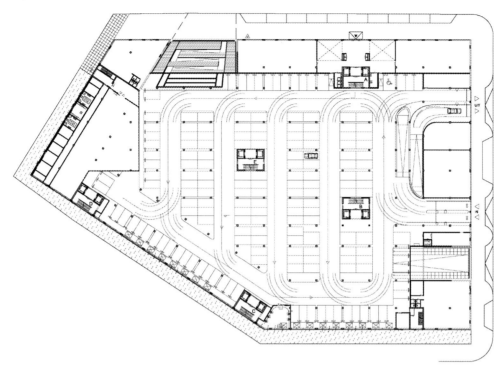

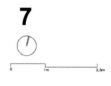

7

Basement story. A unified car-park occupying the entirety of the site.

Ground floor. The floors with multiple access alternate areas of building with areas of courtyard.

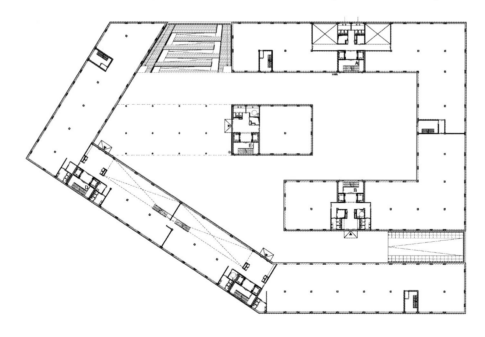

8

termining the height grading of the administrative building. This macro-building handles the 23,000 m² of offices and services by subdividing the premises into layers of height, showing a clear will to relate the parts to the outside space.

Internal courts are generated, empty spaces resulting from a plan in which the ranges partially invade the occupation of the site, freeing a partly-enclosed inner court. A courtyard with a fretwork shape, which leads us through the interior towards the multiple

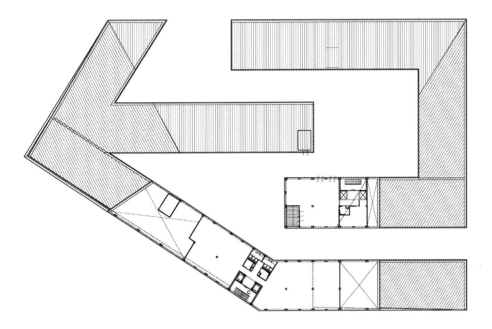

█ Third floor. Vertical means of circulation are interrupted in the same proportion as the offices.

█ Fourth floor. The roofing levels are made variable by means of folds.

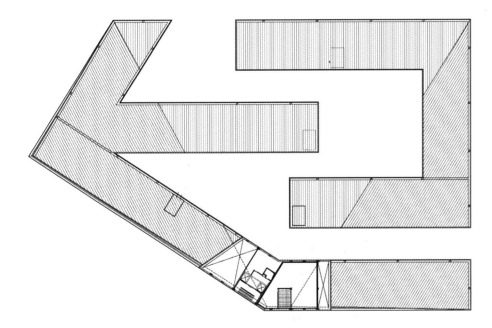

entrances and creates a new route between the city and the existing park. The car-park story of 15,000 m2 occupies the entirety of the site at basement level, unifying all the access points of the different wings in which the firms and businesses are distributed.

The large number of entry-points underlines the accessibility and flexibility in the complex functioning of the business building, also securing the needs for evacuation and sectorization of the areas.

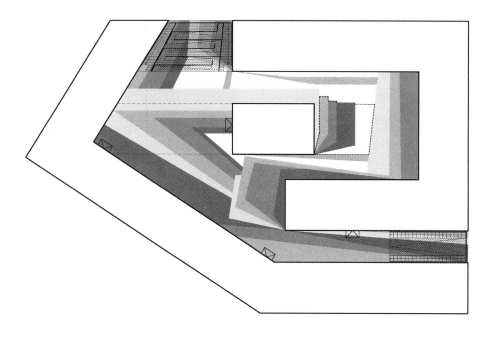

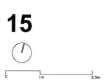

15

▨ Roof level. The play of sunlight reflections is taken into account in the finish.

▨ The angle at which the sunlight falls creates a play of multicolored reflections.

The density grading of the planning according to height simplifies the constructional complexity of the building, a feature which results in a favorable relation of end value per square meter built, thus making this corporate center affordable to a greater number of businesses and the participation of local bodies in the financing of the project. The neutral layout of the building minimizes its occupation according to height, up to the irregular roofing level, expressed in a finish of aluminum panels which contribute to the total

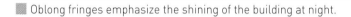
Aerial view of the working model simulating the final materials

Oblong fringes emphasize the shining of the building at night.

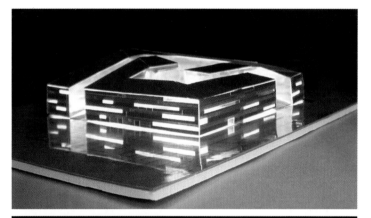

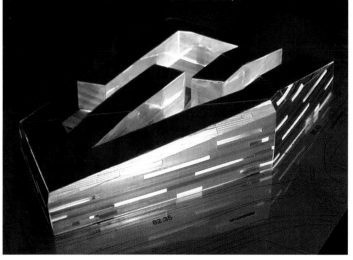

glittering appearance. At night, the play of reflections is activated again by the arrangement of linear openings in the façade, distributed in an alternating pattern which creates a dance of multicolored reflections, now under the impact of artificial light.

"living_tomorrow"
(pavilion_Amsterdam)

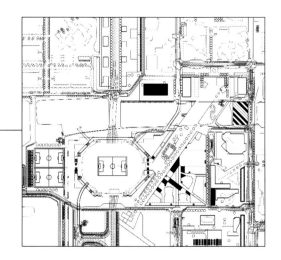

TECHNICAL DATA

Location Amsterdam South-Axis, near the Arena Stadium, Holland.
Architects Ben van Berkel.
Collaborators Igor Kebel, Aad Krom, Martin Kuitert, Markus Berger, Ron Roos, Andreas Bogenschütz.
Supervision of works Werner Claes, Bart Thijs.
Date of project 2000-2003.
Building area 4000 m².

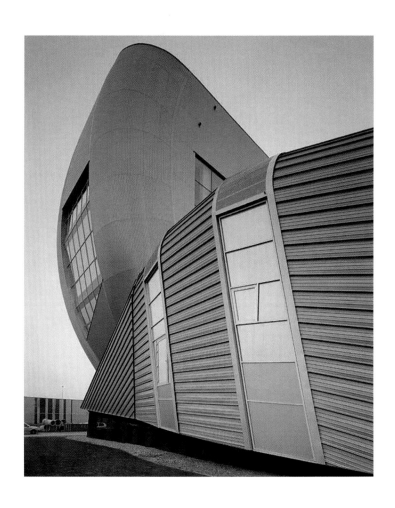

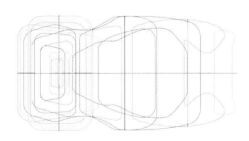
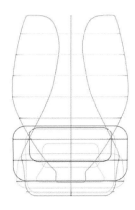
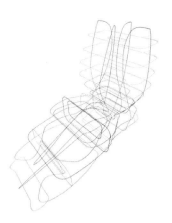

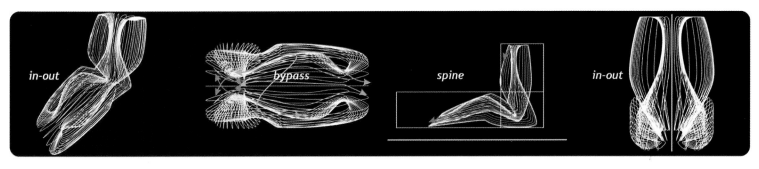

in-out   bypass   spine   in-out

■ Study of three-dimensional modeling.

■ Volumetric rendering of the project.

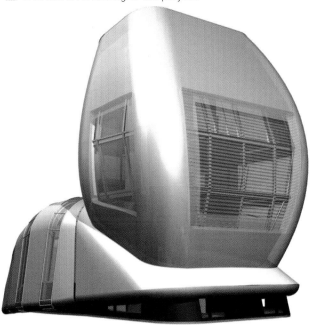
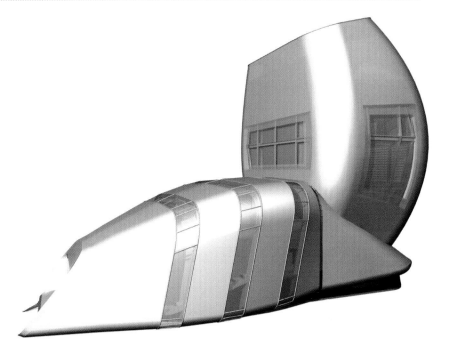

The building materializes a show-room, a pavilion for the exhibition of products and prototypes housing two temporary exhibitions, "The house of the future" and "The office of the future", where the visitor has the opportunity to travel in time to enjoy the technological advances and innovative concepts that will become part of our lives within about the next 5 years.

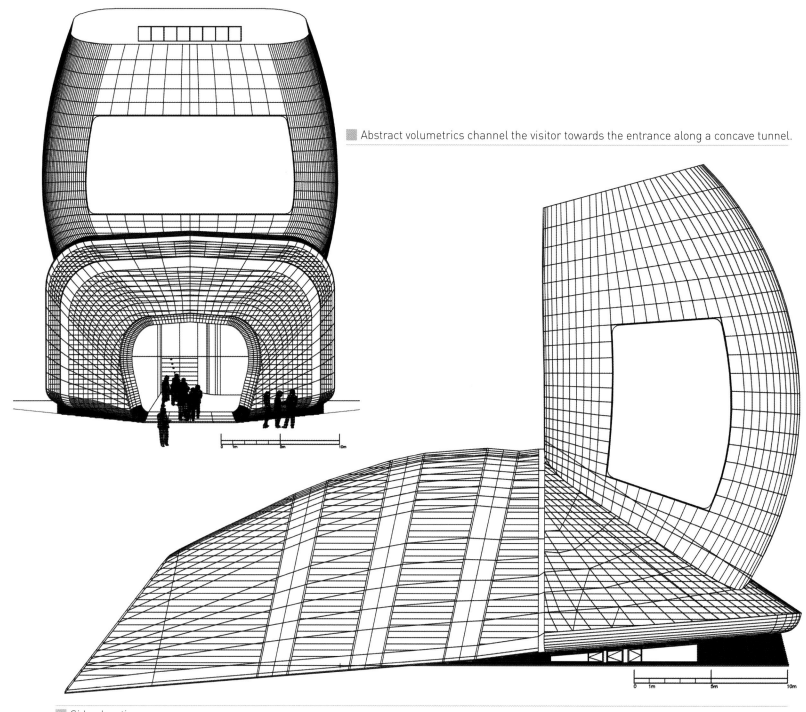

Abstract volumetrics channel the visitor towards the entrance along a concave tunnel.

Side elevation.

The building is a great machine, a dynamic entity designed virtually through the use of the most advanced technology. The result is strongly innovative: a soft shape which is generated by the rotation of an assembly of curved, irregular directions turning around an axis. From the study of three-dimensional movement emerges a body formed by a spatial mesh, which becomes the milestone of a more complex, faster-moving and computerized future society. The complex process of virtual materialization determines an organic, almost anthropomorphic shape of continuous surfaces. There is no break, and the discontinuity of the access is

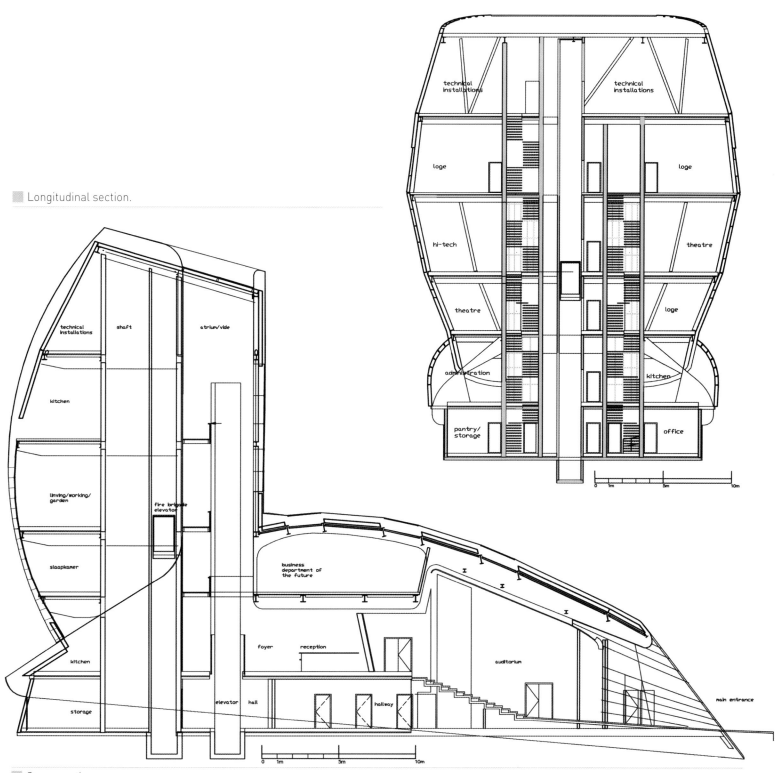

technical installations

technical installations

loge

loge

hi-tech

theatre

theatre

loge

administration

kitchen

pantry/ storage

office

0 1m   5m   10m

technical installations

shaft

atrium/vide

kitchen

living/working/ garden

fire brigade elevator

slaapkamer

business department of the future

kitchen

foyer

reception

auditorium

elevator hall

hallway

storage

main entrance

0 1m   5m   10m

Cross section.

expressed in a point of inflexion in which the visitor is absorbed by a fluid trajectory of soft shapes.

The façade of metal sheeting and glass keeps up the concept of futuristic curves in which the interior and the exterior form a single continuous skin which folds in space, a Moebius strip along which one can travel infinitely. Inside, the organism of futuristic curves breaks up into autonomous service spaces such as the reception, the staircases and the access elevators and the showrooms. The internal layout receives in its 3500 m^2 the exhibition of innovative products of major companies and business groups specializing in

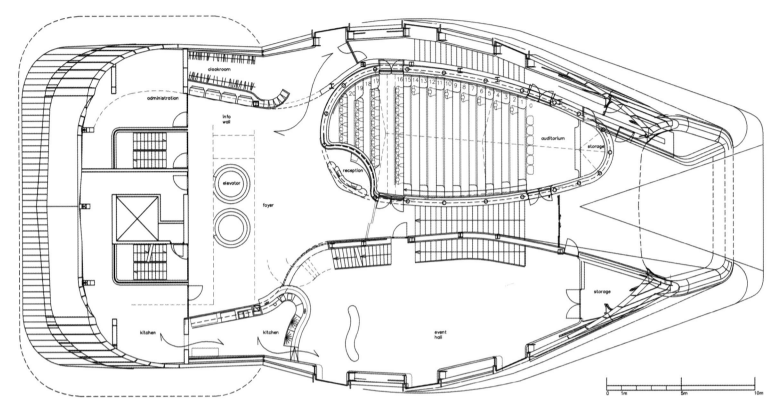

■ Ground floor of the Pavilion "Living Tomorrow".

■ The curved shapes of the pavilion are handled with recyclable materials.

IT and technological development such as HP, Microsoft, Telfort, Philips and Unilever.

The pavilion includes all the customary features. The functioning exhibition areas, symbolically located in the 33-meter tower, are supported by a large "foyer"-type lobby, an auditorium and a restaurant which complement the public uses and various internal administration offices.

The experimental work defined by complex computer calculations bears fruit in a stimulating formal result. The building aims at being a prototype for the future, in addition to the ones exhibited within it. The architect, the city and the individual by necessity or by the use of their imagination define "the shape of the future".

The curious project of the pavilion "Living Tomorrow" raises new questions and reflections; an intelligent excuse to initiate debates on the definition of the term "future". Its design clearly incorporates the guidelines for action in the immediate future of a society in the process of globalization, which shows its concern for

sustainable development and a growing respect for the environment. It incorporates the principle of eco-sustainable design, using a power-system of solar panels, a water conservation system and a temperature-control system which extracts surplus warmth from one room and transmits it to another. Overall, the materials used are recyclable and with a high environment-friendly factor.

cap_sabadell

EMBA.
MASSIP-BOSCH
ARQUITECTES

Emba. Massip-Bosch Arquitectes is a Barcelona based architectural studio that was set up by Enric Massip-Bosch in 1991. The philosophy with which the firm was established, freedom in its approaches towards its projects, has allowed it to develop its undertakings in a multidisciplinary way and to incorporate experiences and knowledge.

Their projects offer highly personalized integrated architectural services and urban planning. In these twelve years of activity, they have accumulated the experience necessary to be able to take on architectural work of great design and managerial complexity.

The studio base includes architects of various nationalities along with eventual specialized collaborators who enrich the results of its work.

Enric Massip has not only developed an outstanding career as an architect, but he has also acquired notable prestige for his the-

parliament_of_andorra

expo_aichi
2005

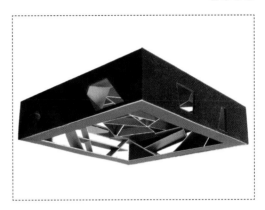

ory and academic practice: Lecturer at the Escuela Técnica Superior de Arquitectura de Barcelona and Valencia, of the Master de Arquitectura y Crítica of the Universidad Politécnica de Barcelona and visiting lecturer in the Polytechnics of Milan, Amsterdam, Venice and Tokyo.

The theoretic work of Enric Massip has been published in specialized books and magazines as well as being presented in seminars and conferences.

The cataloging of their designs can be subdivided into three large areas of study: sustainability and the environment, functional requirements and heritage and urban intervention.

The theoretic work carried out on the subject of the home, the new technologies and accessibility complete the line of work that has been formalized in a technically adequate and constructively rigorous way.

1st prize	Prizewinning Projects.
2004	Spanish Pavilion in the Expo of Japan.
2004	Extension and refurbishing of Sants Station (Barcelona).
2003	Remodeling of Gambetta Square, Carcasonne (France).
2003	Mixed-use building (market, offices, residences) in Sant Cugat (Barcelona).
2002	Central bus station and annexed car park building in Sant Feliu de Guíxols.
2002	Retail center and 92 residences in Montcada i Reixach (Barcelona).
2001	29 residences for IMPSOL in Tiana.
2001	CAP of Sabadell.
2000	Hotel Plaça Forum 2004 in Barcelona.
1997	University building for the UPC. Manresa.
1996	Remodeling Plaza Inmaculada. Manresa.

cap_sabadell

TECHNICAL DATA	
Location	Sabadell (Barcelona).
Architect	Enric Massip-Bosch.
Client	Servei Català de la Salut, Generalitat of Catalonia.
Colaboradores	*Structure:* Manel Fernández. *Installations:* Joan González. *Building engineer:* Xavier Aumedes. Marc Rifá, Vera Schmidt, Architects. Arantxa Manrique, architectural student.
Project date	2001.
Completion date	2004.
Built area	1351 m².

CARRER SABONERIA

PLAÇA DE CASTELAO

▓ The ground floor entrance frees as much space as possible and participates in the plaza.

Sited next to other installations used for municipal services, it was decided that this new building would be aligned to the east and, in this way, contribute to defining the northern façade of the square in which it is located. Along the same lines, the scale of the new CAP and that of the existing service building were to be of the same order. The result is a two-story building with a ground floor that offers an elongation of the exterior space.

The two floors of the building correspond to two differentiated parts of the program of uses.

On the lower floor, we find the entrance and the program for the administration and building maintenance. These spaces are illuminated by light wells. The entrance to the building has been conceived in such a way as to integrate the entrance hall with the exterior, the square enters the building.

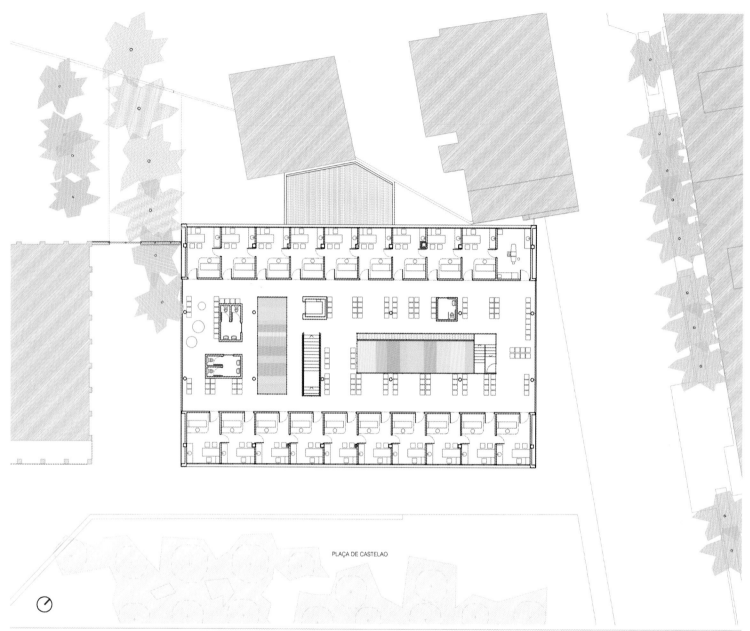

PLAÇA DE CASTELAO

First floor. The waiting room occupies a space surrounded by the consulting booths.

In the upper part, all of the consulting and waiting areas are grouped in a unique space in a systematic way. This facilitates the differentiation of zones that respond to different medical specialties. The waiting room is fragmented by the interruptions provoked by the patios for illumination and ventilation for the lower floor. The transparency of the interior patios allows for an overall perception of the area and helps users orientate themselves. The general sensation is one of a certain well being which is achieved by this open fluid space in which light plays an important role. The screens uniform the hollows and allow for a rational use of light to

The perception from the interior is that of a comfortable space in which light takes on a leading role.

be made as well as resolving the privacy of the consulting booths. The design has been cataloged within the group of works that base their principal objective on the resolution of the functional requirements of a specific program. A typological solution for a health clinic in which neutrality by definition in the finishes and details, a simplicity in volumes with a precise constructive resolution that does not corrupt the priority of fulfilling the function and optimizing its spaces has been chosen.

The entrance materializes as a link between the new and the existent.

The form of the exterior offers a play on a set of simple volumes that have been treated with great subtlety. The hollows in the siding and the siding itself have been ordered in a modular and repetitive way. The constructive technique is organized and clear. It makes the superfluous obvious and the priority in the programmatic resolution evident. In addition, it groups the elements in a clean way, in large hollows that are unified in the façade in a coherent and, above all, functional form.

■ The northern façade of the plaza is organized along the existing line.

■ The light wells establish the program on each level.

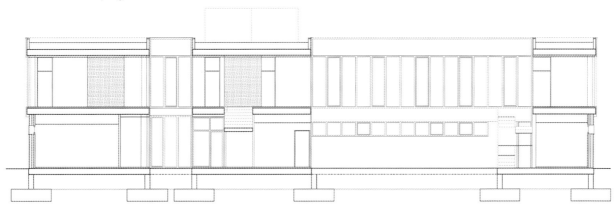

The siting of the building frees a large amount of public exterior space that maximizes the volumetric perception of the construction.

A peripheral plaza resolves the constant flow of movement with the arrangement of itineraries that consolidate a constant dialogue with the urban surroundings.

parliament
of_Andorra

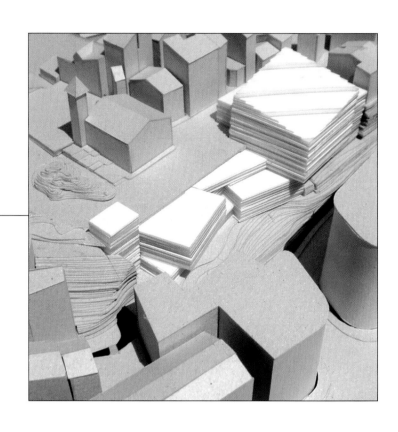

TECHNICAL DATA

Location Andorra La Vella.
Architect Enric Massip-Bosch.
Client Síndic Gral. (Government of Andorra).
Collaborators Aleix Antillach, Sanja Belli, Marc Rifà, Minoru Suzuki, architects.
Per Mejer Johansen, architectural student.
Project date 2002.
Completion date 2002.
Built area 1101 m².

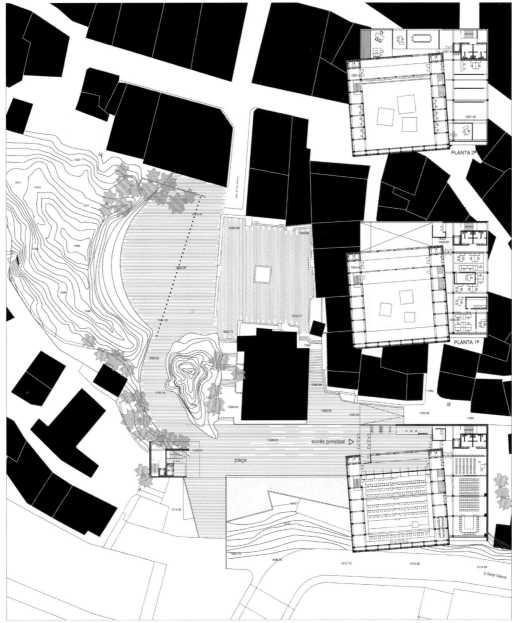

Location of the new complex showing how it fits into the existing urban surroundings.

The design for the General Council of Andorra building is cataloged along with the group of designs that act over preexisting urban conditions. Accordingly, its design is that of a building that intends to be an open balcony onto the landscape and the valley on a complex plot over a cliff partially colonized by the intervention of man.

The concept is that of a building with a solid base that integrates into the silhouette of the mountain along with volumes in the rock of its same proportion and which marks its presence by means of the inclusion of a volume of a great height, the Parliament building which rises in a symbolic way as a landmark in the complex. The resulting plaza that lies among the volumes that make up the Council building constitutes a space formed by existing and new buildings.

The dimensions of this plaza define a public space superior in continuity than that existing over the Government building.

A new access is assured from the lower level by means of a public system of vertical communication.

The proposal to change the planned route for the entrance of vehicles to the area behind the mountain in order to conserve the continuity of the plaza has been carried out and this has created a new public space of greater dimensions.

Cross section through the volumes of the Council Building.

Cross section through the Parliament Chambers.

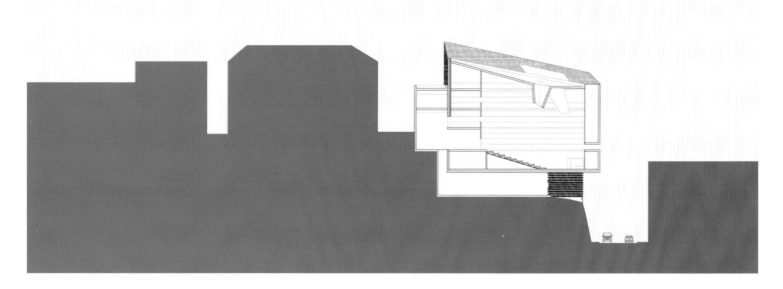

With the intention of integrating the complex into the landscape, a group of volumes that mix in amongst themselves and with the wall of rock have been proposed. Longer visuals have been sought that avoid a continual façade and that make the most of the different parts of the program in order to define variations in height and position. Due to its form, position and dimension, the council's meeting room materializes the symbolic value of the complex.

The other elements are strategically situated to achieve a continuity of the urban scale which is more domestic that the immediate surroundings. The materials and roof forms of the old building called the Casa de la Vall have been recovered in order to define the materials and shape of the new project. It therefore consists of a slate cube with a pitched roof, also covered in slate which is also used in the rest of the buildings in a double façade as a material to offer protection from the sun.

Interior of the meeting room.

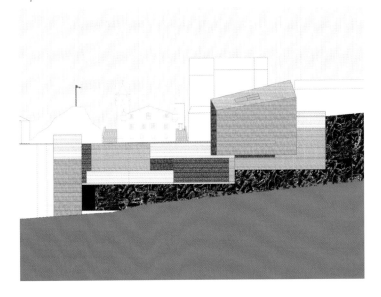
Elevation of the volumetric group.

The interior of the chambers is an uncluttered space of great dimensions that breaks its purity of form by means of the powerful intersection of a large skylight made up of three "cannons" that direct light towards the interior.

The overall perception is that of a static auditorium that includes the chambers, the public gallery and the press gallery. Everything becomes united by the subtle warm unifying wooden paneling which creates a stately aspect all of which is flooded by natural light.

expo_aichi
2005

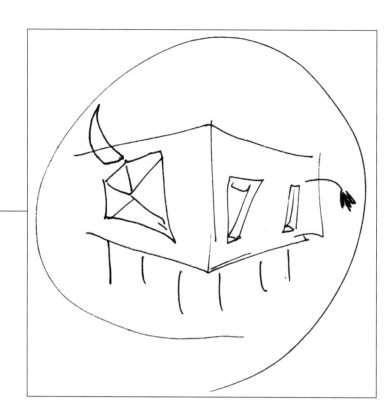

TECHNICAL DATA

Location Aichi, Japan.

Architects Enric Massip-Bosch – emba, arquitectos.

Client SEEI - National Society for International Expositions.

Collaborators *Scriptwriter and press agent:* Jesús
Alvira.
Architects: Hug Alemany, Minoru Su-
zuki, Marta Budó.
Graphics and 3D modeling: Rupert
Maurus. *Photograpy:* Pau Guerrero.

Project date 2004.

Built area 1850 m².

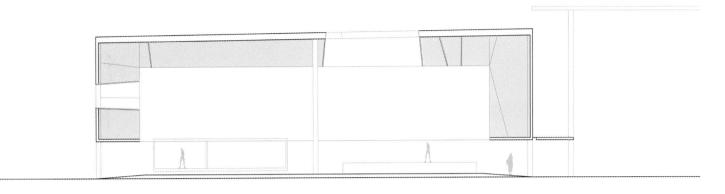

Cross section.

Longitudinal section.

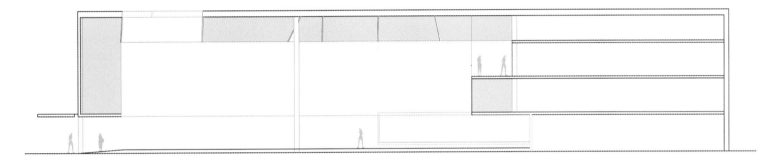

Volumetric scale model.

The proposal for the Spanish pavilion in the universal exhibition in Aichi, Japan is based on the idea of an archetype plaza as a meeting point, a place of experiences, exchange and information, a place where a different experience to those found in the other spaces of the Expo can be found.

The building is situated in a space defined by the organization and materializes in a volume of a square form which is raised from the plane of the ground by slender supports which create a completely open ground floor. A covered plaza where life and ac- tivity is carried on. The entrance porch marks the routes for pedestrian transit and invites the visitors to enter the confines of the pavilion.

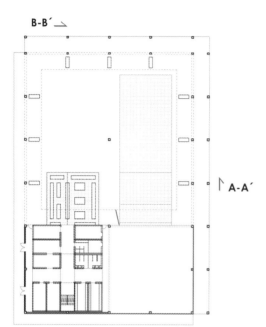
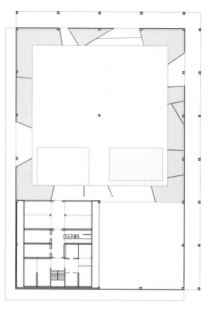
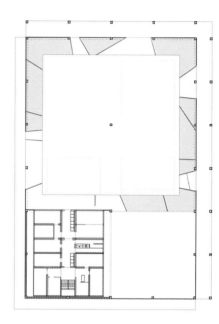

■ The interior square unifies the activity that takes place in it.

■ Interior perspective. Play on materials, light and color.

In the interior the essence of Spain is displayed. The visitor is immersed in a dynamic space which is exceptional, a large-scale festival in the principal square of a town.

The explosion of forms, colors and textures torment, create undefined flows, a large place for exchanges of experiences unified by a panel of irregular cells that make up a large three dimensional screen. This panel has been made up of pressed paper planes in gold and blood red over which images are partially projected. It is the living reflection of a direct reference to the most traditional forms of Spanish art and architecture.

Artistry is felt, coffered ceilings Mozarabic filigrees, modernist mosaics, screens, wrought iron work... all conceptually blended together in a play ins and outs, light and shade, colors and textures.

▨ Detail of the large screen covered with paper panels in gold and blood red.

▨ Volumetric scale model that features the black skin of the exterior siding.

The exterior volume is perceived as a clean silhouette, a tumbler of brilliant colors, a skin of black plastic filament that rises symbolizing the national icon of the bull... a majestic threatening bull that invites participation in the great festival that is going on in the interior.

One of the objects of the proposal is that of clearly using in its materialization the sustainable concept of the 3Rs (Reduce, Reuse, Recycle), in such a way that a small number of elements are used and those that are used are reusable or recyclable, an important aspect of the Expo of d'Aichi. Consequently, few elements have been used and those used are reusable or recyclable in the same way as the constructions where the restaurant, kitchen and offices have been located are rented or can be unassembled.

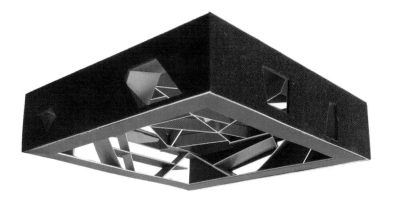

EXPOSURE|
ARCHITECTS|

Oliviero Godi and Dorit Mizrahi were the founders of this architectural studio in 1997, with its office in Bergamo, near Milan (Italy). The two of them have a similar academic background, New York and Milan, a professional career which includes work in the United States, Great Britain, Spain, Israel and Japan, carrying out projects of very diverse complexity and type: design of interiors, industrial design, residential design, large-scale service buildings... Their record is notable for their participation in the technical team of well-established professional offices such as Pierce & Allen in New York, Zaha Hadid in London and the Obayashi Co. Center of Technical Research in Japan.

This experience accumulated all over the world caused them to define themselves as "exposure architects" when they came to establish their own office. Exposing by offering the tools before the answers, asking for the involvement of the user taking part in the project and not as a mere observer.

octospider

The beginning of their projects starts from an exhaustive analysis of their historical, social and natural context. The final result must be a work coherent with the facilities requested, but it also needs to meet the necessary conditions to be considered an integrated space at every level. The participation of the user in the program is also basic, without forcing situations but seeking an interaction, an active participation that will make a dynamic language possible.

Their architecture is conscious of a role in creating spaces, available for the use it has been designed for, without forgetting flexibility of arrangement; the space at the end of the day is defined by the user himself. "the right thing is for many users to act proactively and dynamically in the project." The end project brings together forms that have been studied, taken apart and reconstructed as many times as was necessary, until the optimum distribution of space has been reached.

First	prizes winner.
1998	Ponte dei Mulini / Comune di Mantova Exposure Architects.
1997	Student complex for Pratt Institute NY. Pasanella+Klein Stolzman+Berg NY.
1997	Best Young architect in the USA Arx studio NY.
1997	Greenport waterfront Arx studio NY.
1996	Zal Barcelona 1995 Arx studio NY.
1995	Spittlemarkt - Berlin Office of Zaha Hadid.

The materials specified need to bring out and support aesthetically the conceptual base of the project. Forms and materials come together for the objectives to be achieved.

octospider

(Workers' cafeteria and
restaurant)

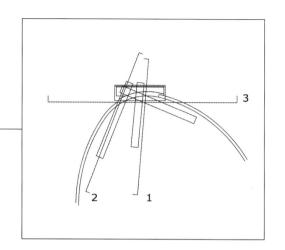

TECHNICAL DATA

Location Klongsarn, Bangkok, Thailand.
Architects Dorit Mizrahi & Oliviero Godi.
Client Mr. Schle Word. Satin Textile, Co.
Collaborators Takeshi Sato, Valter Gilberto.
Consulting firms Structural Engineering: Eng. Marco Verdina. Local architect: Mhun Srire-untong. Civil Tech Design and Consul-tants Co, Ltd.
Works supervision Sita Karnkriangkrai.
Mr. Sita Karnkriangkrai.
Atis Build Co., Ltd. Bangkok-Thailand
Date of project 2000-2001.
Completion of work 2003.

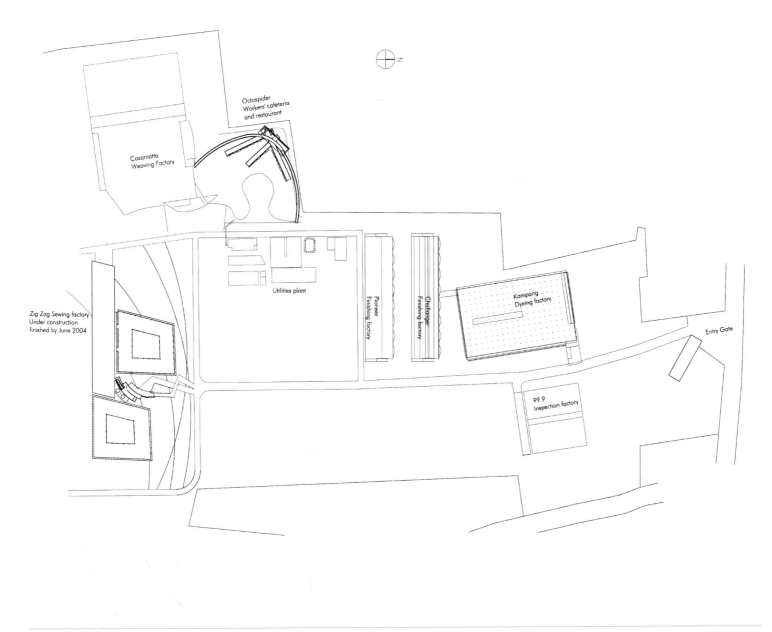

Octospider
Workers' cafeteria
and restaurant

Casamatta
Weaving Factory

Zig Zag Sewing factory
Under construction
finished by June 2004

Utilities plant

Pioneer
Finishing factory

Challenger
Finishing factory

Kampang
Dyeing factory

Entry Gate

99.9
Inspection factory

▨ The location of the building blends into the industrial estate..

Octospider, as its name suggests, is a magnificent observatory, a facility which serves a strictly functional and necessary purpose, providing a restaurant-cafeteria which will offer its services mainly to the workers in a textile industrial estate in their rest hours. The concept of the project aims at reclaiming a certain quality of life for the social act of eating, especially bearing in mind that this is an hour of rest, of switching-off for the customers, who lack the time to leave the workplace-context.

The building stands half-way between the factory and the production buildings, in the middle of an existing lake.

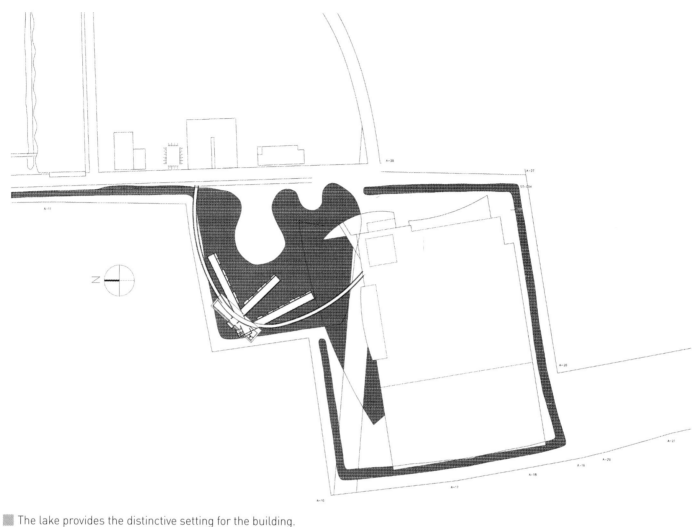

■ The lake provides the distinctive setting for the building.

The building floats upon the lake, raised on slim circular supports which suggest natural elements. They are like a plantation of slim bulrushes which hold up simple boxes in the air. The complex assumes a majestic air, rising eight meters above ground level and thus assuring outstanding views over the distant landscape, while simultaneously sketching between its supports the more immediate decor of the adjacent textile factory. The shape of its ground-plan, of great simplicity, is made up of three straight bars radiating from a single point, resting on a lake-dwelling type of structure of slim concrete cylinders. The angular curve of the ramp contrasts with the lightness and regularity of the prisms which contain the working area.

The 3 dining-rooms are articulated from a single point, stretching out over the lake.

The access to the building is a ceremonial pedestrian way. A footbridge which marks a well-defined shape, a long curving trajectory rising above the lake and drawing us progressively deeper into the complex. This suggestive route implies entry into a world of well-marked identity removed from the context of its immediate environment.

At its highest point, a simple, narrow volume meets at a tangent the curve of the ramp and welcomes the visitor. This is the main nucleus containing the kitchen services, the food-handling area and the self-service counter.

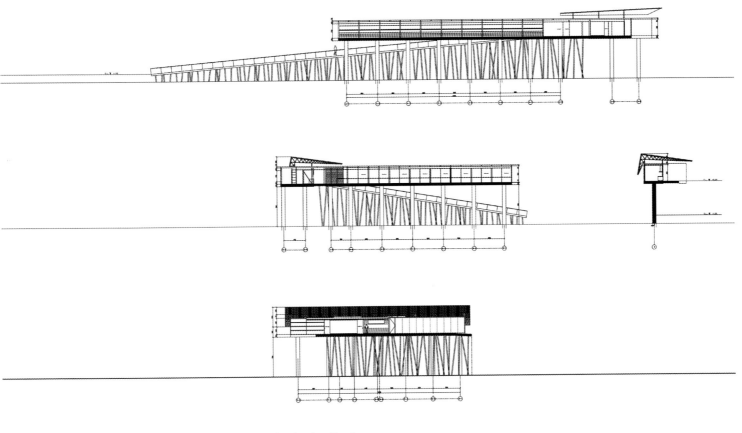

■ General sections. The prisms are articulated from the food-collection area.

■ West and South elevations. The dining-rooms rise to the topmost contour.

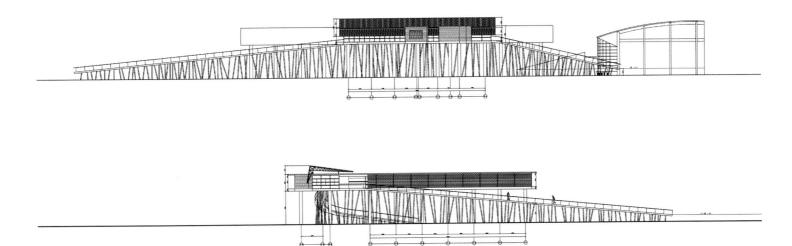

The customer collects his meal and heads for the eating area, expressed as three slim prisms which, articulated from the collection point, stretch over the lake in the manner of three jetties, standing on cylindrical reinforced-concrete supports like the main prism itself.

The dining-rooms, eight meters above ground level, convey a pleasing sense of isolation and of exceptional contact with nature. The approach ramp continues through the main volume, which completes its trajectory serving as an entry-exit to the complex and return journey to work.

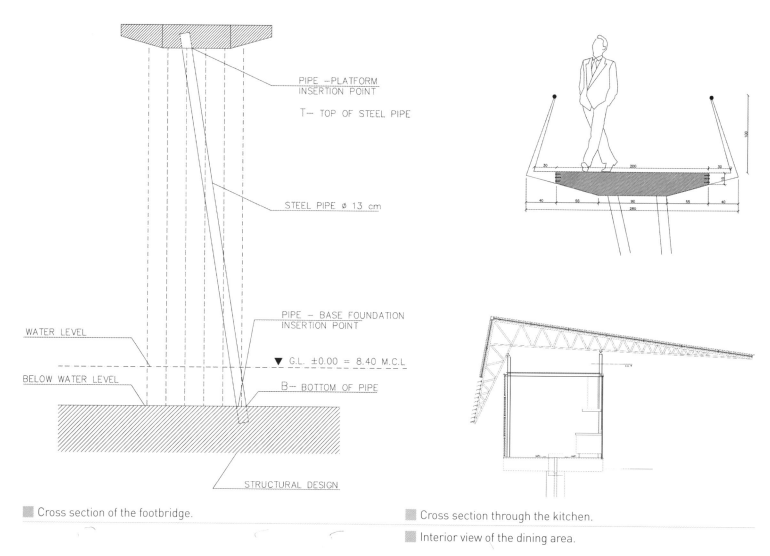

PIPE —PLATFORM
INSERTION POINT

T— TOP OF STEEL PIPE

STEEL PIPE Ø 13 cm

WATER LEVEL

PIPE — BASE FOUNDATION
INSERTION POINT

▼ G.L. ±0.00 = 8.40 M.C.L

BELOW WATER LEVEL

B— BOTTOM OF PIPE

STRUCTURAL DESIGN

▨ Cross section of the footbridge.

▨ Cross section through the kitchen.

▨ Interior view of the dining area.

Each of the dining-rooms is subdivided into independent booths, partitioned by thin wooden panels to form private areas for 6 diners.

The construction of the walls is handled differently from the main volume. The location of the building over water is an effective solution to the refrigeration of the area in the climate of Bangkok. The façades, made up of panels whose orientation can be changed, enable the interior to be protected from sun and rain, and at the same time let the air through to allow ventilation.

The ceiling design is based on simple fretted aluminum sandwich panels and internal thermal isolation.

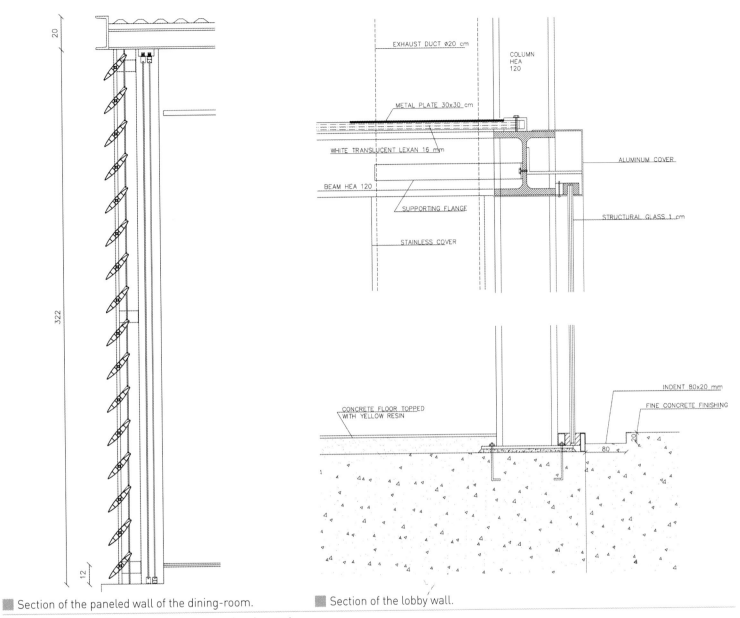

EXHAUST DUCT Ø20 cm

COLUMN HEA 120

METAL PLATE 30x30 cm

WHITE TRANSLUCENT LEXAN 16 mm

ALUMINUM COVER

BEAM HEA 120

SUPPORTING FLANGE

STRUCTURAL GLASS 1 cm

STAINLESS COVER

INDENT 80x20 mm

FINE CONCRETE FINISHING

CONCRETE FLOOR TOPPED WITH YELLOW RESIN

80

20

Section of the paneled wall of the dining-room.

Section of the lobby wall.

Detail of the panels whose orientation can be changed.

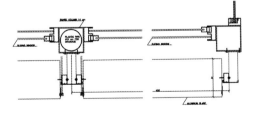

The kitchen block has a double enclosing skin on the roof. A triangular metal structure serves the outer skin, and the inner one takes the form of a translucent honeycombed polycarbonate envelope which filters light, so that a spectacular sight is given of the building lit up at night.

The project achieves its purpose, which is not purely functional. The worker receives a small prize, a reward for his daily work and effort. A small distant oasis isolates him from his routine for a little while, open to fascinating views to enjoy while eating and chatting.

gürtel_boulevard

SILJA TILLNER
ARCHITECT

Silja Tillner (1960) studied at the University of Technology of Vienna and in the Academy of Fine Arts. She also undertook a postgraduate course in town planning in the University of UCLA (Los Angeles).

In 1995, she set up her studio in Vienna.

Her work, in which she combines the strictest of architectural experience with sociological, geographical, cultural and political studies, is centered on, above all, complex urbanistic actions and in the implantation of new buildings in historical contexts.

retractable_cover

edificio de oficinas "skyline"

She was responsible for the revitalization of the zone of Gürtel Urbion for which she was awarded the Bauhaus Prize in 2000.

She has also been awarded the IFAI (International Fabric Association) Prize and the 'ar+d' (architecture and design) prize for the project of the retractable membrane of the City Hall of Vienna.

She has participated in numerous conferences in Vienna, Zurich and Bern as well as in the Texas University of Austin, in the Ecole d'Architecture of Nancy and in the Center of Architecture in Strasburg.

First	prize in the following competitions.
2001	'Office complex Senngasse', Vienna.
2002	'Office complex Spittelau', Vienna.
2003	'Head office ÖGB', Vienna.

She has been a visiting lecturer at the Ecole d' Architecture in Nancy and she presently gives classes in town planning at the Technical University of Innsbruck, as a visiting lecturer.

gürtel-urbion
(revitalization of gürtel boulevard)

TECHNICAL DATA
Location Vienna.
Architect Silja Tillner.
Client MA 19, MA 21A.
Collaborators Hannes Achammer, Christopher Lottersberger, Beate Lubitz, Bernhard Anderl, Martin Ritter.
Project date 1998.

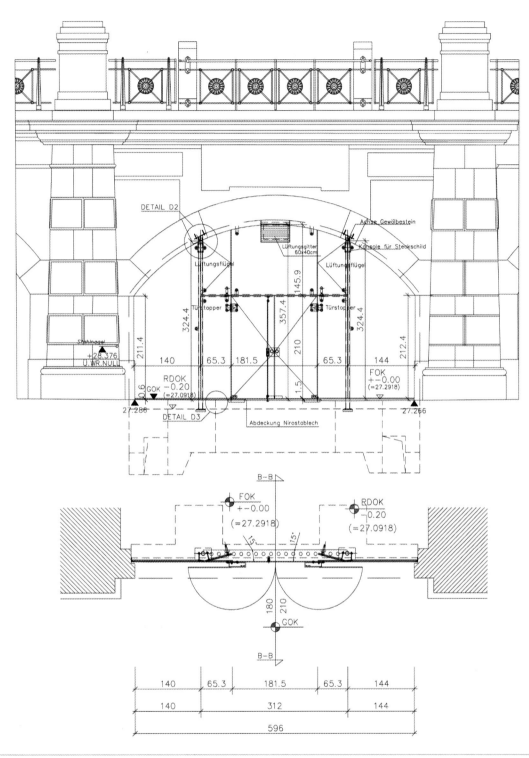

DETAIL D2
Achse Gewölbestein
Lüftungsgitter 60x40cm
Konsole für Steckschild
Lüftungsflügel
Lüftungsflügel
Türstopper
Türstopper
Stahlnagel
+28.376
U.WR.NULL
RDOK -0.20
(=27.0918)
GOK -0.20
FOK +-0.00
(=27.2918)
DETAIL D3
Abdeckung Nirostoblech
27.286
27.266

B-B
FOK +-0.00 (=27.2918)
RDOK -0.20 (=27.0918)
GOK
B-B

145.9
324.4
357.4
324.4
211.4
212.4
140 65.3 181.5 210 65.3 144

180 210

140 65.3 181.5 65.3 144
140 312 144
596

Recuperation of the arches.

Gürtel makes up the backbone of an area that extends some six kilometers; it is the most important traffic artery in Vienna and it carries a volume of some 100,000 cars/day. It is also crossed by the railway line (nowadays a metro) installed by Otto Wagner in 1890. This sector is the object of a revitalization program developed in cooperation with the municipal administration of Vienna that proposes to resolve the unavoidable coexistence of public and vehicle spaces and seeks a change of image which is

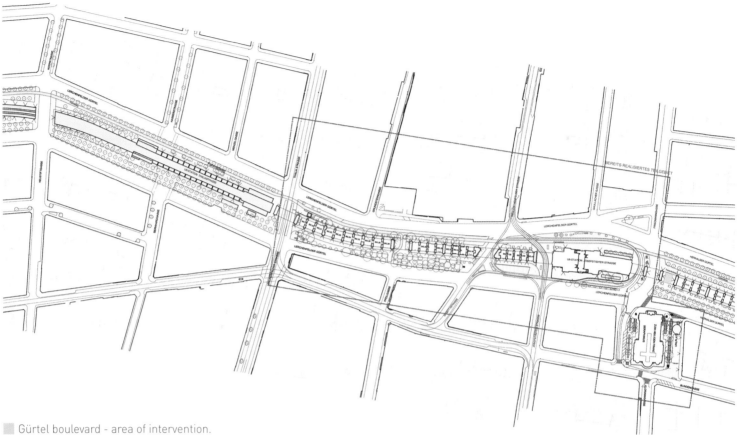

Gürtel boulevard - area of intervention.

Details of the enclosure section.

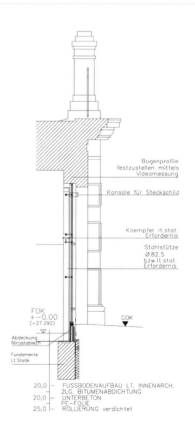

both lasting and respectful with the architectural inheritance. The intervention is centered on the improvement of, as much from an aesthetic as from a functional point of view, the intermediate strip of the Gürtel that reappears as a space for man and offers a great variety of services, retail premises, restaurants and bars thanks to the recovery of approximately 50 arches of the bridge.

■ Before and after the refurbishing of the arches.

In order to improve its transparency and increment visibility, a uniform glass enclosing has been chosen: a light steel and glass structure formed by two pillars situated below the keystones of the arch and a beam following the line of its base. A modular system for doors, windows and supports for signs gives the enclosed space the necessary flexibility for it to be adapted to the requirements of the different commercial activities that are carried out.

The illumination achieved by means of spotlights over each arch that reduce the visual and urbanistic impact to a minimum contribute to improving visibility and security in the area as well as emphasizing the architecture inherited from Otto Wagner.

retractable_cover

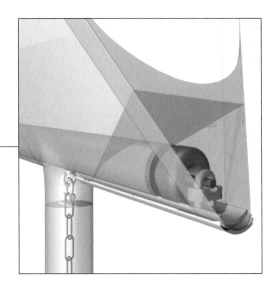

TECHNICAL DATA
Location Vienna.
Architects Silja Tillner.
Client MA 19, MA 23, City of Vienna.
Collaborators Rudolf Bergermann.
Structural eng. Schlaich Bergermann & Partner, Vasko & Partner.
Project date 2000.
Area 1000 m².

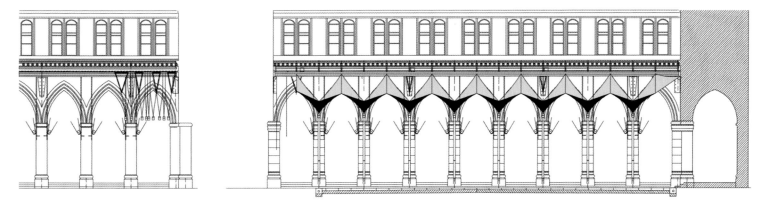

Longitudinal section.

Cross section.

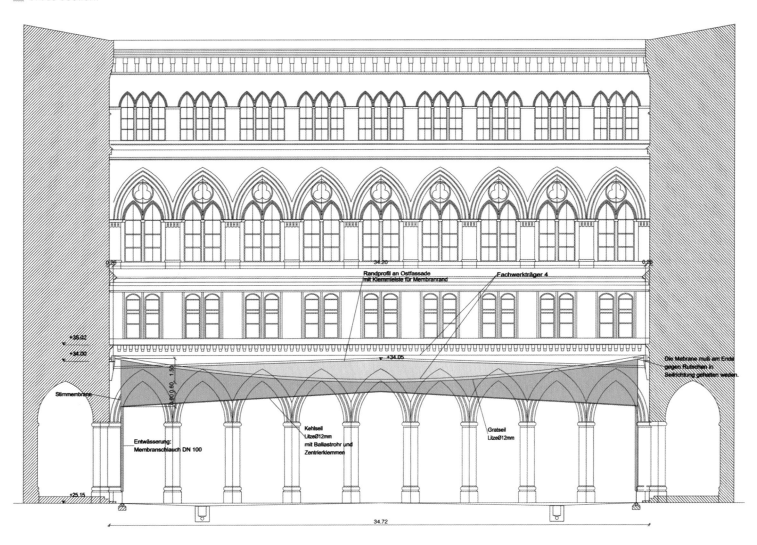

The project contemplates the installation of a retractable covering 34.2 x 32.5 m to cover the courtyard of the City Hall of Vienna and protect it from bad weather when used for the celebration of public and cultural activities. For this, a structure made up of a translucent retractable membrane of polyester is proposed. This would allow the courtyard to be partially or completely covered ac-

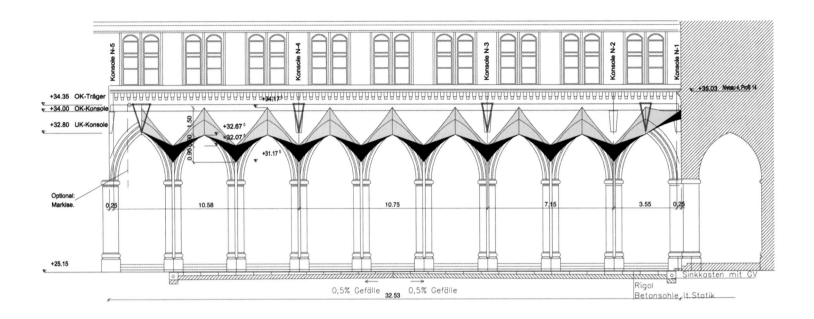

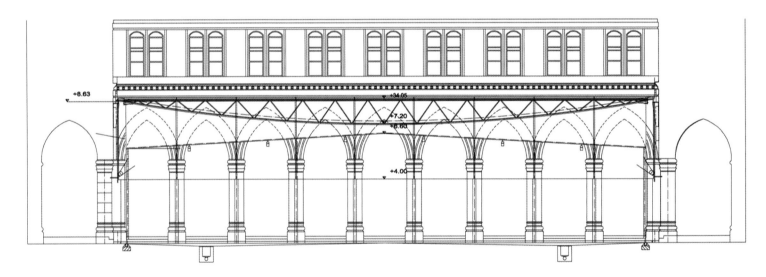

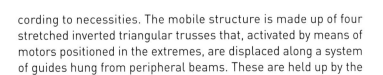
Longitudinal and cross sections.

cording to necessities. The mobile structure is made up of four stretched inverted triangular trusses that, activated by means of motors positioned in the extremes, are displaced along a system of guides hung from peripheral beams. These are held up by the

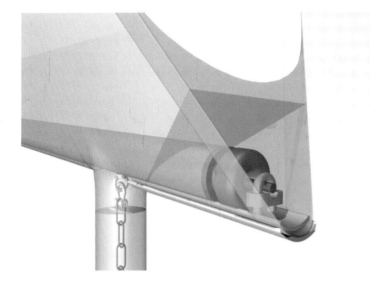
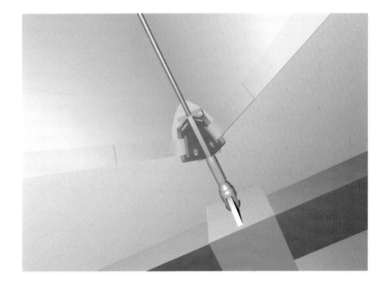
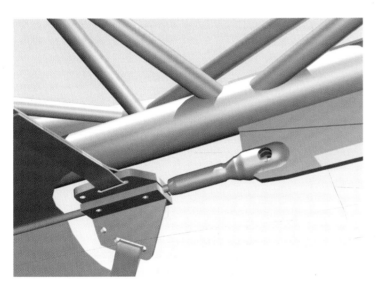

walls of the courtyard by means of supports that resist the horizontal strain on the stonewalls and only transmit the weight vertically. The membrane is kept tight in its upper parts by cables

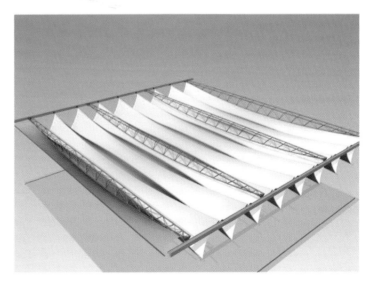

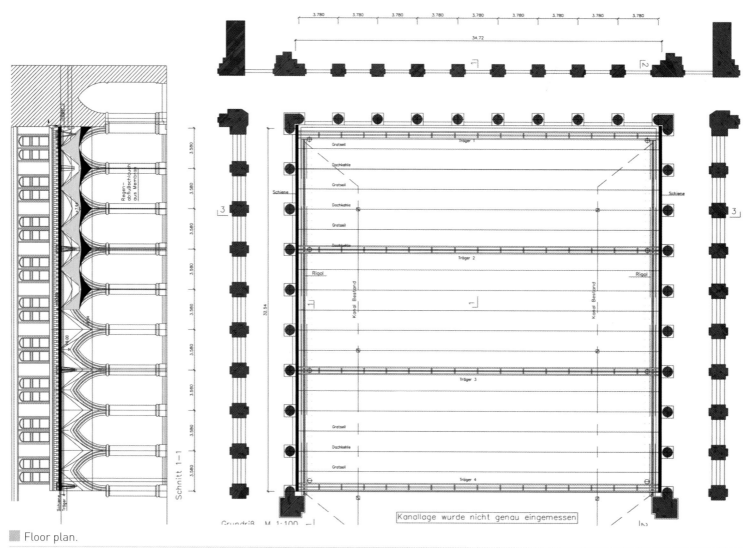

Floor plan.

The folds highlight the form of the arches.

Cover folded away.
Extension of the moveable cover.

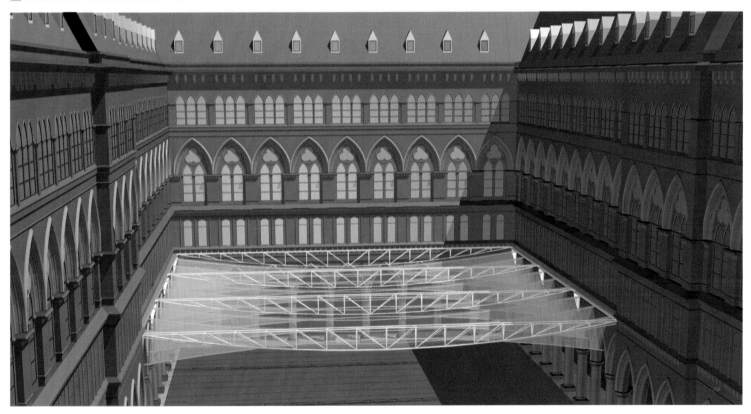

that hold it to the guides by means of moveable joints and in its lower part by chains that slide along the tubes used to drain rainwater. Due to the different heights between the cables, the folds of the cloth seem to highlight the form of the neo-Gothic arches of the courtyard and create an undulation that is acoustically most advantageous.

office_building
"skyline" (spittelau)

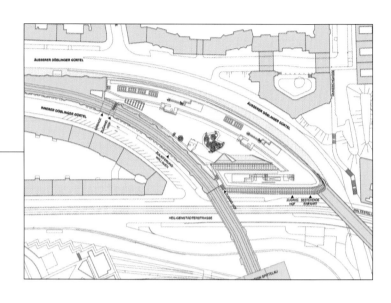

TECHNICAL DATA

Location Spittelau, Vienna.
Architect Silja Tillner.
Client Porr Immoprojekt.
Collaborators RAHM Architekten.
Structural eng. Werkraum Zt-OEG.
Competition date 2002.
Commencement date 2004.
Built area 3474 m².

The building that is found situated in the 'Gürtel Boulevard' intersection of the principal traffic routes in and out of the city. The intervention is contained within the overall framework of a general urban plan for the recuperation of the area which is a transition zone between the administrative center and a residential district.

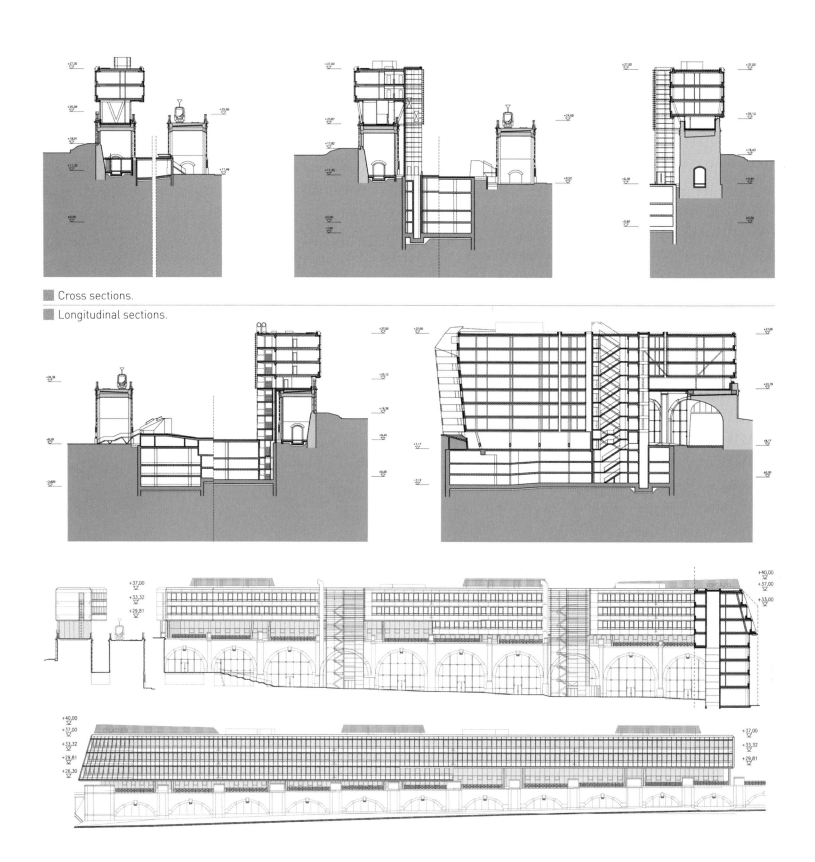

Cross sections.

Longitudinal sections.

The project consists of a superstructure of a curved form which, situated over a section of an abandoned railway line, follows the tracks and integrates into the existing structure of the bridge. This takes on a new meaning and acts as a support for a new volume conceived as an element of transition that connects the two neighborhoods separated by the stretch of tracks.

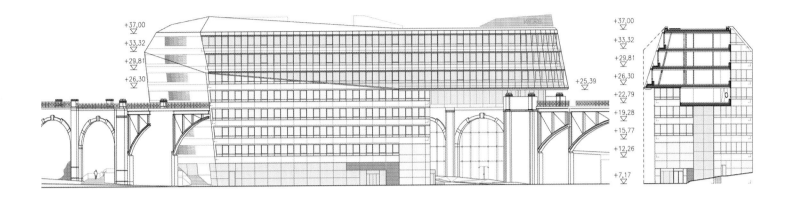

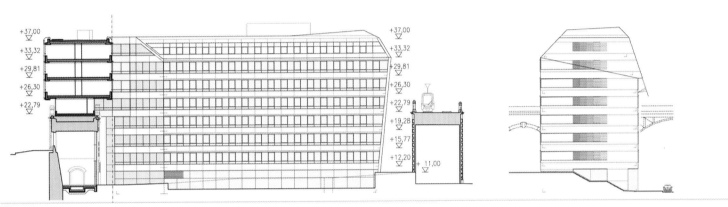

Elevations of the complex.

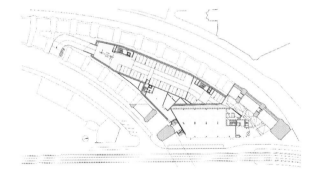

Basement floor - parking lot.

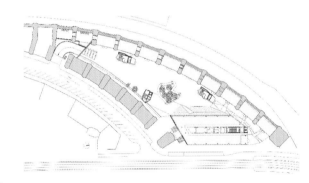

Ground floor - accesses.

Standard floor plan.

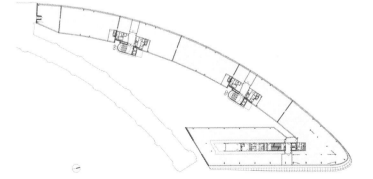

Its materials, glass and steel, clearly differentiate it from the mass of the existing bridge while at the same time reducing to a minimum the weight that the inclined pillars transmit to the arches.

Its mixed structure, its curved front and its enclosing exhibit all of its visual impact and create a renewed environment in which the new dialogs with the historic.

BAAS|
ARQUITECTES|

ordi Badia is the founder member of the studio BAAS-Arquitectes based in Barcelona. He graduated in architecture from the ETSAB (Escuela Técnica Superior de Arquitectura de Barcelona) of the Polytechnic University of Barcelona (U.P.C.). He worked in partnership with the architect Tonet Sunyer until 1993.

In 1994, he set up BAAS, a studio created with the objective of making the collaboration of professionals from different disciplines possible on architectural and design projects. Alongside his professional activity, his academic practice also stands out. He is a teacher at the School of Design ELISAVA, he was associate teacher in the Department of Architectural Projects at the Escuela Técnica

morgue_of_terrassa

morgue_of_leon

Superior de Arquitectura del Vallés (ETSAV) from 1994 to 2001 and he has been associate teacher in the Department of Architectural Projects of the Escuela Técnica Superior de Arquitectura de Barcelona (ETSAB) since 2001. Another important aspect developed by Jordi Badia is his participation in numerous conferences, courses and seminars.

Of the numerous projects undertaken by BAAS the following stand out: Morgue of Leon, the house CH, the Morgue of Terrassa, the Clinic Orto, the stand of IBERCON or the offices of IBERCON in Palma Majorca. More recently, a judicial building in Sant Boi de Llobregat (Barcelona) and the CEIP Ferrer i Guàrdia in Granollers (Barcelona).

Prizes	Prizewinning projects
2002	House CH. Prize FAD Architecture.
2001	Morgue of Leon. International prize AR+D
2001	Morgue of Terrassa. 1st prize
1997	Enlargement cemetery of Salvador.

BAAS has been awarded with a number of important prizes such as the international AR+D 2001 for their design of the Morgue of Leon and a special mention and the FAD Prize for Architecture 2002 for their project for the House CH.

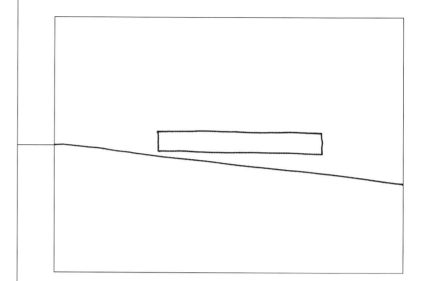

morgue_of_terrassa

TECHNICAL DATA

Location Funeral complex of Terrassa, Barcelona.

Architect BAAS Jordi Badia.

Client Municipal Morgue of Terrassa.

Collaborators Sergi Serrat, Marcos Catalán, Santi Vinuesa, Rafael Berenjena, Bárbara Camarero, Ginés Egea.

Consultant companies *Structure:* Eduard Doce, architect. *Installations:* Consulting Lluis Duart. *Building engineer:* Francesc Belart.

Constr. management Jordi Badia, architect. Francescs Belart, building engineer. Lluis Duart, installations engineer.

Project date 2001.

Completion date 2002.

Built area 3000 m².

Construction company Construcciones Peñarroya. Agustí Peñarroya.

Ground floor. The administrative program of private use is independent from the rest of the building.

The Morgue of Terrassa is a building created to house a ceremonial and spiritual program which achieves a tremendous amount of symbolism in its formalization.

The concept of the building is clear and honest. A white elemental volume occupies the space in which it has delicately been placed. Like a feather, it lightly rests on a slope with a gentle gradient. The pure form rises apparently suspended in the air and

defying gravity while it maintains its horizontality in contrast to the fall of the land. The lie of the land has allowed for the inclusion of a semi basement floor located below the principal form of the building in which a private administrative program has been installed. This acts independently from the rest of the program and opens onto a side patio and can be accessed directly from the street by means of an external stairway.

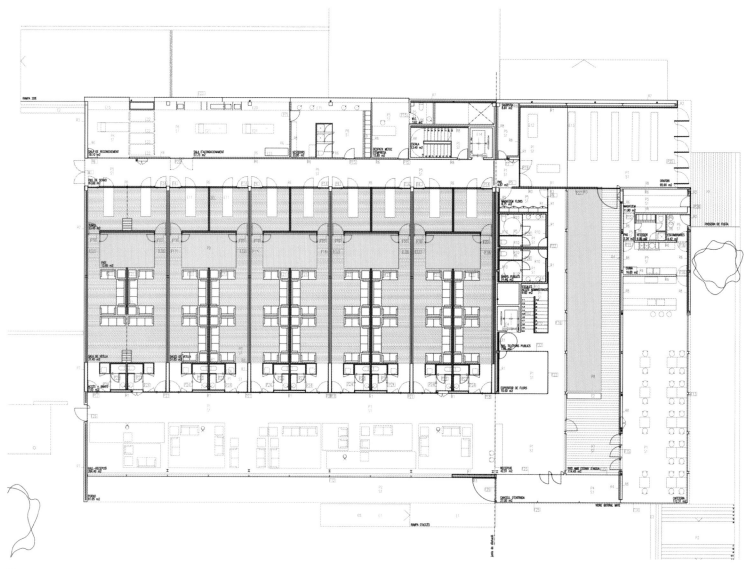

The public program is laid out around the water patio.

The large entrance porch gives the welcome.

In the interior of the volume the rest of the program of a public use in contained. It is subdivided into three areas grouped by modules. The vigil room, the chapel and the cafeteria are connected around an interior patio in which water is present as a symbolic element.

The interpretation of the space shows a desire to integrate natural phenomena into the simple pure forms of the architecture in neutral finishes. Light, shade, the sky, water... are all featured in the space, a solemn area. An elegant place which is discrete and in which emotions and the transmissions of sensations play

The lower floor is independent and opens onto a side patio.

The principal volume of the building seems to be suspended in the air.

an essential role. The building highlights this exchange in its surroundings. In this way, it breaks its own hermeticism of pure volumes and creates a porch open onto the landscape in its principal façade and that is framed by the clean profile of the principal horizontal volume. The light floods the building, not only through the façades, but it is also silently filtered through the interior patios to give life to the visiting rooms distributed in line and successively next to the hall.

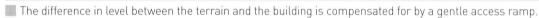
The large porch opens onto the landscape framed by the cleanliness of the main volume of the building.

The difference in level between the terrain and the building is compensated for by a gentle access ramp.

The main access is produced in a sequential way. First, it is approached along a ramp with a gentle gradient that compensates for a small change of levels between the terrain and the base of the building. The large porch welcomes us and directs us into the interior of the installations through a large door.

From the entrance, the large water patio, which communicates the entire complex, is perceived. We finally reach this area that is immersed in green light produced by the stained glass of the partitioned area. Once in the water patio, we perceive the chapel that symbolically rises in a second plane. We reach this point by

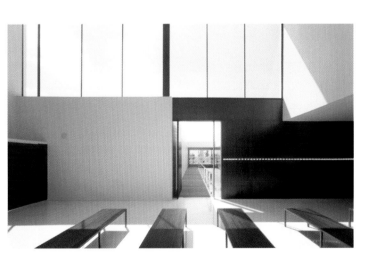

going over a wooden walkway suspended over calm clean water. Advancing towards the area of reflection, the view of the sky takes on a leading role. Finally, we find ourselves in a clean space, minimalist in which the superfluous is unnecessary, in which the important thing is to search for peace, rest, faith. A place in which light and the sky welcomes and comforts us.

municipal_morgue
of_leon

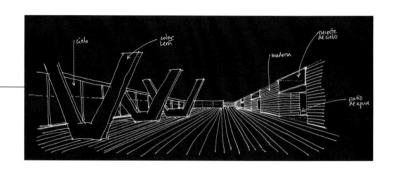

TECHNICAL DATA

Location	Municipal Morgue of Leon.
Architects	BAAS Jordi Badia / Josep Val.
Client	SERFUNLE. Funeral Services of Leon.
Collaborators	Elena Valls, Tirma Balagué, Albert Cívica, Marcos Catalán, Juan Carlos Castro, Frans Massana, Lorena Maristany, Rafael Berenjena, Francesc Belart, Santi Vinuesa, Bárbar Camarero, Ginés Egea, Josep Martínez, Luis Victori, Sergi Serrat, Lluis Carreras, Jordi Mercadé.
Consultant companies	*Install.:* Consulting Luis Duart, S.L. *Structures:* Engineering Workshop
Construction manag.	Jordi Badia / Josep Val, architects. Miguel Martínez, architect. Mariano Fernández, José Manuel Pérez, building engineers.
Project date	2001.
Built area	3074 m².
Construction company	BEGAR.

The site lies within an urban context.

BAAS TANATORIO MUNICIPAL DE LEÓN 2000

The skylights scratch the sky in search of light.

The result is of a minimal visual impact. The building is completely buried and it offers a roof converted into a sheet of clean water in which the sky is reflected like a mirror of the city.

The roof is the only façade of the building. Its continuity is interrupted by some mysterious and imposing irregular volumes that, in a tentacle like way, reach for the sky in order to pull in natural light through their cavities into the interior of the building.

The roof of the building is integrated into the exterior space.

Some imposing volumes transport light into the interior.

Light wells also appear is a discrete order and break the superficial plane of the sheet of water so as to become patios that are indispensable to the functioning of the internal program.

The entrance to the building is resolved in a subtle way. It is integrated into the green zone progressively in its penetration towards the interior.

The building manages to impose a minimal visual impact on its surroundings.

A long slope covered in ivy and birch trees that allows for the incorporation of a large window in the access has been created. In the interior, the play of light and shade delimits the forms of the spaces and the furniture that chooses the same language, that of pure lines. The building has been constructed entirely in concrete the color of which pays homage to the stone of Boñar autochtho-

The interior areas are illuminated through the light wells.

nous to the zone and used in a great many building in the city. The interior flooring has been resolved by the use of continuous sheeting of iroko wood which brings warmth to the interior.

The wood of the floors folds back on itself to cover the divisions that separate the vigil rooms from the lobby. Details in black appear spread around in no particular order and dress the interior

■ The weight of the slab is made evident by the imposing structure.

respectfully symbolizing a display of mourning. The lobby chooses simplicity in the conception of its space which is clean and fluid. The structural design of the supports achieves the uncluttered spaces required for its use and at the same time express in an imposing way the weight of the higher slab that accommodates the pool of water.

The work space is neutral and functional.

The perimeters of the building immaterialize in continuous planes open to the light wells and, without interference, the buried building communicates with the open sky and pursues the necessity of obtaining fluid spaces. In contrast, the working areas are hermetic, discrete and private. The functionality continues to dominate in the selection of forms and materials.

ARCHI-
TECTONICS

ARCHI-TECTONICS was founded in New York in 1994. The studio functions as a research and development laboratory in which the computer, integrated more as a tool for creation than merely an instrument used for drawing, is an active ingredient in the design process. The use of 3D software facilitates the visualization of the projects as well as the fabrication of the constructive elements.

ARCHI-TECTONICS' designs have been published in various magazines. Some of those that stand out are: installations for the Digital Image in Midtown Manhattan, the offices for the magazine Gear, art galleries in Chelsea along with various refurbished lofts

spaces_for_art

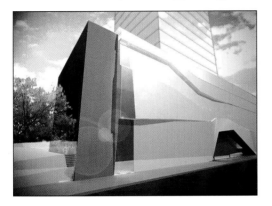

project_in_greenwich_street

and retail areas in Manhattan. And, recently completed: a residency and a guest house in Upstate New York, an eleven-story building for mixed-use in Soho and a gymnasium-spa in New York.

Their work has been shown in various monographic exhibitions: Form Zero Gallery in Los Angeles (1994), Kunsthal in Rotterdam (1996), Parsons Gallery NYC (2000), Frederieke Taylor Gallery in Chelsea and HW&SF in Mexico D.F. (2004)

The visible head of Archi-Tectonics is the New York based Dutch architect Winka Dubbeldam. Winka graduated from the

Faculty of Architecture in Rotterdam (1990) and took a master in 'Advanced Architectural Design' in the University of Colombia (New York). She has worked in the offices of Steven Holl, Bernard Tschumi and Peter Eisenman and she has also been an auxiliary lecturer in the University of Colombia (New York) as well as in the University of Harvard. She presently gives classes at the University of Pennsylvania (Philadelphia).

She has received various prizes and grants for the development of her investigation such as the "Emerging Voice" prize awarded by the Architectural League of New York (2001).

schoonhoven

TECHNICAL DATA
Location Schoonhoven, Holand.
Architect Winka Dubbeldam.
Competition date 2003.

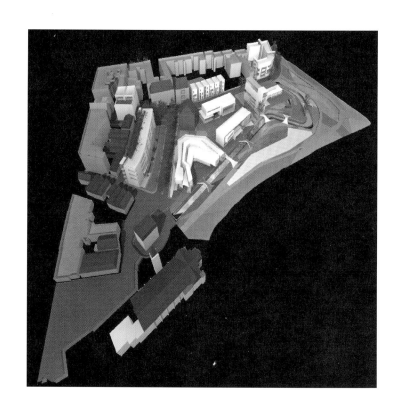

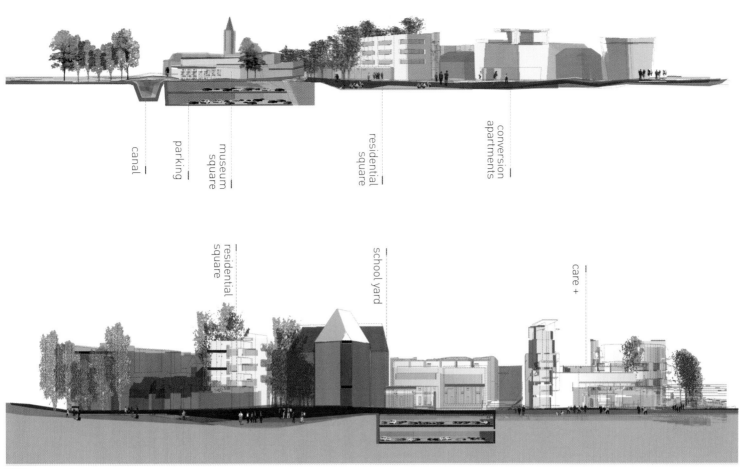

residential square

school yard

care +

canal

parking

museum square

residential square

conversion apartments

Trasversales.

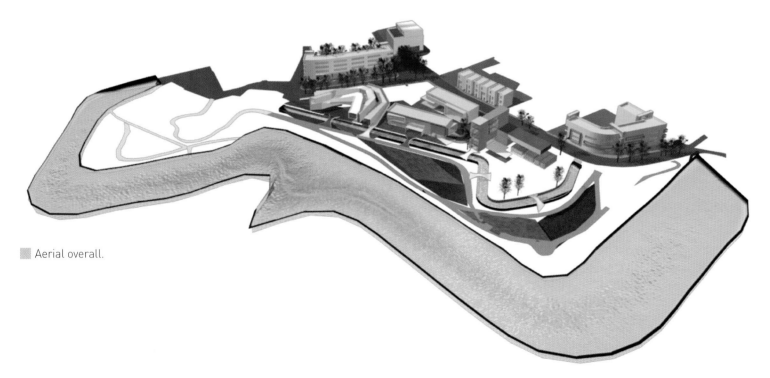

Aerial overall.

The decision made by the Dutch government to protect the 'green heart' of the center of the country has had direct consequences on city limits.

The council of Schoonhoven, accepting the fact that the city could not continue to expand, has opted to promote the Requalification of an area of the old center: a forgotten space that is

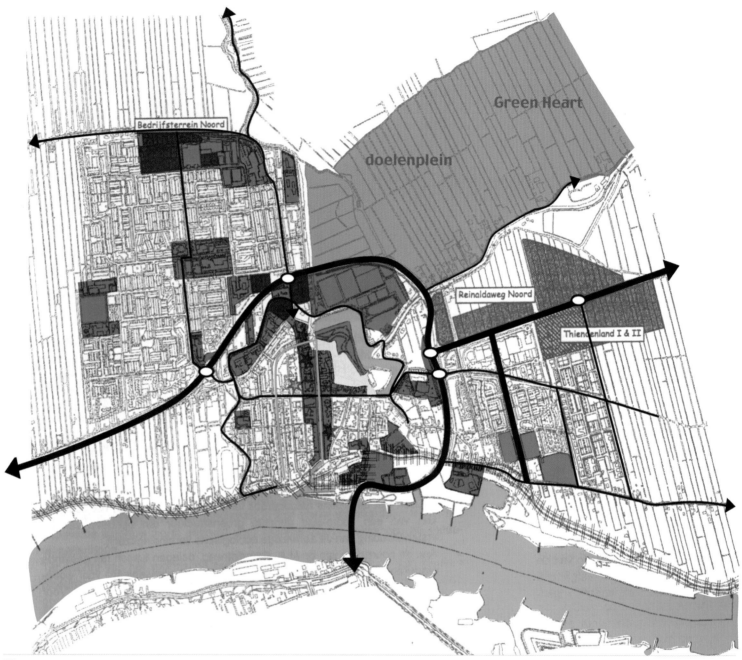

Green Heart

doelenplein

Bedrijfsterrein Noord

Reinaldaweg Noord

Thiendenland I & II

Urban diagram.

presently used as a parking lot. The proposal is to give it back its original structure of streets and canals, to connect it once again with the center and to intensify its densities and uses.

The strategy of the project consists in redefining the urban infrastructure by widening the principal paths to transform them into tree-lined streets with shops and restaurants and to assign

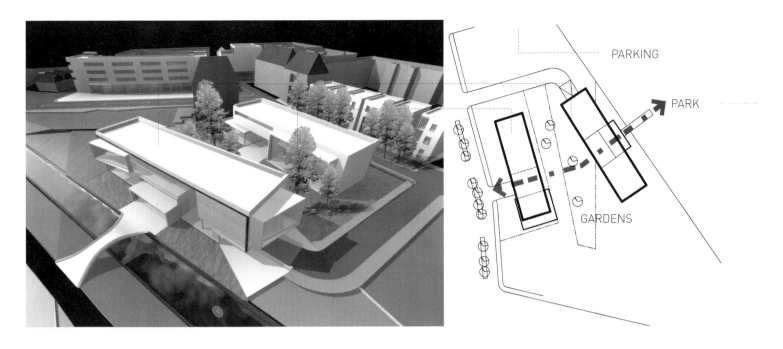

PARKING

PARK

GARDENS

Entrances.

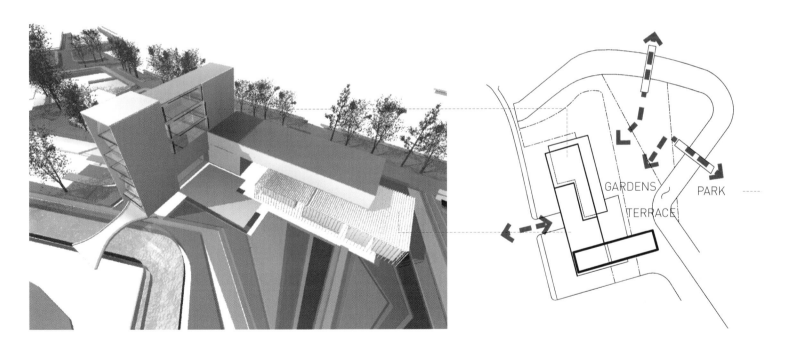

GARDENS

PARK

TERRACE

a specific function to the area that takes over this forgotten green zone. The park has been laid out in three basic built-up areas of influence: a new museum situated in one of the extremes and which strengthens the cultural connection between the new neighborhood and the city; some schools grouped around the center and directly linked to the park and a

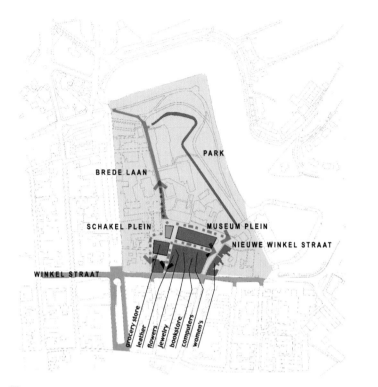
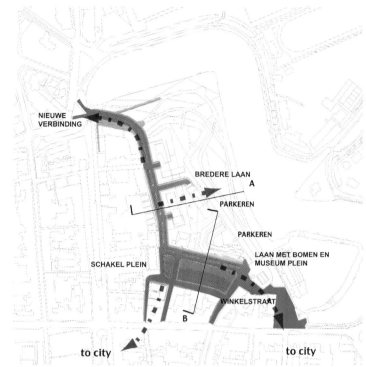

Urban diagrams.

Museum.

residential zone that incorporates a gardened area with direct access to the park and to the retail area around the museum.

This last element acts as a filter and connects the new urban structure with the low density of the old center.

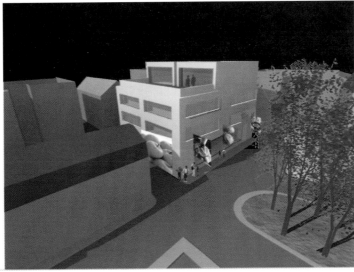

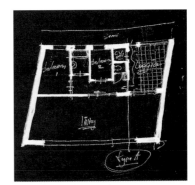

Conversion apartments.

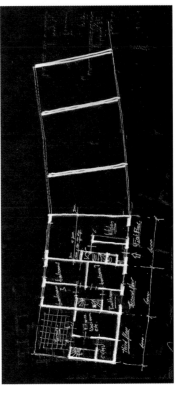

New single family housing.

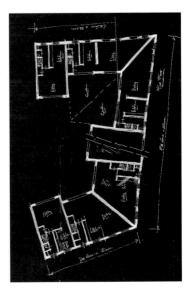

New flexible housing units.

spaces_for
the_art

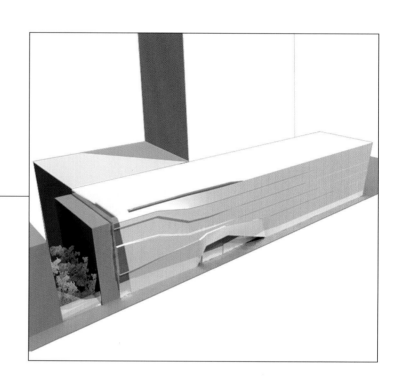

TECHNICAL **DATA**
Location 42nd street, NYC
Architect Winka Dubbeldam
Collaborators Ana Zatezalo, Brooks Atwood, Alex
Pincus

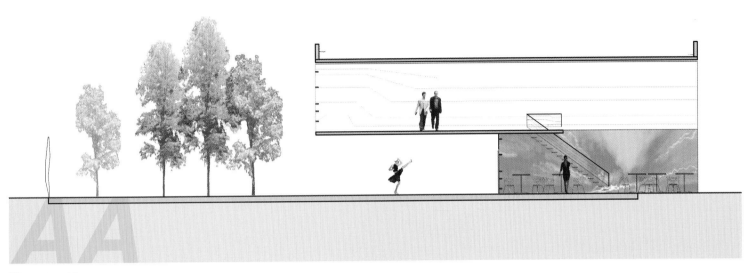

Section AA.

Plan diagram AA.

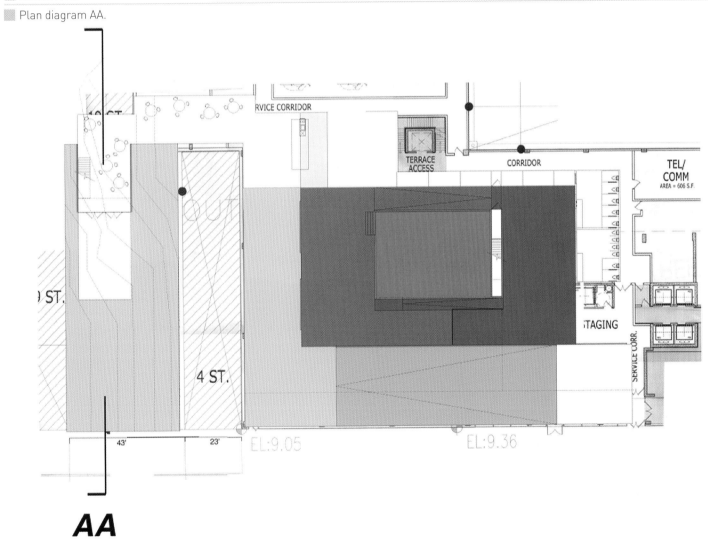

AA

The project consists of the design for an Art Center: a flexible space situated in the base of a newly constructed residential tower.

The gallery program, situated below three floors of parking, has been completed with a bookshop, offices, storage area and exterior patio which offers the possibility of being used as part of

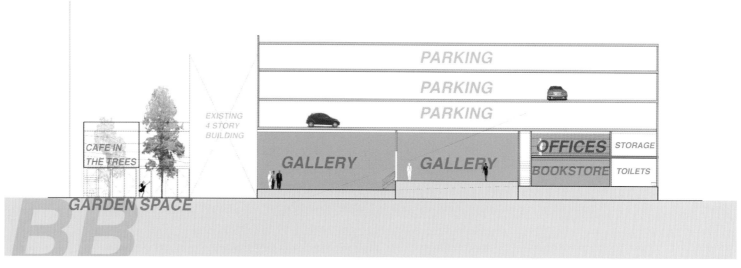

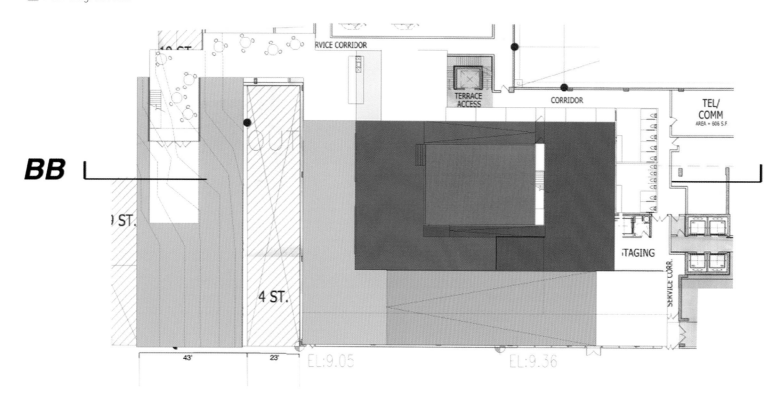

Section BB.

Plan diagram BB.

the exhibiting space. With the objective of strengthening its identity as cultural center in Manhattan, it was decided to distort the façade of the gallery: starting from the rhythm of the curtainwall, the siding gently deforms until it reaches the entrance to the building. Opaque and transparent stripes filter the exterior light and form hollows that offer slanted views of the interior and

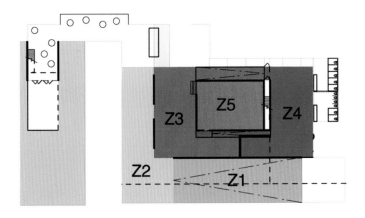
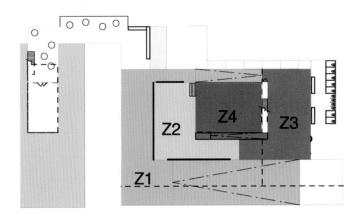
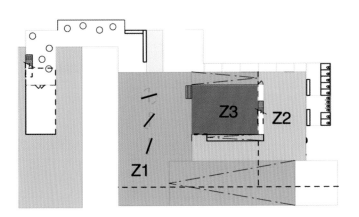
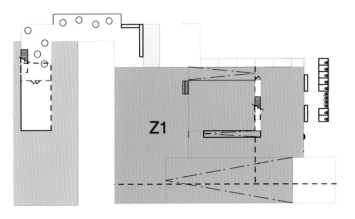

Plans density.

Elevation diagram.

invite the exhibition area to be discovered. The movement of transformation of the façade is translated to the formalization of the program: a system of ramps ascending in spiral organizes

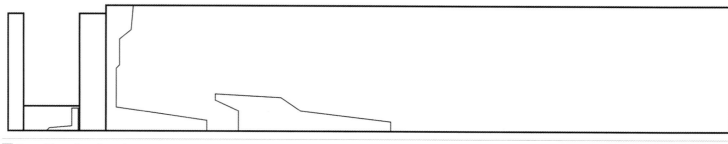

Recodify gallery façade

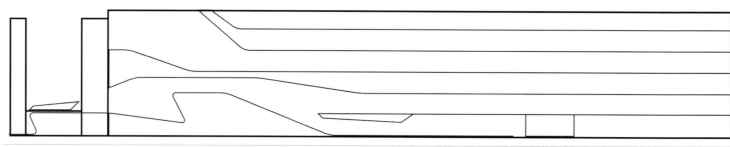

Deregulate mullions.

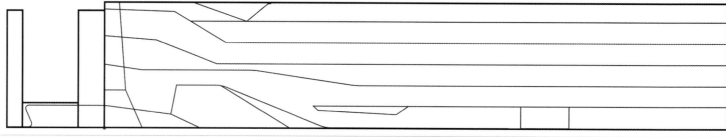

Generate façade topography.

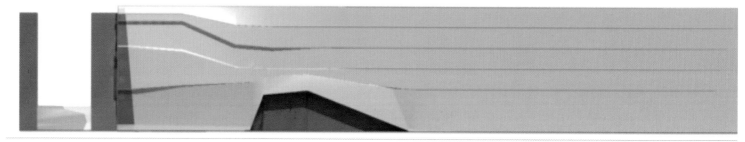

Potential façade variation (2^n deformation)

Process of distortion of the façade.

the interior space in five levels and brings a visual continuity to the gallery. The use of sliding panels produces many possible distributions. The floor can be used as just one large exhibition space or broken down into five differentiated areas. The route goes on to the level of the bar which leans out over the patio in projection.

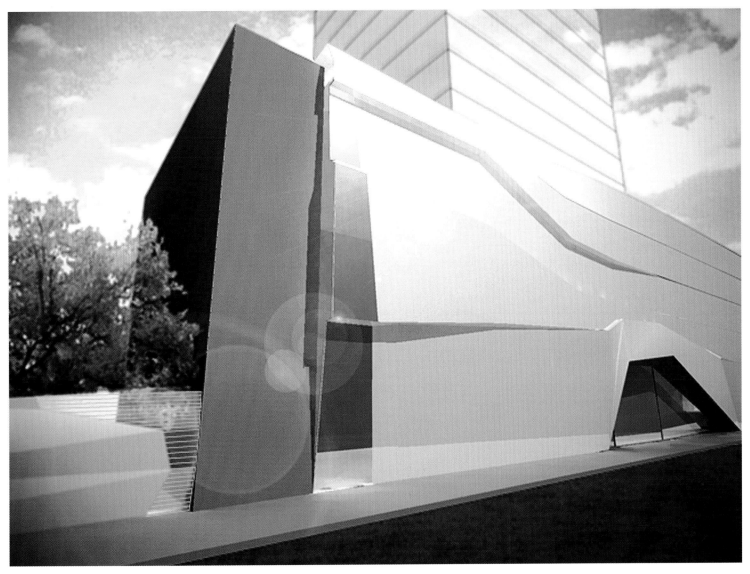

Final render.

Final elevation.

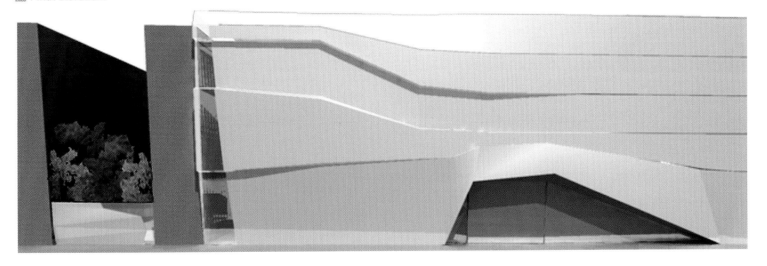

project_in greenwich_street

TECHNICAL DATA
Location Soho, New York.
Architects Winka Dubbeldam, Ana Sotrel.
Client Take One LLC.
Collaborators David Hotson, Michael Hundsnursch-
er, Nicola Bauman, Amy Farina, Ana
Zatezalo, Deborah Kully, Stacey Mari-
ash, Ty Tikari, Leo Yung, Beatrice
Witzgall, Tanja Bitzer.
Project date 2000.
Completion date 2003.
Built area 6000 m².

Large-sect. night.

Penthouse view.

Situated to the south of Soho, an old warehouse with six floors has been converted into an eleven-story building with a mixed program. The abandoned state of the factory has been revitalized

Exploded-view.

by the implantation of new uses: an art gallery and retail premises on the ground floor and 22 open-plan apartments in loft style
on the higher floors.

Vertical communication is achieved by means of a central nucleus that contains the services and installations and which ties
the hybrid program together in an efficient way.

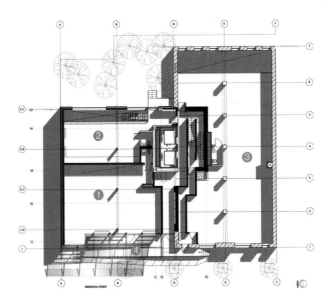

Main floor plan: 1. art galery; 2. office space; 3. retail; 4. entry.

6th floor plan: 5. loft space; kitchenette; 7. bath; elevator-stair core; balcony.

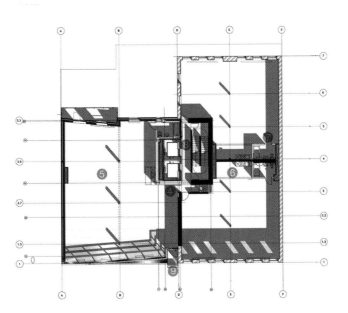

The principal interest in the new building lies in its façade: a cascade of inclined glass panels that embrace the brick enclosure of the warehouse.

The integration of a new glass and steel structure in the existing building establishes a bridge between the past and present and reinterprets in this way the code of the traditional New York

■ Night-south.

■ Penthouse detail.

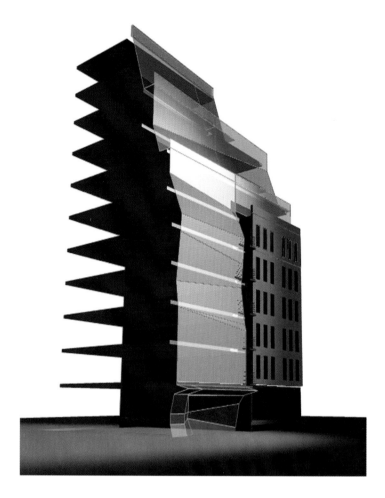

■ Curtainwall diagram.

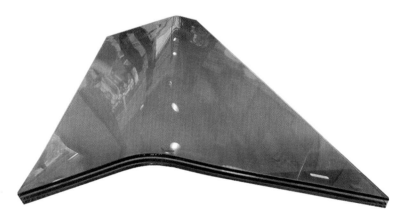

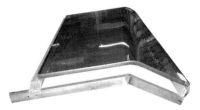

constructions. Some balconies in projection in the union between the two emphasize the distinction between the old and the new, between the private and the urban.

On the ground floor, the glazed façade doubles outwards and offers shelter to the art gallery and to the entrance hall to the res-

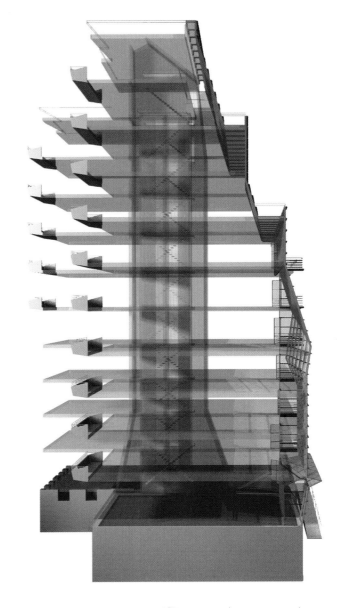

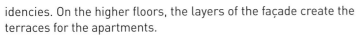
Curtanwaill + elev.

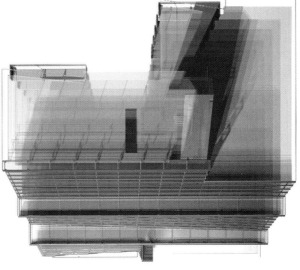

idencies. On the higher floors, the layers of the façade create the terraces for the apartments.

The curtainwall is made up of panels of curved glass, tailor made in Barcelona, and extrusion steel profiles that come from Hong Kong.

Ext gallery.

Sky exposure plan

| Setback code | Setback variation | 2.7 to 1 | Inflection 1 | Inflection 2 |

Penthouse view. NJ.

In contrast, the walls are made of concrete blocks, aluminum profiles and wooden windows.

The fold as mediation between past and present, and the glass inflections as a device for spatial composition materialize the urban complexity within a discrete architectural object.

palazzo_gioberti

UdA
ufficio di architettura

Walter Camagna, Massimiliano Camoletto and Andrea Marcante set up UdA (Ufficio di Architettura) in 1992 in Turín, after having worked in Spain, the USA and Germany. Since 1999, they have also been able to count on the collaboration of the architect Davide Volpe with whom they have developed various projects such as the Levis House, the Adidas Outlet in Nuremburg or the assembly for the Basel Jewelry Fair.

The studio presently has offices in Italy (Turin) and France (Nice) and is made up of architects, engineers, graphic designers and consultants.

levis_house

house_in_revigliasco

In 1988, they won first prize ex-aequo in the international competition for the extension of Hospital Molinette in Turin.

In addition, their projects 'Ilti Luce' and 'Levis House' have been selected on various occasions.

Their work has been published in numerous specialized magazines among which the publication by AV Monografías "20 Young European Architects for the 21st Century" edited in 2000 stands out.

They participated in the VII Venice Biennale of Architecture in the exhibition dedicated to "The City of the Third Millennium".

In 2002, the studio was invited by Toyo Ito, Alejandro Zaera-Polo and Bob Van Reeth to represent Italy in the exhibition "New Trends of Architecture in Europe and Japan 2002" that was taken to the cities of Tokyo, Gantes, Bordeaux, Salamanca, Lisbon and Madrid.

These young architects were visiting lecturers at the Chiba University of Tokyo in 2002 and they were invited to exhibit their project 'Palazzo Gioberti' in the exhibition "GA Houses Project" organized by the GA Gallery of Tokyo in 2003.

pàllazzo_gioberti
(house_for_a_video_art
collector)

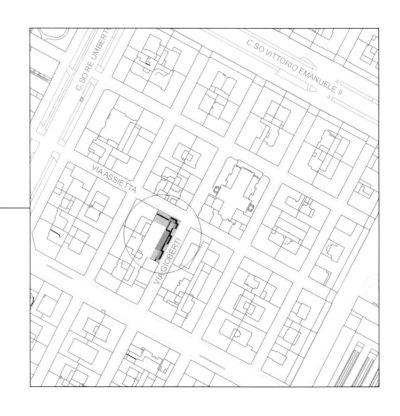

TECHNICAL DATA
Location Turin.
Architects Andrea Marcante, Walter Campagna.
Collaborators Marco Luciano, Luca Talarico.
Project date 2003.

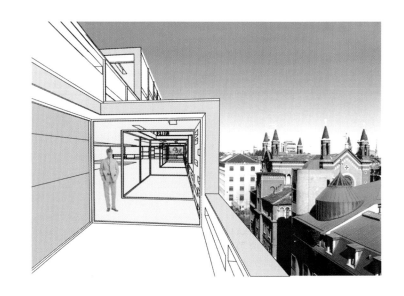

■ Elevation Gioberti-street.

■ Elevation Assieta-street.

The building lies in an orthogonal interweave of urban extension in the center of Turin. It was constructed as a suburban residence and later enlarged, during the second part of the 19th century, until it became a small three-story palace. At the end of the 1950's, two new levels were added and the building became a block of offices.

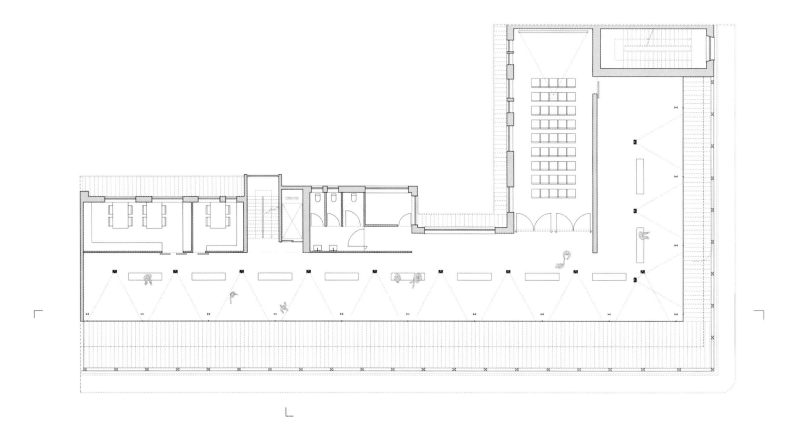

Sixth floor - art gallery.

Section.

The project consisted of remodeling the higher floors and the creation of a residence and a gallery for a video art collector. The gallery, in addition to accommodating the collection of videos, was conceived as a space in which to hold exhibitions and cultural acts related to the world of art. Its glazed perimeter, over which the videos are projected, acts as an element that relates

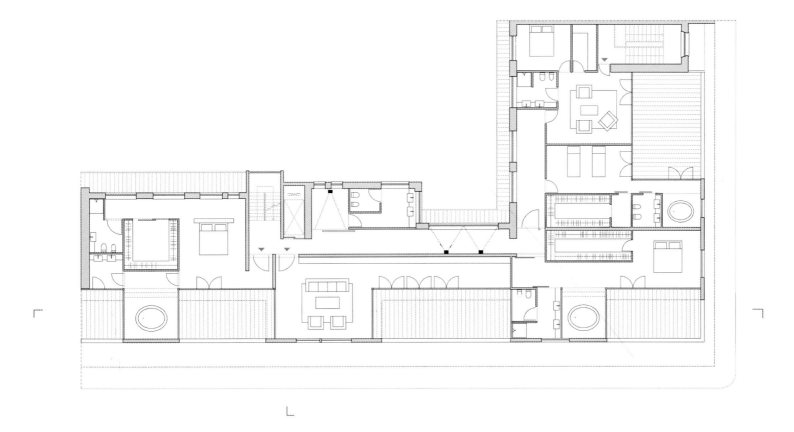

Seventh floor - night area of residence.

Eighth floor - day area of residence.

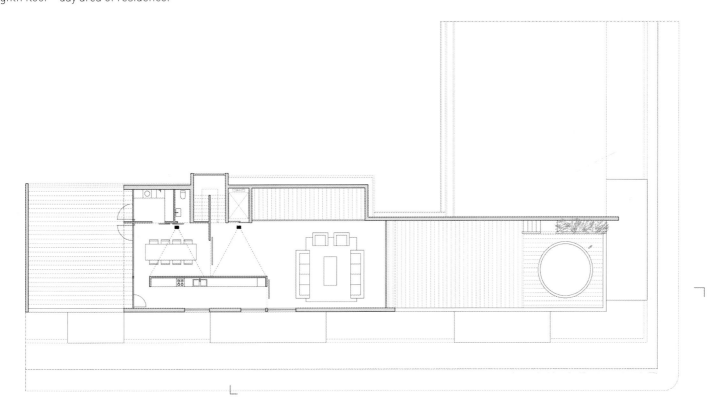

■ Overall view.

and unifies the new intervention with the existing historical building. The residence, situated on the two higher levels, is offset and forms terraces that establish a play on views and spatial relations that question the ambiguity and duality between the public and the private, between seeing and being seen, as an echo of the rites of contemporary art.

View from the terrace.

Overall view.

The façade is enclosed with translucent Plexiglas panels that hide a structure of openings through which the light filters.

The sophistication of the façade's covering represents the contemporary ornamentation that converses with the friezes, stucco and columns of the historic "palazzo".

levis_house

TECHNICAL DATA
Location Valdorno, Biella.
Architects Andrea Marcante, Walter Campagna and Davide Volpe.
Collaborators Luca Ramello.
Project date 1998.
Built area 85 m² and 35 m² of terrace.

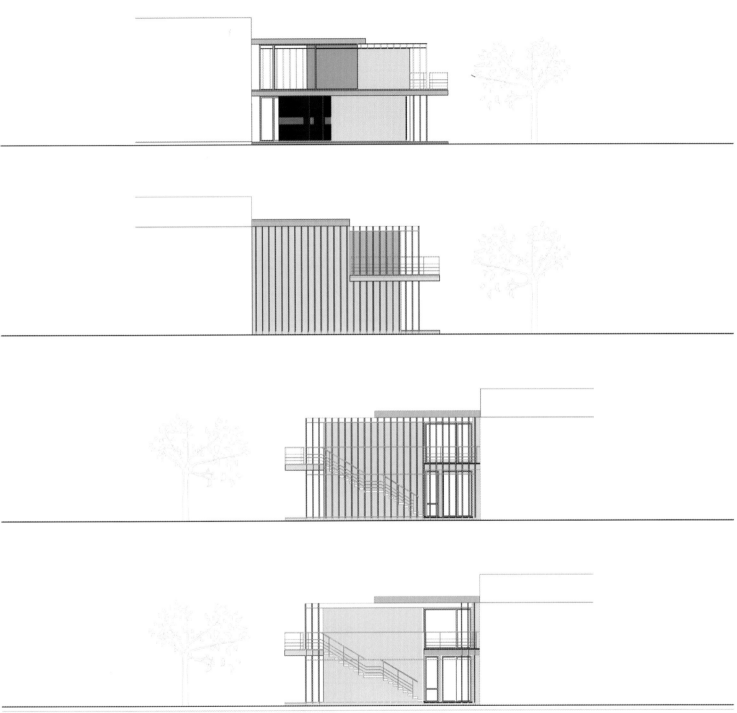

Elevations.

The project came about due to the need to enlarge a rural house in the north of Italy. In one of the extremes, in the place that was occupied by a small hay loft, a new two-story volume has been sited that is reached by means of an exterior ladder which links the interior directly with the rooms of the existing building.

Interior view.

Staircase that units the two floors.

The new construction, in which steel reinforced concrete walls have been combined with large glazed openings, lies protected behind a screen of vertical laminated wooden strips that filter the light and the landscape.

■ View of terrace.

■ Dining room on the ground floor.

This enclosing reinterprets the hollows and the balconies of the traditional buildings in the surroundings, screening the space, the present and one's memory.

In the interior, the different areas (kitchen, dining room and bathroom on the ground floor, and living room with terrace on

Laminated wood ribs.

Night view.

the higher) were conceived as a sequence of filters that from the closed spaces of the original building gradually open towards the landscape of the Alps. The architecture is manifested here not only as a means of organization of the physical space, but as a projection of a sensory relationship with the exterior environment.

house
in_revigliasco

TECHNICAL DATA
Location Revigliasco, Turin.
Architects Andrea Marcante, Walter Campagna and Mariabeatrice Picco.
Collaborators Marco Luciano, Luca Malavolta and Curti Corrado.
Project date 2003.
Built area 300 m².

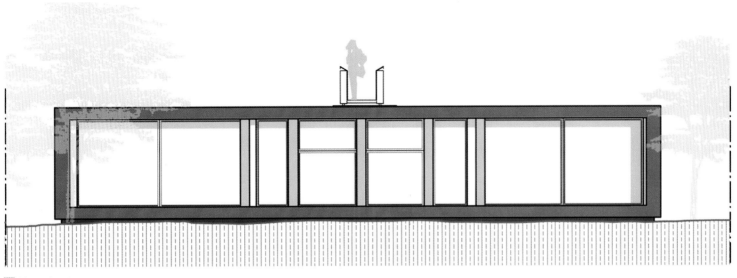

■ Elevation from access.

■ Elevation from garden.

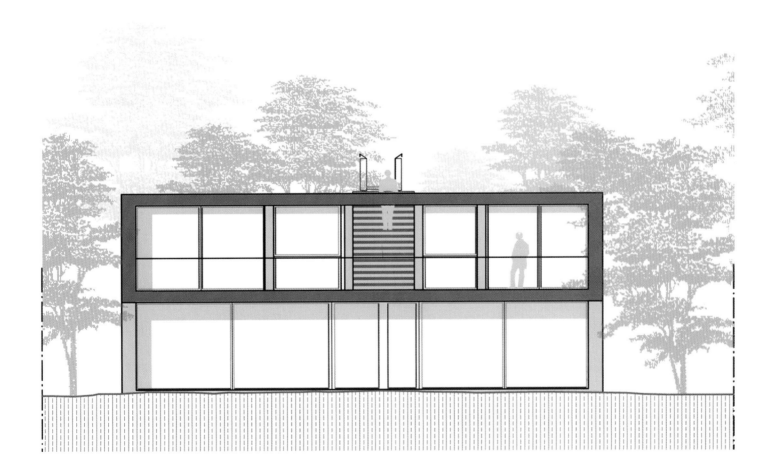

The house oriented to the south, is situated in the higher part of a plot with a marked gradient. Although it was conceived to be shared by two families, it manifests itself as a single unit, one volume that rests over an elevated terrain. It stretches out towards the landscape in the way of a lookout point. The entrance begins with a walkway situated in the upper part of the plot. From

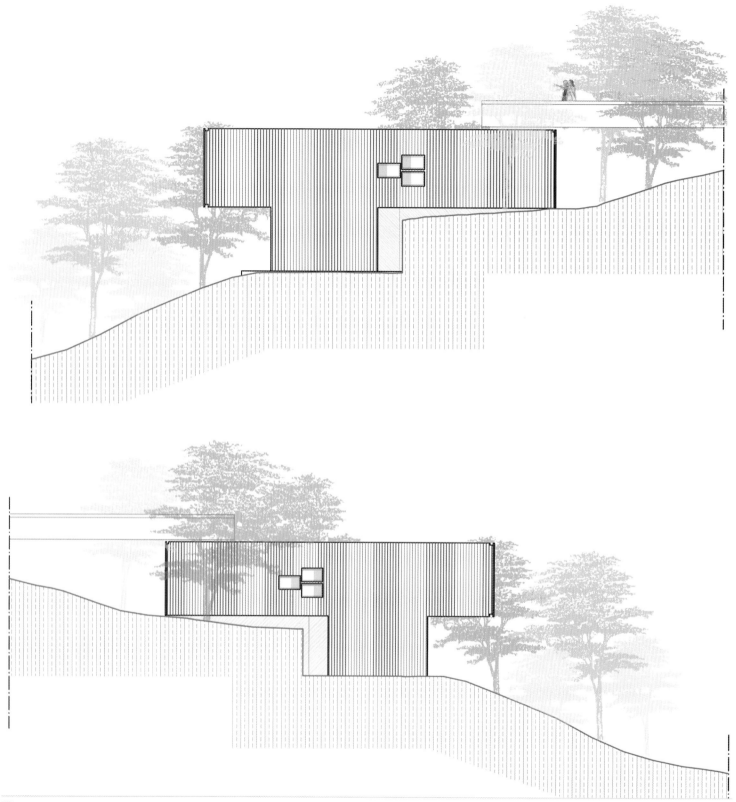

Elevation from behind.

here, the covered plane is the only perceptible element; its horizontal development dominates and redefines the landscape. Steps lead to the first level of the residences in which the access-es to the bedrooms are situated. On the lower level, the living rooms open out onto the garden which has been conceived as a natural extension of the interior space. The organization of the

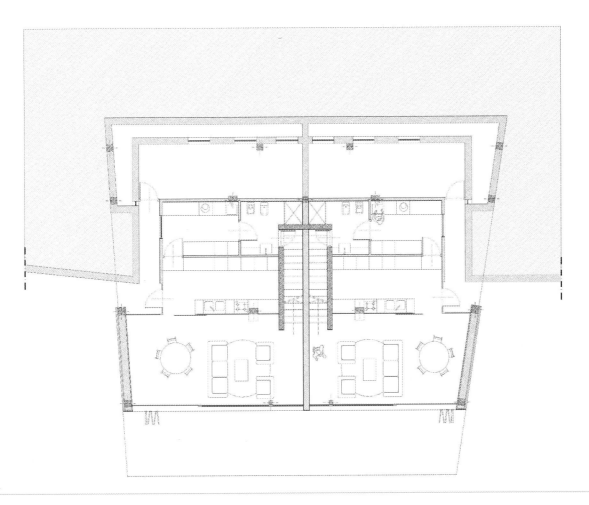

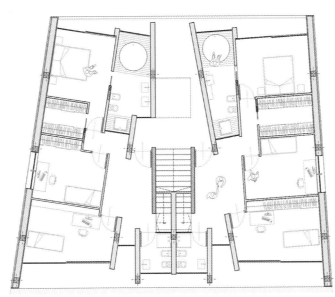

■ Lower level.
■ Upper level.

spaces offers a visual and spatial openness that emphasizes the link between man and nature, between the house and the land on which it has been constructed. The marked relationship estab-

lished with the immediate surroundings specifically manifests it-self in the exterior where the wooden siding becomes a mosaic of abstract textures but familiar: that of the two cultivated fields, that

█ View from the access walkway.

█ Scale model of complex.

of the human work which transforms nature into landscape. In this way, the house does not impose, but it allows itself to be contaminated by the characteristics of incertitude and the intrinsic

Mosaic of abstract textures in the roofing and sidings.

View of the scale model.

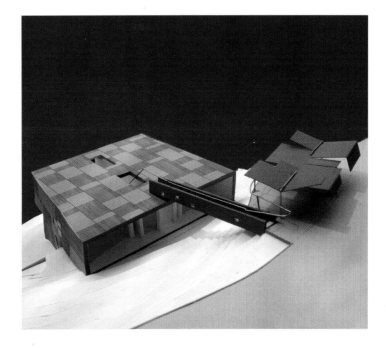

transformation of the landscape all of which it absorbs. As it camouflages itself, it reflects the way nature has been manipulated by the hand of man.

house_D

BULANT &WAILZER
Architekturstudio

The architects Aneta Bulant-Kamenova and Klaus Wailzer formed their company in 1996 and established Architekturstudio Bulant & Wailzer in Vienna with the intention of encouraging architectural practice and experimentation with new materials and construction techniques (freestanding aluminum enclosures, constructions in glass, etc.).

Bulant & Wailzer work in the abstraction and in the formal reduction of the visible structure in order to maximize the space with the intention of providing greater sensory freedom and extending

wien_west

ful_house

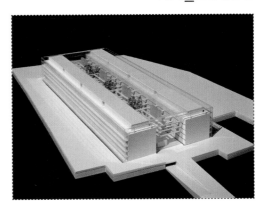

observation beyond the predictable. In order to do this, they see the possibility of extending the substantial limits of architecture and offering an indefinable secret and unpredictable poetry in the use of glass. In spite of their interest in the possibilities of the new technologies, the artistic aspect often dominates the ideas of the two architects. In the search of apparently simple structures, their attention oscillates between the object and architectural conditions.

The quality of their designs has led to them winning various national and international competitions and being awarded with prizes by a number of institutes around the world (in Austria, the USA, France, Germany and Bulgaria).

Their proposals have been presented in numerous publications and international exhibitions and they have both been invited to many conferences and workshops.

Aneta Bulant - Kamenova and Klaus Wailzer give conferences in the University of Technology of Vienna and they are visiting lecturers at the Academy of Fine Arts of Vienna.

house_D
(glass_space in_the_garden)

TECHNICAL DATA
Location Vienna.
Architects Aneta Bulant and Klaus Wailzer.
Completion date 2002.

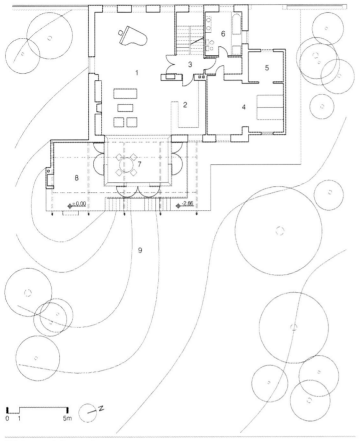

Overall floor plan.

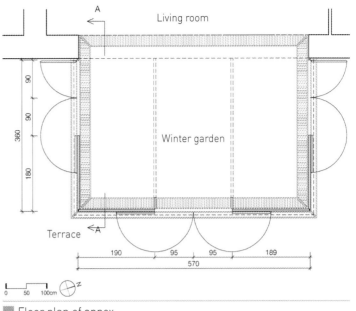

Floor plan of annex.

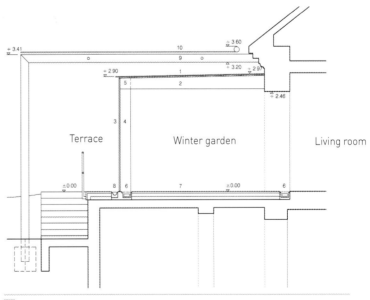

Section of the glazed room.

The project consists of the construction of a room on the terrace of a 169-year-old house situated in a residential area of Vienna.

The owners decided to extend the space of the living room so as to improve the relationship with the exterior and communication with the garden. With this objective, it was decided to eliminate the wall that communicated with the terrace and add over this a glass volume. The pure cubic form of this transparent body brings autonomy and allows the annex to exist without entering into conflict with the traditional architecture of the old house.

Over the glass volume, a pergola formed by aluminum masts that support sliding cloth panels that filter the light and emphasis the transition between the house and garden has been installed. The objective is to obtain a graduation of spaces with zones that are climatically different one to another.

The wall of the living room, the glass room, the intermediate space of the terrace situated below the pergola and the open garden form a multi-layer membrane in which the transparent box

■ Overall view.

assumes a central position in this chain so as to make it belong as much to the house as to the garden. It is an integrated space of the exterior onto the interior in which "even the autumn rains and the winter snow storms are transformed here from inconvenience to poetry..." This small building, Solutia Design 2003 prize of the AIA (American Institute of Architects) for architecture in lami-

▨ Details of the joints.

▨ Construction details.

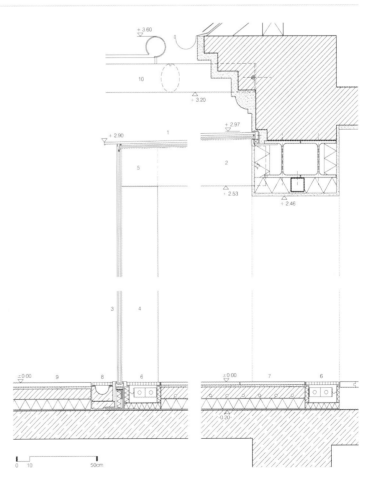

nated glass, displays the structural capacities of this material and represents a pioneering work in the use of glass laminates.

In Austria, construction in glass fixed with silicone without the reinforcement of mechanical elements is prohibited. However, these architects have created a new technique that uses adhesive connections between the glass beams and the pillars which allows them to avoid the use of screwed metal plaques.

wien_west

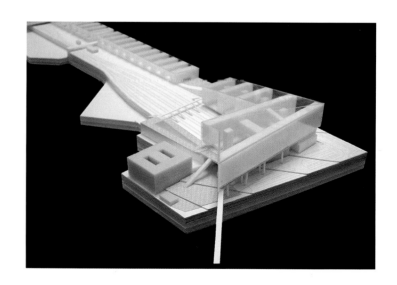

TECHNICAL DATA
Location West Vienna .
Architects Bulant & Wailzer.
Client Town planning Competition, Station area, City of Vienna.
Built area 135,000 m² (public space).
15,000m² (retail area).
150,000 m² (buildings).

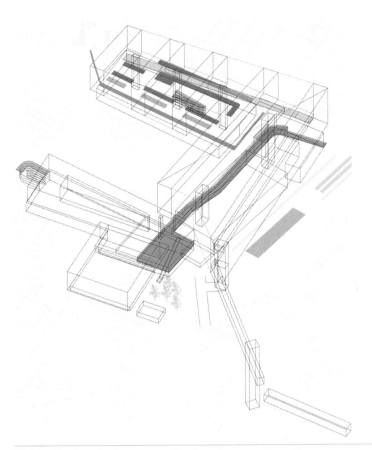

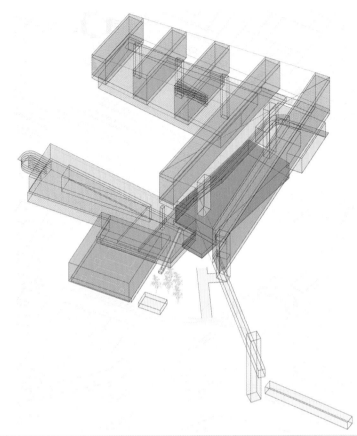

Distribution of volumes, zonification of use and transit routes.

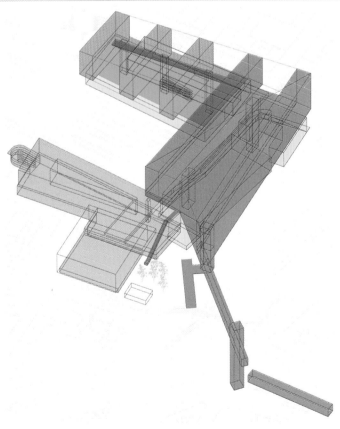

The project responds to the pressing need of territorial reorganization of the urban area that incorporates the aggressive imposition and interferences of the extensive railway infrastructure existent in the central station of West Vienna. The present implantation causes a harsh environmental incidence in the urban area, an abrupt discontinuity of the pedestrian flow and the prolongation of the zone in its more domestic scale.

The area is presented as a new business center with a dynamic civic activity. The objective consists in uniting this with the existing urban area and reflecting on the necessities and formal language that should be used in this new urban sector.

The achievement of a distancing from the existing infrastructures, a solution to the problem of a lack of space and the creation of spectacular panoramic views over the city are the principal objectives of the design.

The complex should be resolved as if it was an autonomous organism integrated into the functioning of the city and that comple-

Upon colonizing the air, a second city is created within the metropolis.

ments its services as well as fulfilling the original proposal of colonizing the plane of the sky. As a result, a city has been constituted over one already in existence, a group that, once again, unites the two urban fronts brusquely fragmented on each side of the railway lines. In this way, a structure that groups in the form of an atrium and that embraces the discontinuous perimeters is born; a complex formed by prototype buildings of great height and compactness conceived as solid elements. These achievements

blend into the flexible transit network that increases or decreases according to demand and that is capable of connecting the different elements as and when necessary.

Sky City, as it will be called, has a large public platform of great dimensions above ground level. Nothing less than 20,000 square meters of public territory to complement that which was already in existence: the great Sky Square. The city has colonized the air by incorporating a complex urban mechanism of large green areas and

TOP **YOUNG** EUROPEAN ARCHITECTS

The buildings are laid out equidistant to one another; this is to say that the volumes have the same value as the voids.

an extensive pedestrian walk along which there are stores, restaurants and leisure installations. The study has been subdivided into two phases of extension to the city. Sector A (situated over the reference plane) consists of 135,000 square meters of new public space and a retail area of some 15,000. In the base, there are two floors dedicated to parking with a capacity for almost 2,000 vehicles which supposes an extension of the urban infrastructure. For the second sector, B and C, the possible planning able to absorb the creation of

150,000 square meters of apartments, business areas and offices along with retail and residential areas that can be extended according to demand have been proposed.

The platform of the raised square creates a series of dispersed posts that look out over the city and proportion a privileged spatial perception. In the extreme north, the terraces of the square offer access limited to taxis, ambulances and firefighter vehicles by means of ramps.

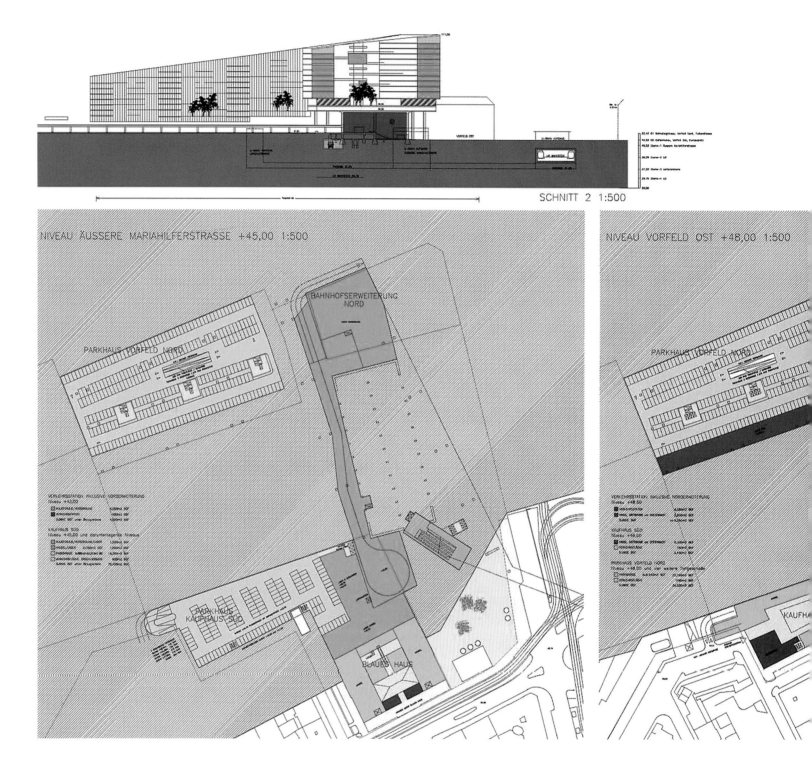

SCHNITT 2 1:500

NIVEAU ÄUSSERE MARIAHILFERSTRASSE +45,00 1:500

NIVEAU VORFELD OST +48,00 1:500

Vehicles and the railway network are integrated into the solid base that acts as the support for Sky Square. In this base, the traffic flows and speeds are controlled in such a way as to obtain total freedom from the urban noise in the elevated city created basically for pedestrians. The pedestrian access is found in the lower square through a first elevator core situated in the southern sec-

tor, or by means of a second point situated in the extreme north and which coincides with the station vestibule and the new commercial boulevard.

Long escalators and pedestrians bridges manage the transit that is found in the different areas where the two levels are connected.

ATRIUM

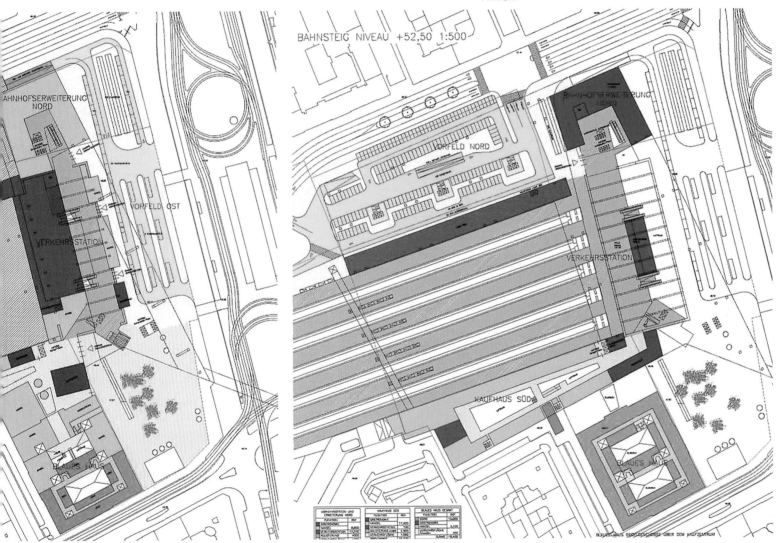

The extensive floors of the high office buildings are connected thanks to the installation of bridges that cross at different heights and which are sectioned in different lengths. These connections lead to the existence of vestibules, cafés, lookout points as well as offering greater flexibility when it comes to possible uses. The structure adapts to the continual changes in the spaces and the office surfaces are extended according to demand. In the highest areas, the location of 50 luxury apartments with impressive views has been proposed. The adaptability of the spaces permits the fourteen-meter-wide galleries to be freed from dividing walls so that cafés and restaurants with panoramic views can be installed on the top floors at any time.

ful_house

(sustainable_architecture
for_the_viennese_suburb
of_simmering)

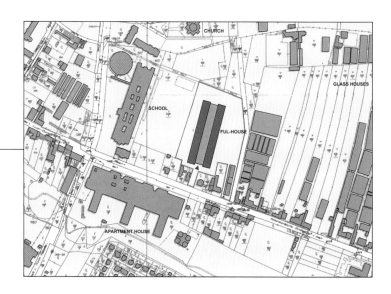

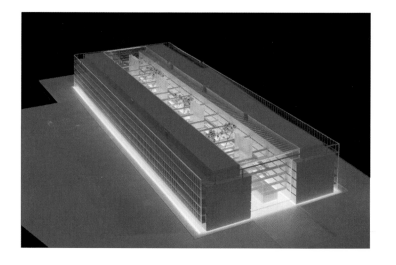

TECHNICAL DATA

Location Simmering, Vienna.
Architects Aneta Bulant and Klaus Wailzer.
Client Exhibition organized by the Center of
Architecture of Vienna .
Project date 2000.

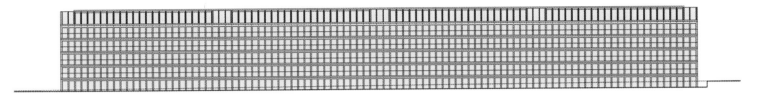

Overall elevation.

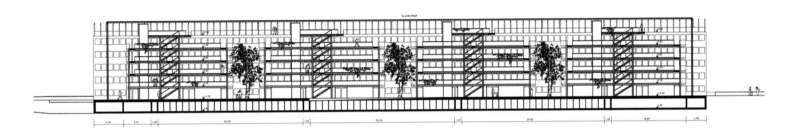

Section through atrium.

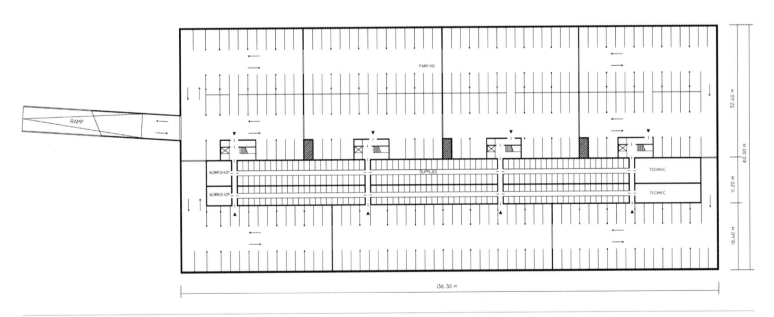

Basement floor - parking.

The project came into being as a result of the exhibition 'Emerging Architecture' organized by the Center of Architecture of Vienna in September 2000.

It is a question of a 300-apartment building situated in the suburb of Simmering on the outskirts of the city of Vienna: an area of a heterogeneous nature with little urban cohesion and insuffi-

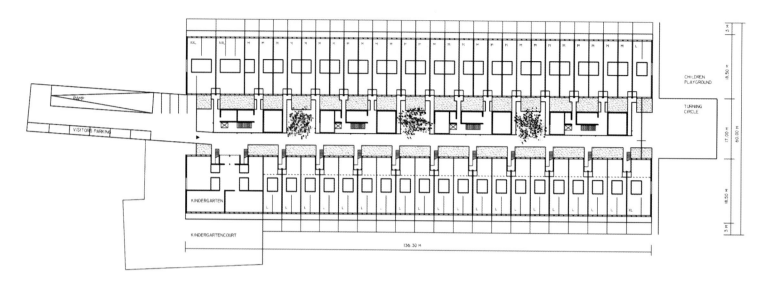

Ground floor plan.

Floor plan level 1.

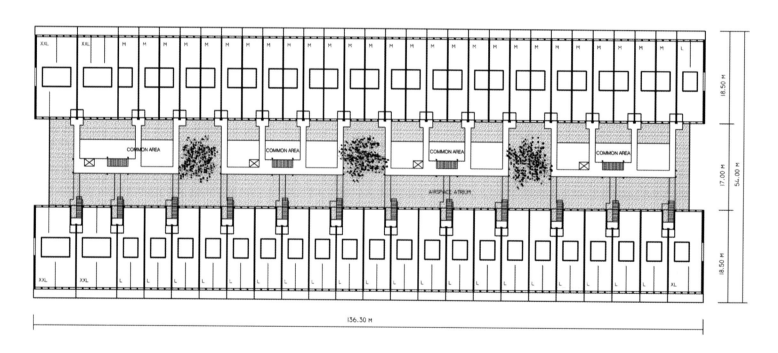

cient public space and infrastructure. Given the minimal possibilities of the surroundings being urbanized in the near future, the project proposes the inverse solution: that of taking the city to the residences. Outside there are the green surroundings, immutable, and, inside, contained between two lines of residential blocks set opposite one another, a street is formed, an atrium cov-

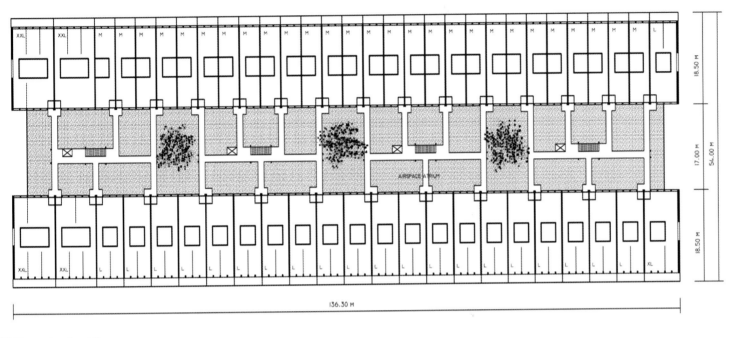

Floor plan level 2.

Floor plan level 3.

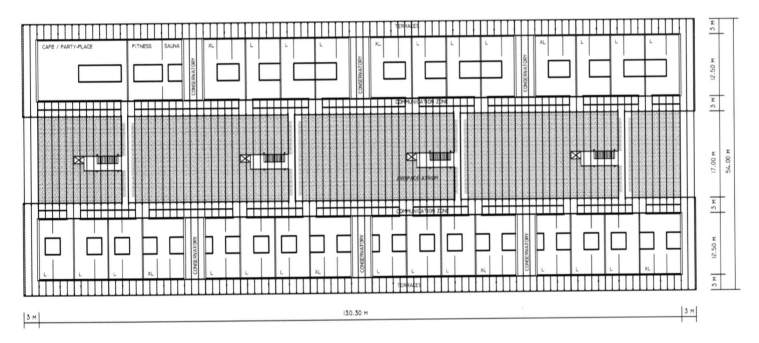

ered by a large skylight. It is a vital interactive vehicle-free central space which accommodates various stores, a nursery school, offices, medical centers and four elevator-stair cores.

The project pays special attention to ecology and energy usage. As a result, the very compactness of the building contributes to minimizing energy loss while the solar panels installed on the

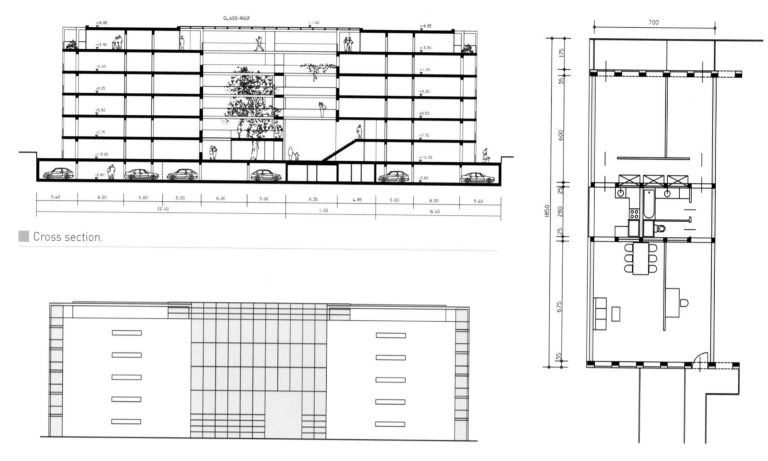

Cross section.

Typologies- examples of grouping.

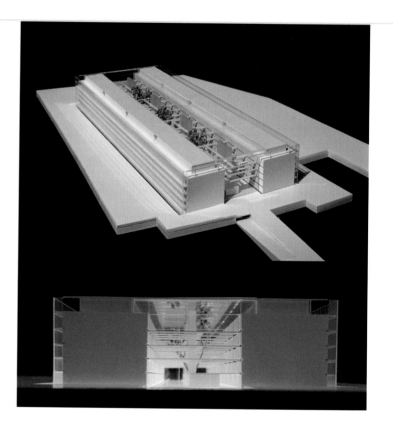

roof provide hot sanitary water. The skylight, with its flexible architectonic structure installed as an autonomous and sustainable unit, paves the way to resolving potential necessities of future development.

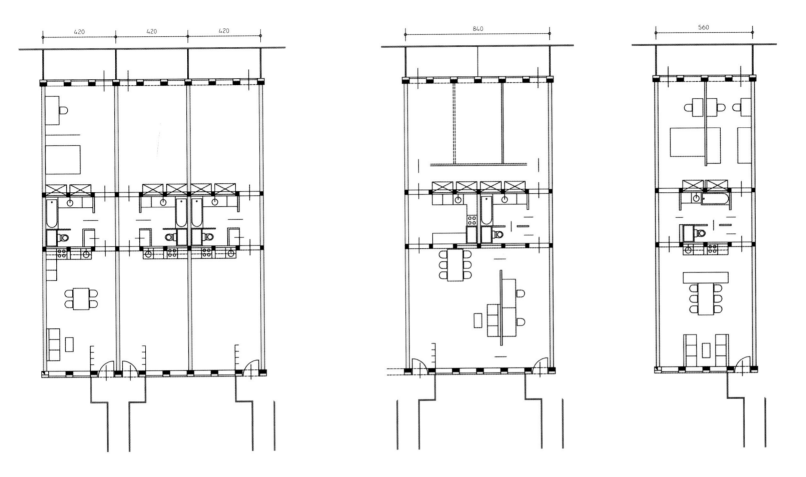

Scale model.

MOUSSAFIR
ARCHITECTES ASSOCIÉS

Jacques Moussafir (1957) graduated in History of Art from the University of Paris in 1984. After having worked in the offices of B. Kohn, C. Hauvette, H. Gaudin, D. Perrault and F. Solier, he set up his own studio in Paris in 1993.

Moussafir Architects Associates' designs have been published in various national and international magazines and selected for various prizes.

Their designs have been exhibited in the following exhibitions: 'Concours Perdus' in the Uzzan Gallery (1996), 'A la recherche de la maison modèle' (1997), 'Hybrid Landscape' presentation of the Berthé House (Rotterdam 2001 and Berlin 2002), 'Constructions de petites échelles' (2001-2002), 'Archilab 2001' and 'Paysages de la mobilité' (Rio 2001 and Mexico 2003).

cabins_for_lock_keepers

maisón_berthé

He has formed part of the Council of Orientation of the National Center of Fine Arts and of the National Commission of 1% of the French Ministry of Culture.

He has also been a visiting lecturer at the Special School of Architecture of Paris and at the School of Architecture, Paris Malaquais.

He has given conferences at the University of Architecture of Paris, La Defènse, Versailles, Dusseldorf and Aix-la-Chapelle as well as at the Escuela Técnica Superior de Arquitectura del Vallès (Barcelona).

Understanding architecture as a phenomena related to experience, Moussafir defines it as the art of the memory: every building produces an infinite number of experiences so that each person

First	first prize in the following competitions.
1999	'Museum of Concrete Art - G. Honegger collection' (Mouans-Sartoux).
2001	'Lock keepers' cabins' (Canal Rhine-Ródano).
2002	'European Center of Chamber Music'.
2004'	'La Luciole, music room' (Alençon).

has a determined image of the physical space that he or she uses; the way we relate to it depends on our memories.

cabins_for_lock keepers

TECHNICAL DATA
Location Canal Ródano - Rhine.
Architects Jacques Moussafir, Bernhard Buch-
berger.
Client Voies Navigables de France.
Structures Batiserf.
Collaborators Lionel Bousquet, Cristiana Floris.
Competition date 2001.
Completion date 2006.
Built area 12 m².

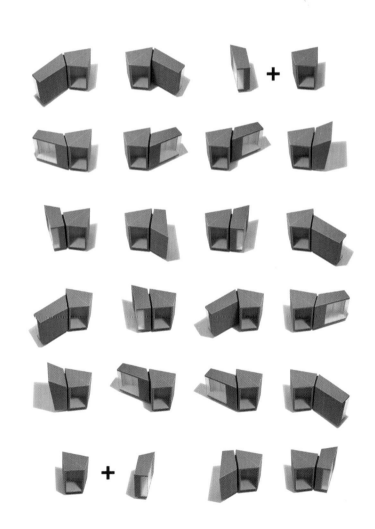

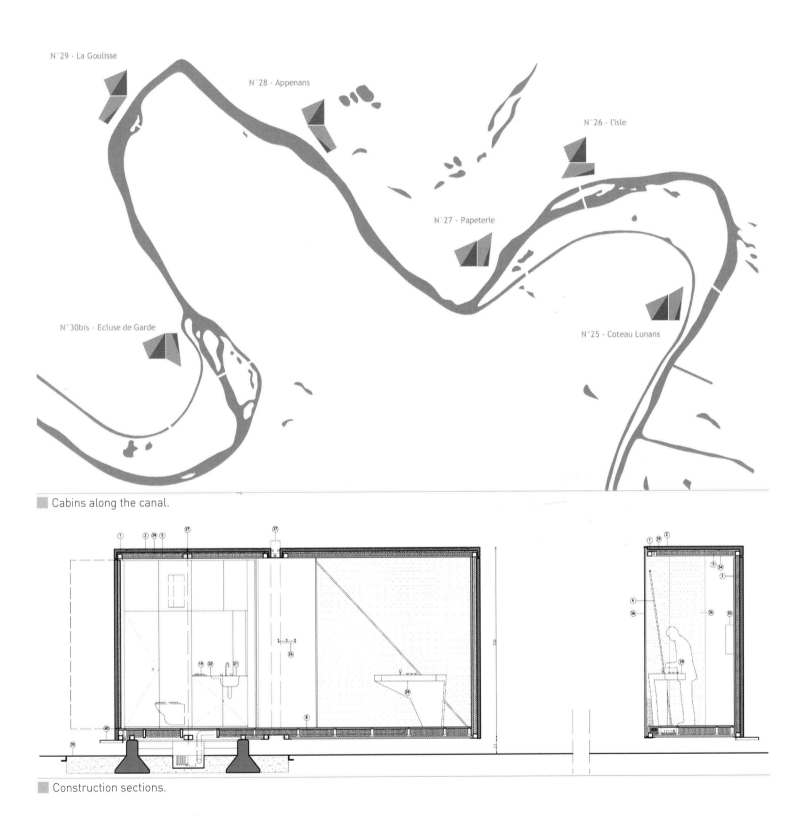

N°29 · La Goulisse

N°28 · Appenans

N°26 · l'Isle

N°27 · Papeterie

N°30bis · Ecluse de Garde

N°25 · Coteau Lunans

Cabins along the canal.

Construction sections.

The objective of the competition was to manifest the existing contradiction between the continuity of the canal, connecting vector between two rivers, and the diversity of the topography of the landscape.

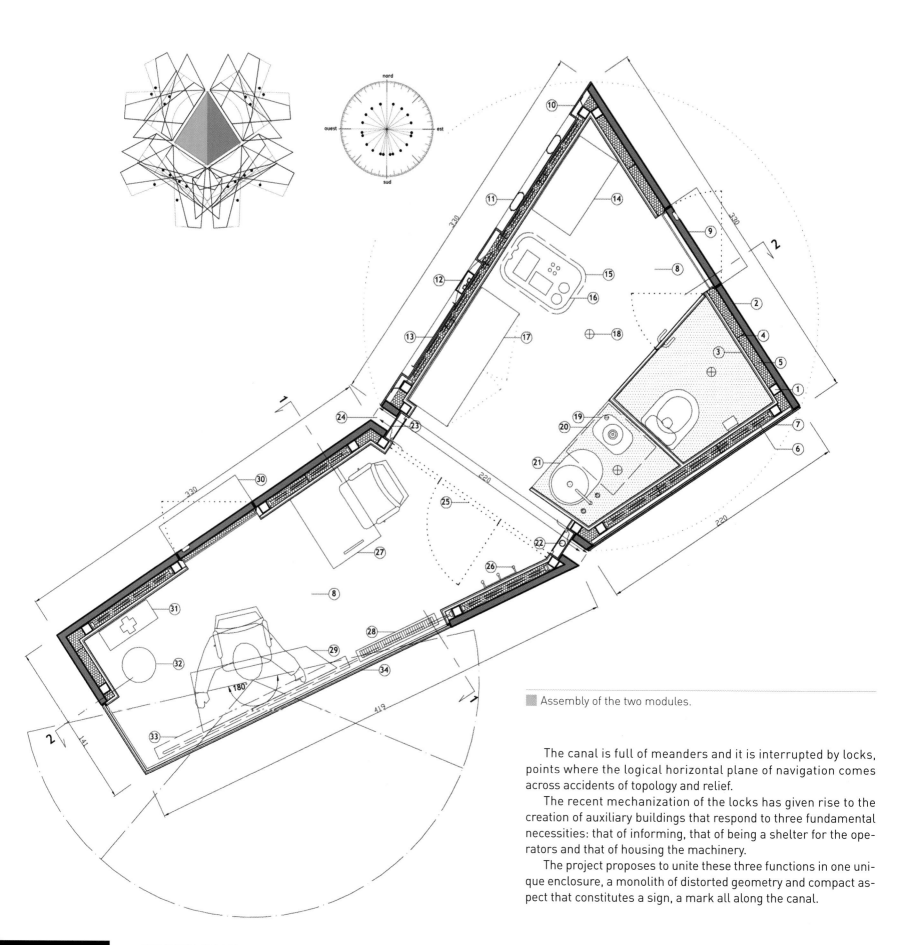

nord
ouest — est
sud

Assembly of the two modules.

The canal is full of meanders and it is interrupted by locks, points where the logical horizontal plane of navigation comes across accidents of topology and relief.

The recent mechanization of the locks has given rise to the creation of auxiliary buildings that respond to three fundamental necessities: that of informing, that of being a shelter for the operators and that of housing the machinery.

The project proposes to unite these three functions in one unique enclosure, a monolith of distorted geometry and compact aspect that constitutes a sign, a mark all along the canal.

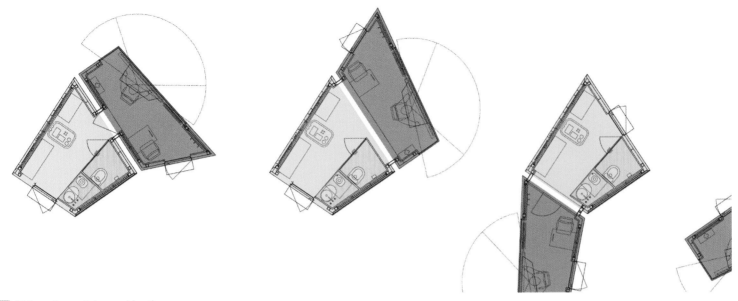

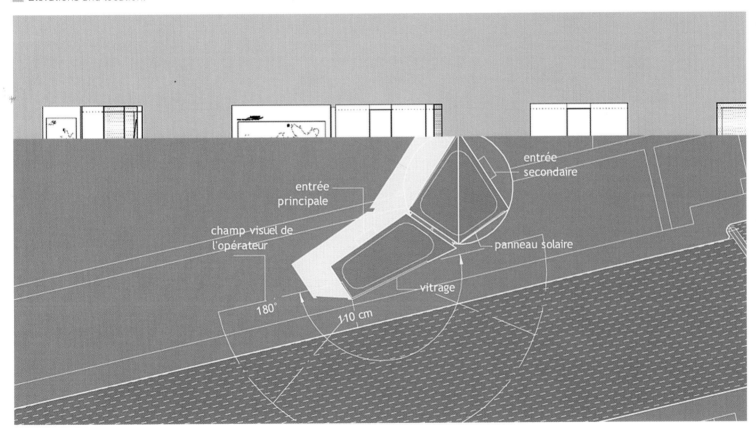

entrée
secondaire

entrée
principale

champ visuel de
l'opérateur

panneau solaire

vitrage

180°

110 cm

Each cabin, reference point in space and time, consists of two plain irregular objects that are connected one to the other. The first is formed by a technical-informative module that is ancho-red to the ground along a north-south axis which indicates the orientation as a weather vane or sun dial would do. Their faces are equipped with solar panels, in order to reduce energy costs, maps

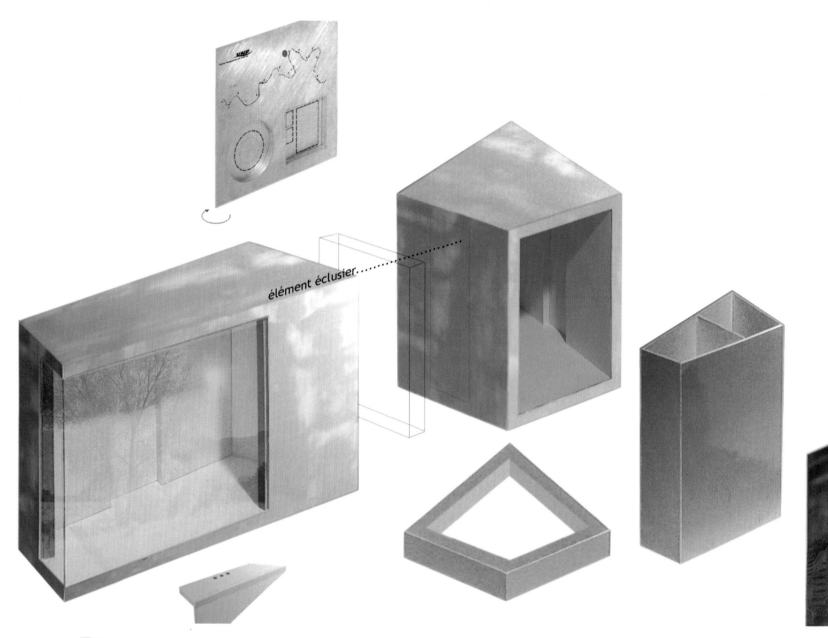

élément éclusier

Prefabricated pieces assembled in situ.

Materials.

and other useful objects (Life rings, telephones...). The second module accommodates the control cabin and the machinery; transparent towards the canal and opaque to the other side, it is supported by the other module in cantilever.

The structure of the cabins is made of prefabricated elements that are easily transportable and assembled in situ that allows for a considerable reduction in costs. The rotation of the control cabin around the technical module offers 26 different combina-

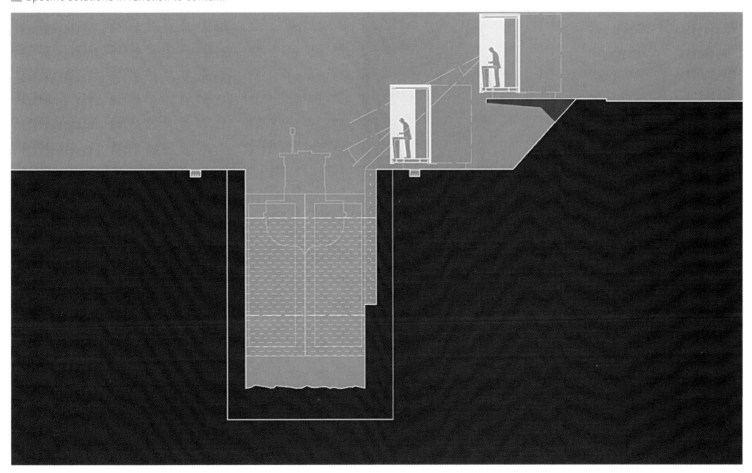

tions of such a manner that, at any point, the first can be situated in line with the canal while the second conserves its north-south orientation.

The flexibility with which it adapts to the differing contexts allows the cabins to integrate easily into the landscape and become habitual sculptures.

berthé_house

TECHNICAL DATA
Location Montreuil.
Architect Jacques Moussafir.
Collaborators Florent Biais, Christiana Floris, Lionel Bousquet, Gilles Poirée, Laëtitia de Lubac, Rémi Schnebelin.
Project date 2001.
Completion date 2004.
Useful surface area 170 m².

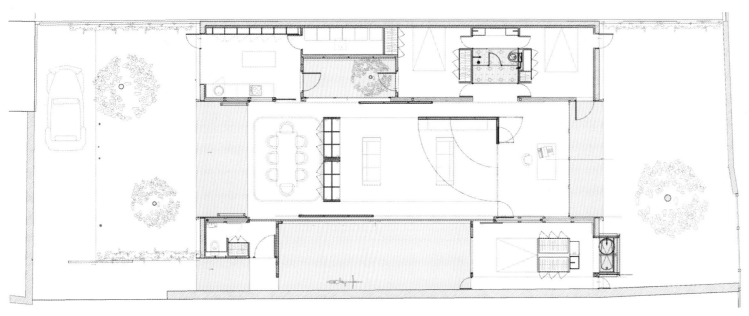

PLAN RDC

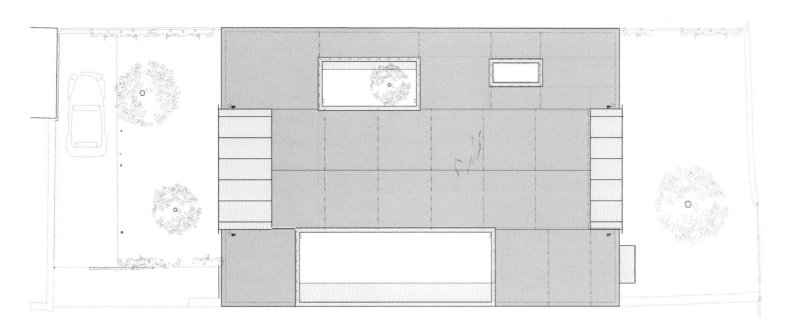

■ The limits of the house become confused with those of the garden.

The residence is situated against an existing wall on a north-south oriented plot and surrounded on three sides by hedge-rows that delimit a vegetable plot. It is a space of silence amidst the urban sprawl of the city. It is a place that was conceived to be experienced from the interior, without enclosures, where its limits become confused with the surrounding garden.

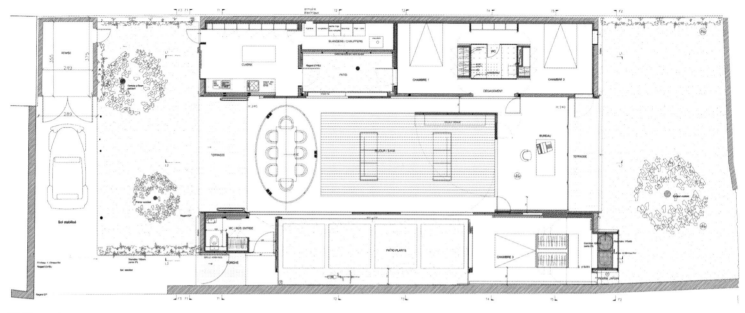

Floor plan.

Interior - exterior.

The walls and the sliding and folding windows hung from the structure of the roof allow for a complete opening of the domestic space onto the exterior.

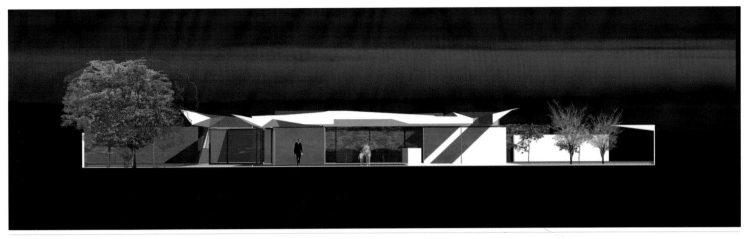

Longitudinal elevation.

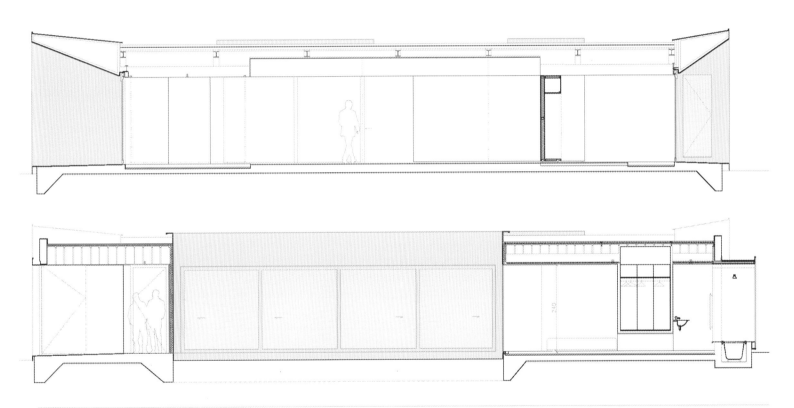

Cross section and elevation.

The house can only be understood as a horizontal plane that comes face to face with the sky and in which the ceiling constitutes the physical and symbolic meeting point between the sky and the ground. The roof becomes the only façade, a laminate of steel with cutouts for the patios and which establishes a vertical relationship with the natural elements.

The vegetable plot as a inhabitable space.

Scale model of the complex.

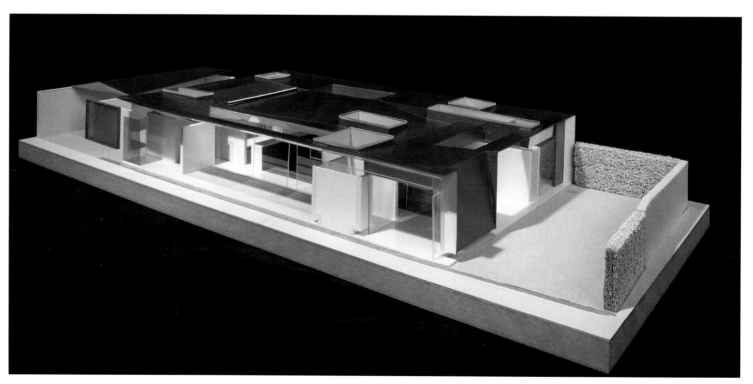

Residence without enclosure.

Space of light and silence.

The limits of the house become confused with those of the garden.

Horizontal plan of the roof with cutouts.

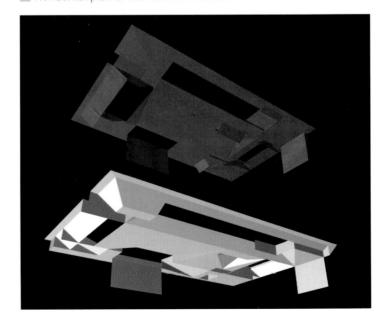

The house has been conceived as a place of silence that contrasts with the excess of information in contemporary life.

Sliding enclosures.

Hollows and patios.

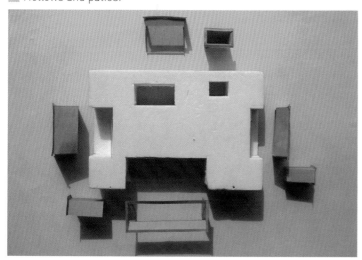
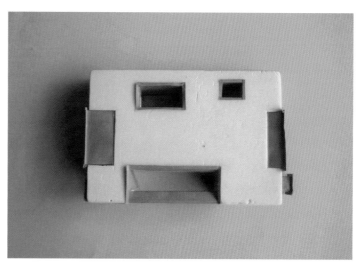

SANAKSENAHO
ARCHITECTS

Matti Sanaksenaho (Helsinki, 1966), graduated from the University of Technology of Helsinki in 1993 and lectured in the university's department of architecture until 1995. He has also been visiting lecturer at universities in Aarhus, Nancy, Copenhague, Estocolmo, Versailles and Trondheim, as well as at the University of Addis Abeba.

He started his career by designing the Finnish pavilion for the Universal Exhibition of Seville as a member of the studio Manark for which he received the State Prize of Architecture of Finland in 1992.

In 1991, he set up his own studio in Helsinki: Sanaksenaho Architects.

In 2000, he was awarded the Reima Pietilä prize for young architects.

ecumenic_art_chapel

villa_cipea

Pirjo Sanaksenaho (Turku, 1966) graduated from the University of Technology of Helsinki in 1993 where she has been a lecturer since the year 2000.

Her collaboration with Matti Sanaksenaho started in 1993 and she was to become his associate four years later.

Sanaksenaho Architects have participated in the following competitions:

The Museum of Modern Art and Architecture of Stockholm (1991), the Finnish Embassy in Berlin (1996), the Ecumenic Chapel (first prize, 1996) and the Helsinki Music Center (1999).

Among their works that particularly stand out are:

The Student House in Vaasa (1998), Stantapark, caves in Rovaniemi (1998), the Family Residence Tammimäki in Espoo (2001), the Old People's Home 'Aurorakoti' in Espoo (2003), Villa in Nanjing for the China International Practical Exhibition of Architecture and the Aho House in Laponia (2003).

Their work has been shown in various exhibitions: the ROM-galleri in Oslo (1992 and 1994), the Stockholm Academy of Fine Arts (1993), the Museum of Finnish Architecture of Helsinki (1992, 1995 and 2004), the Festival of Helsinki (1995), the Nordic Pavilion in the Biennial of Architecture of Venice (1996), the University of Navarra (2000), the Art Front Galley in Tokyo ('New Trends of Architecture in Europe' 2002), the GA Gallery in Tokyo (2004) and in the 9th Biennial International of Architecture of Venice (2004).

The projects taken on by Sanaksenaho Architects range from interior design to urban planning.

Pure materials and sculptural forms are often a reference point for their work.

ecumenic_art chapel

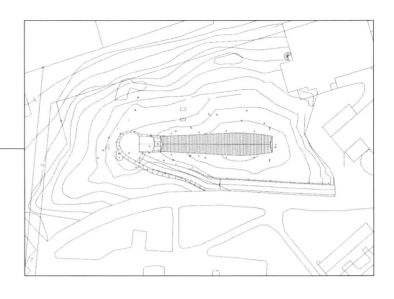

TECHNICAL DATA
Location Turku, Finland.
Arquitect Matti Sanaksenaho
Client Association St. Henrik's Chapel
Collaborators Pirjo Sanaksenaho, Enrico Garbin, Sari Lehtonen, Teemu Kurkela, Juha Jääskeläinen, Maria Isotupa, Jaana Hellinen, Hannu Konola, Kain Tapper.
Project date 1997 (1995 competition)
Completion date 2005.
Built area 300 m².

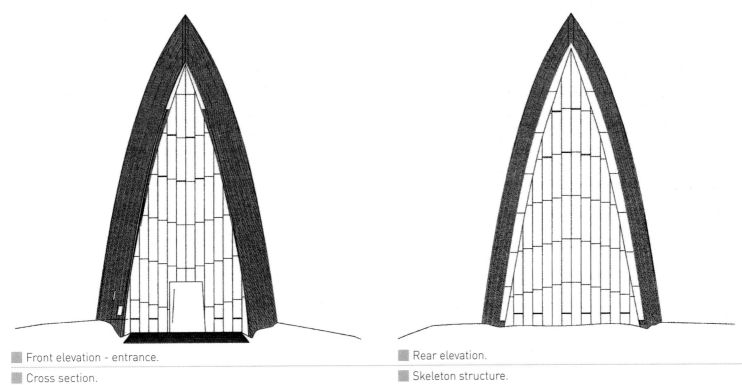

■ Front elevation - entrance.

■ Cross section.

■ Rear elevation.

■ Skeleton structure.

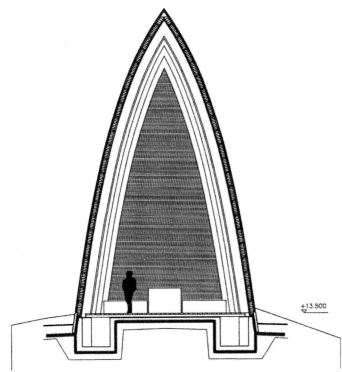

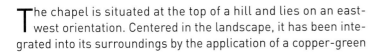

The chapel is situated at the top of a hill and lies on an east-west orientation. Centered in the landscape, it has been integrated into its surroundings by the application of a copper-green

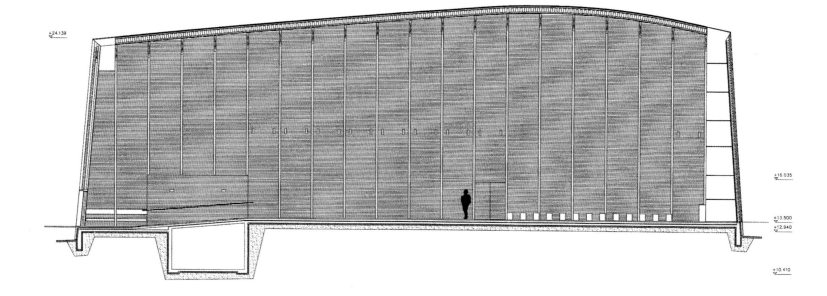

+24.139

+16.035

+13.500
+12.940

+10.410

■ Longitudinal section.

■ South elevation

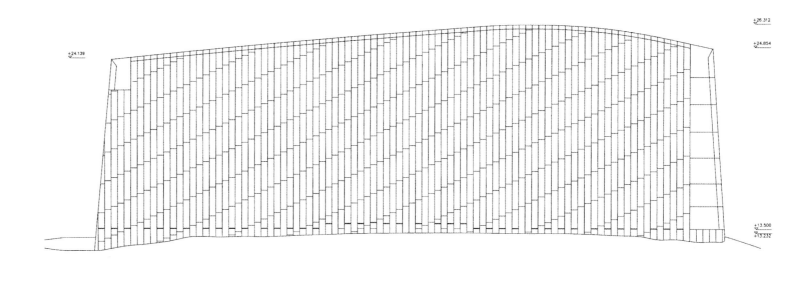

+26.312

+24.854

+24.139

+13.500
+13.232

patina which completely covers it. A close harmony between the architecture and the landscape has been established. Its conception has a sculptural starting point: an art object deposited amidst

nature, a formal piece that goes far beyond a mere architectural model. From the entrance, and through a small hall illuminated by a skylight, a passage leads to a large space 12 meters in height

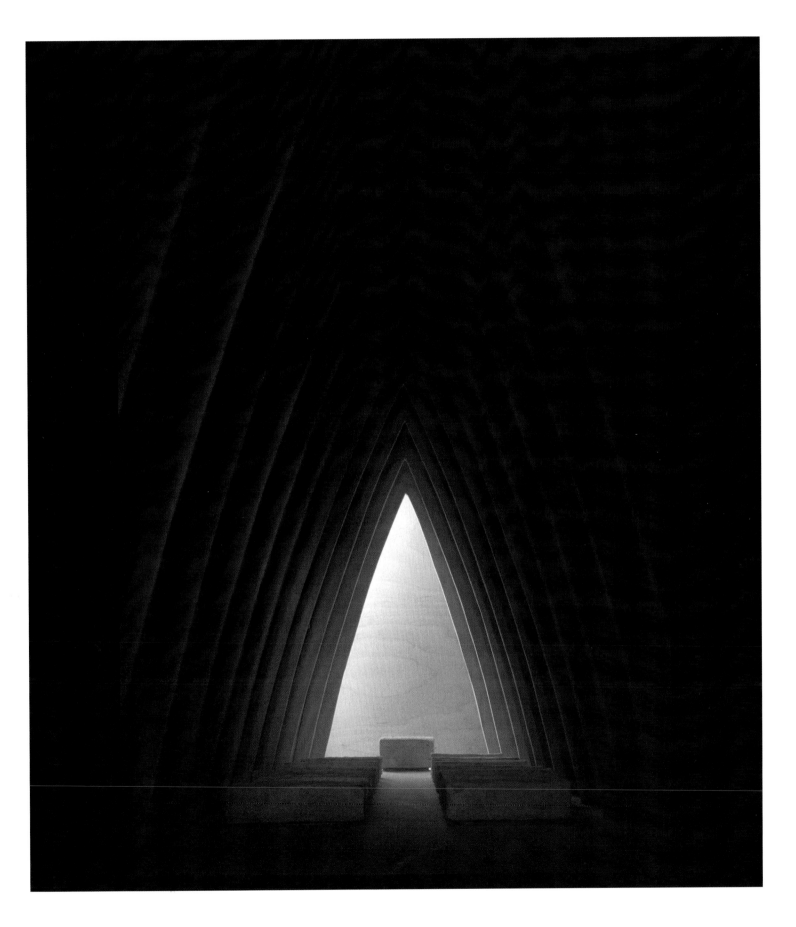

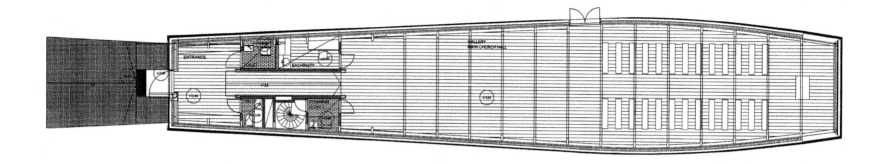

■ Floor plan

■ Side elevation.

in which, following the axis, a gallery is situated in the foreground and the chapel in the background. The wooden ribs that form its structure evoke the organic form of an enormous marine skeleton.

From its interior, a strong indirect light that floods the chapel can be enjoyed. In one of its extremes, two lateral windows in painted glass, a creation of the artist Hannu Konola, illuminate the altar.

TOP **YOUNG** EUROPEAN ARCHITECTS

The entire interior has been paneled in wood and as much the benches as the altar are solid pieces carved by the sculptor Kain Tapper.

In spite of the fact that the competition was won in 1995, it was not until February of 2004 that work began. The chapel is expected to be open to the public in the spring of 2005.

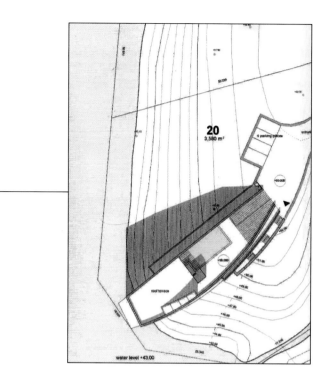

house_in_Nanjing

TECHNICAL DATA
Location Nanjing, China
Architect Matti Sanaksenaho.
Client Nanjing Sifang Educational Enterprise, China International Practical Exhibition of Architecture
Investor / client Nanjing Sifang Educational Enterprise, China International Practical Exhibition of Architecture
Project date 2003-2004
Completion date 2005
Built area 80 m².

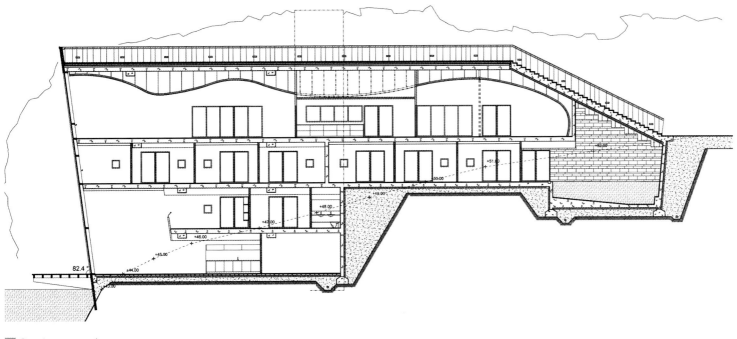

Southeast section

Southeast façade

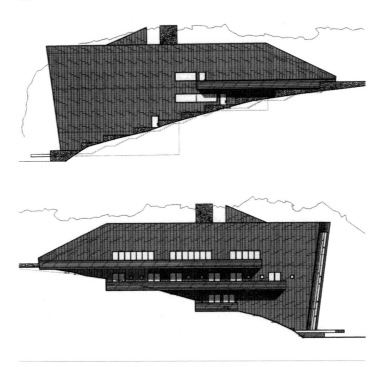

Northeast façade

The house forms part of the China International Practical Exhibition of Architecture (CIPEA) and constitutes one of the objects exhibited.

It is situated in the center of the exhibition area on the shores of a lake and surrounded by dense vegetation.

The copper-green patina with which it is covered camouflages its presence among the trees of the forest. In this way, the surroundings into which it has been inserted are emphasized.

The house was conceived as a holiday home and it combines this use with that of being a temporary workshop for passing-through artists, a space for meetings and seminars, or a resting place for small groups and families.

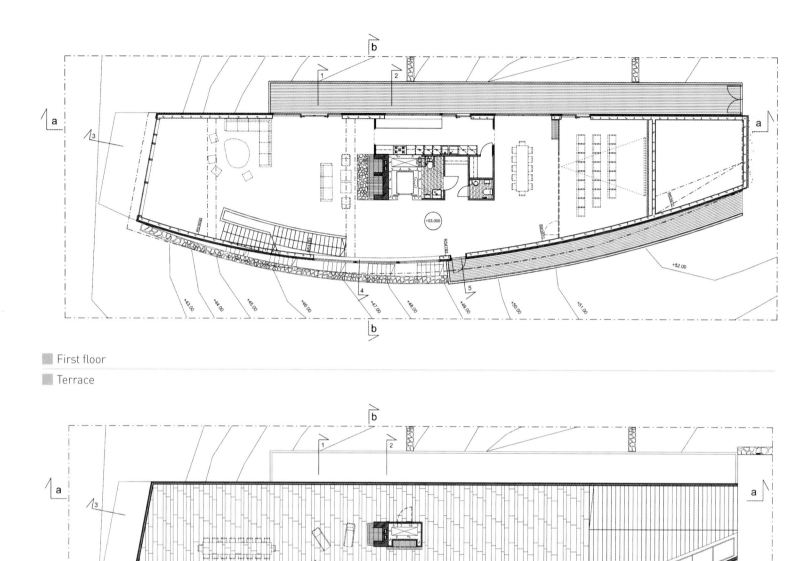

First floor

Terrace

The program has been organized over five levels. The two lower floors are occupied by a suite that can be used as a workshop. On the intermediate floor (level 3) the bedrooms are situated.

The fourth floor, which coincides with the main entrance, groups most of the public functions. In the extreme of this floor, a room that opens onto the lake by means of a large window is situated. Some sliding panels allow this space to be unified with the conference room which strengthens its flexibility.

Lastly, the terrace situated on the top level accommodates the activities that are carried out in the open air.

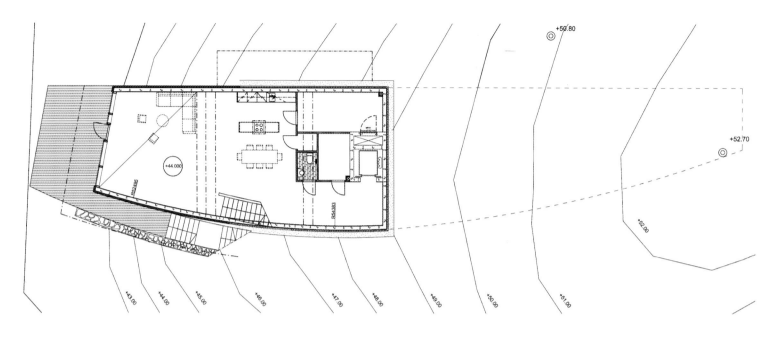

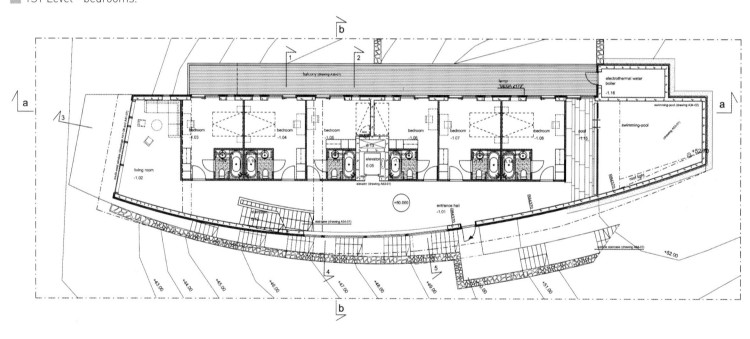

2ND Level - entrance.

1ST Level - bedrooms.

All of the materials used have clear references to the surroundings: the interior is paneled in wood and natural local stone has been used to cover the volume of the elevator, the fireplace and to pave the terrace. The house evokes a boat aground in the lake. Its volume, its materials and its reflections seek the conception of a space for activities in tune with nature.

■ Mezzanine - suite/workshop.

■ Ground floor - suite/workshop.

■ Roof floor - terrace.

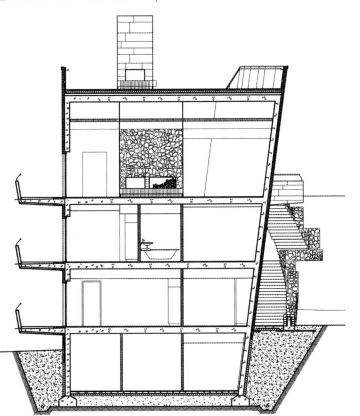

EBNER- ULLMAN
ARCHITECTS

Peter Ebner graduated from the University of Technology of Graz. In 1995, and after collaborating in the studio of the architect Mark Mack in Los Angeles, he set up his own office in Salzburg.

From then, and until 2003, he combined this activity with that of being the president of the Initiative Architektur of Salzburg.

In 1998, he opened a studio in Vienna in collaboration with the architect Franziska Ullmann.

student_hostel

house_b

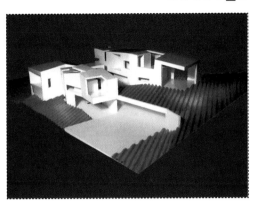

He has lectured at the Universities of Salzburg, Rome and Boston and, since 2003, he has given classes at the University of Munich. Franziska Ullmann graduated from the University of Technology of Vienna, city in which she established her own studio in 1993. In 1998, she associated with Peter Ebner. She has taught at the University of Applied Arts of Vienna and she has been a visiting teacher at the School of Design in Harvard in Boston. Since 1995, she has given classes at the University of Stuttgart.

PETER EBNER + FRANZISKA ULLMANN have taken part in numerous conferences in Universities in Europe, Asia and America.

Their work has been published in 16 countries and their projects have been included in various exhibitions among which the following stand out: 'Emerging Austrian Architecture' (Vienna, Frankfurt, Copenhagen, Budapest, Rome), 'Frische Fische' (Vienna, Oslo, Dornbirn, Graz), 'Housing and friends' (Munich, Koblenz, Klagenfurt, Moscow) and 'GA Houses Projects' 2002 and 2004 (Tokyo).

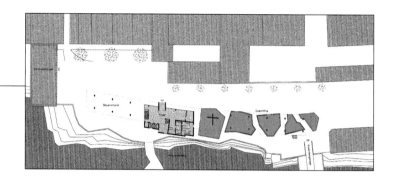

student_hostel

TECHNICAL DATA

Location Salzburg, Austria.
Architects Peter Ebner and Günter Eckerstorfer.
Client Österreichische Studentenförde-rungsstiftung Wenzl-Hartl.
Collaborators Wilhelm Brugger, Peter Schurz, Mi-chael Petschner, Schmid + Schmid, Bischofshofen.
Project date 1995.
Completion date 1999.

South façade facing mountain.

South elevation.

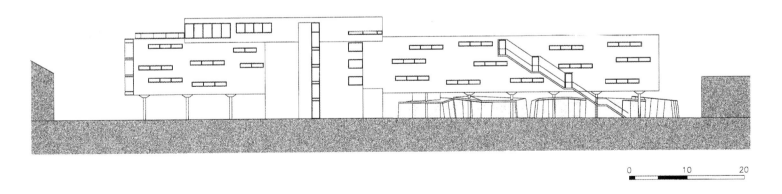

0   10   20

The rugged faces of Kapuziner Mountain make up the backdrop for many of the buildings in the center of Salzburg. They establish a reciprocal dialog amongst themselves which creates a very particular leitmotiv in the architecture of the city. The student hostel is situated on a narrow band, between the precipice and the old quarter, where it had been molded by the curvature

■ View of the terrace.

■ Standard floor plan.

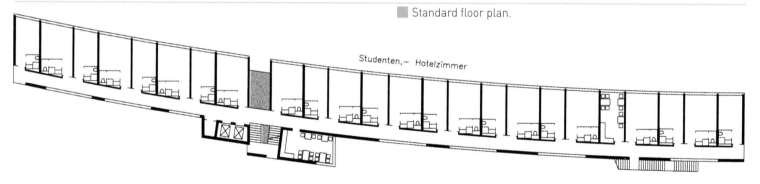

Studenten,— Hotelzimmer

of the mountain. Its implantation inverts the characteristics of the traditional architecture: if the buildings in the old quarter give a weighty appearance emphasized by the continuous base over which they are supported, the hostel, in contrast, is raised over piles that dematerialize its base.

View of access by means of tunnel.

Ground floor - communal areas.

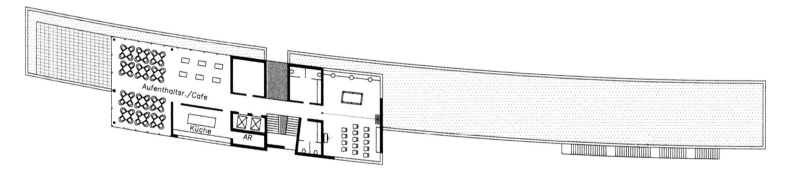

On this open floor, various autonomous glass boxes have been situated in an irregular way to accommodate retail premises. Like stones fallen from the mountains, they intend to attract the attention and interest of the tourists that visit the area.

Vertical communications core.

View of the south façade and details of staircase.

In one of the extremes, there is also an area that is used for a weekly agricultural market. The access to the residence is produced in the form of a tunnel and is indicated by means of a vertical glazed cut in the façade that frames the vertical communi-

cations core and which offers carefully calculated views of the mountain. The homogeneous glass skin of the north face reflects the parallel sequence of the rooms and combines transparent parts and translucent parapets. The south façade, facing

TOP **YOUNG** EUROPEAN ARCHITECTS

■ Details of staircase.

the mountain, is painted in cobalt blue and is free of any tectonic reference. The building is used as a hotel during the summer in order to reduce renting costs for the students throughout the academic year.

house_b

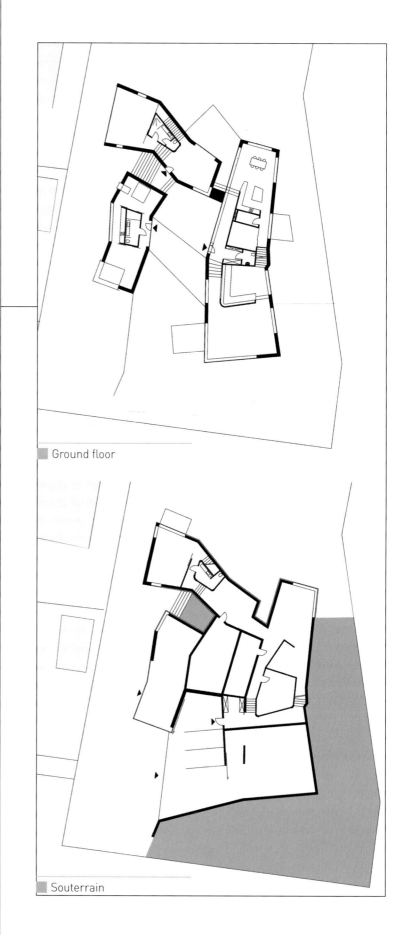

Ground floor

Souterrain

TECHNICAL DATA
Location Hallwang, Austria.
Architects Peter Ebner + Franziska Ullmann.
Client Mr. B.
Collaborators Markus Zilker, Sebastian Maevers.
Landscape gardening Auböck + Karasz.
Project date 2003-2004.
Completion date 2006.
Built area 935 m².

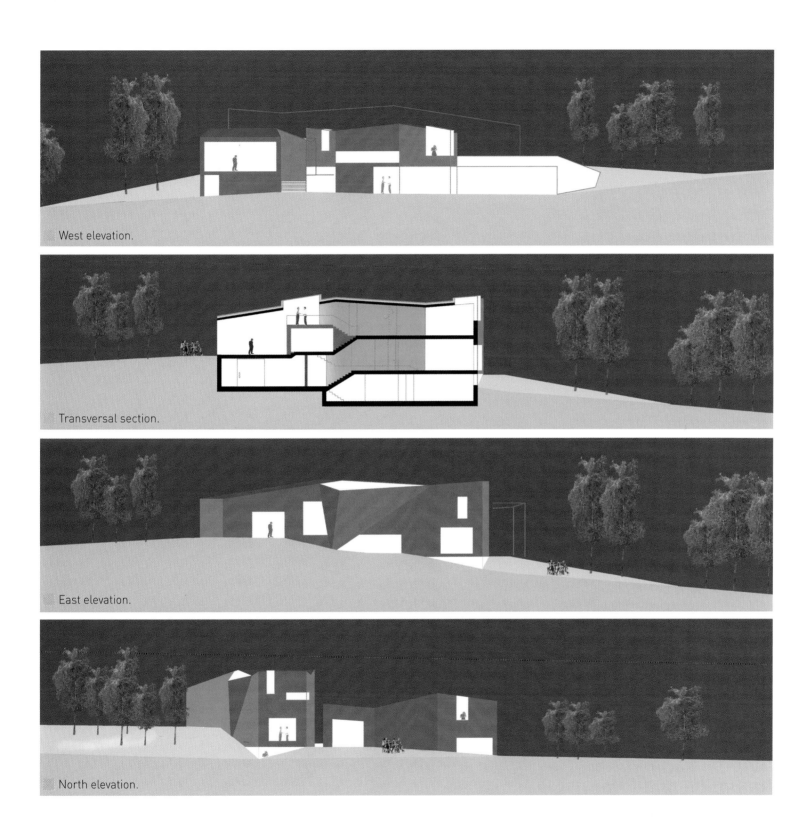

West elevation.

Transversal section.

East elevation.

North elevation.

In 1930, The Viennese architect Josef Frank wrote in his essay on the home: "a well organized house needs to be presented like a city with streets and pedestrian crossings that inevitably lead to traffic free squares, places where one can rest.' Peter Ebner uses this quotation to reflect on the close collaboration that he maintained with the client and which lead to the idea of designing not a

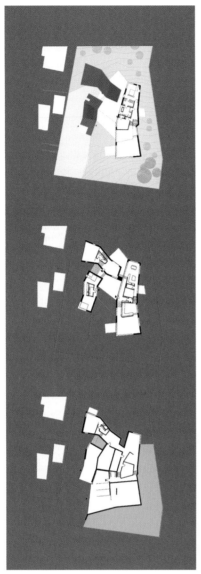

Floor sequence.

First floor.

Scale model.

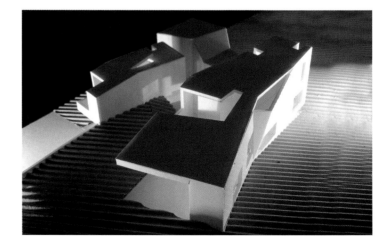

house, but diverse separate volumes that combine the different programs: an office and two residences, one for the parents and another for the children.

The plot is almost completely surrounded by meadows and willow trees. The three volumes of the house have been placed on the plot in a seemingly casual way, they look like uncut diamonds.

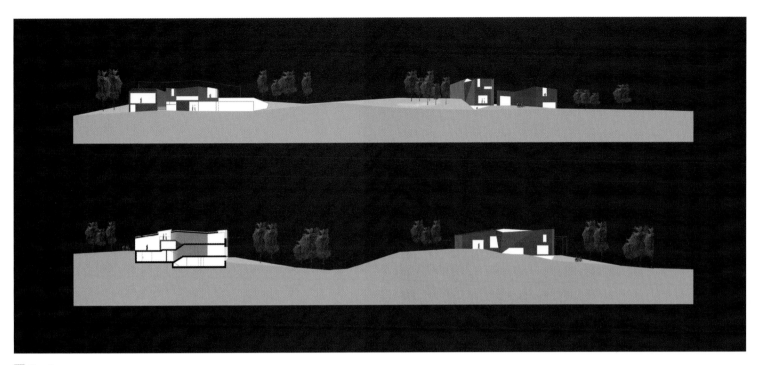

Sections.

Scale models.

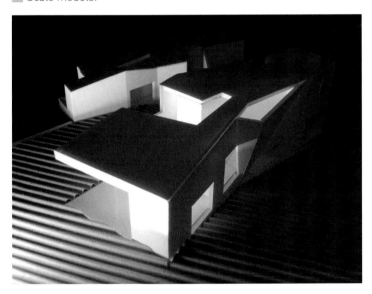
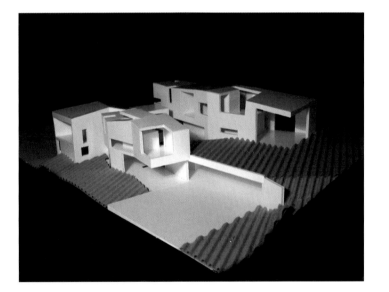

Located in a town with no more than 200 inhabitants, a style that closely relates to the surrounding farms was sought so as to establish a dialog with the existing constructions. In response to the topography of the area, the program has been distributed on different floors which help define different atmospheres on each level.

The lay out contributes to the fluidity of the spaces and allows for the client to experience the house as separate parts of the same space. The construction was carried out by means of traditional brick walls which have been painted in a rusted steel color in order to make the points of intersection between the building and the landscape stand out.

MANSILLA + TUÑÓN

Arquitectos

Emilio Tuñón Álvarez (Madrid, 1958) and Luis Moreno Mansilla (Madrid, 1959) set up the office MANSILLA + TUÑÓN ARCHITECTS in 1992 with the intention of not only dedicating themselves to the design and building activity, but to the confrontation of theory and academic practice as well.

From 1990 to 1992 they sat on the editing committee of the magazine ARQUITECTURA of the C.O.A.M. and since 1998 they have been members of the editorial committee for the magazine PASAJES.

In 1993, along with Luis Rojo, they set up the thinking exchange cooperative CIRCO and published a bulletin by the same name (C.O.A.M. prizewinner 1995, and awarded with the 3rd Latin-American Architecture and Engineering Biennial Publication Prize in 2002).

nanijing

ilidio_pinho_foundation

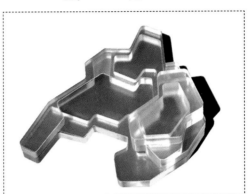

Currently, they are both lecturers in the architectural design department of the Architecture School of Madrid and they have been visiting lecturers to universities in Lausanne, Barcelona, Frankfurt, Navarra and Puerto Rico.

They have received the following prizes: the Architecti Award 1996, the CEOE Foundation Award 1997, the Excellent Work Award 2000, the COACV Award 2000, the FAD Award 2001, the COAM Award 2003 and the Spanish Architecture Award 2003.

Mansilla + Tuñón have won the following competitions: Madrid's Regional Cultural Center in the former El Aguila factory (1995), Leon's Concert Hall (1996), the Castellón Fine Arts Museum (1998), the Cultural Center in Bescia (2000), the Sanfermines Museum in Pamplona (2001), the Museum of Cantabria (2002), the Spanish Royal Collections Museum (2002), Urban planning for

Valbuena in Logroño (2003), Public Library in Calle de los Artistas in Madrid (2003) and Lalín City Hall which is presently under construction. Among their works that particularly stand out are: the Archeological and Fine Arts Museum of Zamora (1996), Indoor Swimming-Pool in San Fernando de Henares (1998), the Fine Arts Museum of Castellón (2000), the Auditorium of León (2003) and MUSAC Museum of Contemporary Art of León (2005).

Over the last few years, MANSILLA + TUÑÓN have developed a diversity of designs in which urban scale along with the problems of occupation have become of great importance.

The Villa 08 in Nanjing and the Ilídio Pinho Foundation contribute to the development of one of the studio's design lines: the integration of a building into its surroundings and the idea of the constructed being an extension of the landscape and an addition to nature.

villa_08
in_Nanjing

TECHNICAL DATA

Location Nanjing. China Continental.

Architects Emilio Tuñón, Luis M. Mansilla y Luis Díaz-Mauriño.

Client China International Practical Exhibition of Architecture.

Local architect Ding Wowo

Collaborators Matilde Peralta, Clara Moneo, Asa Nakano, Catherine Cotting, Andrés Regueiro, Ricardo Lorenzana and María Langarita.

Date of the Project November 2003.

Builded area 400 m².

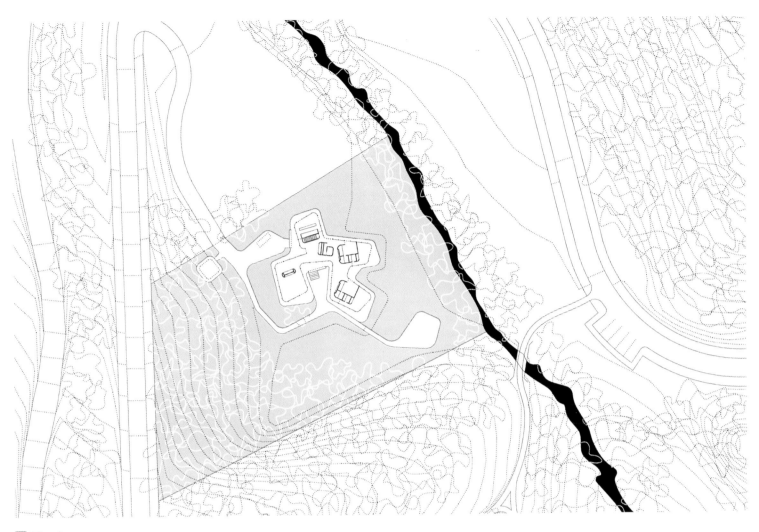

Site plan.

Scale model of location.

The house is situated on a plot with a gentle gradient and it is surrounded by trees. A double skin defines its outer limits: a glazed perimeter that encircles and delimits the interior space and a screen of cut bamboo that shields the house from the outside and filters the light. The residence is the place that is inside this band of a variable width.

The house twists and turns over on itself as if it were a living changing organism while directing the eye towards the forest outside.

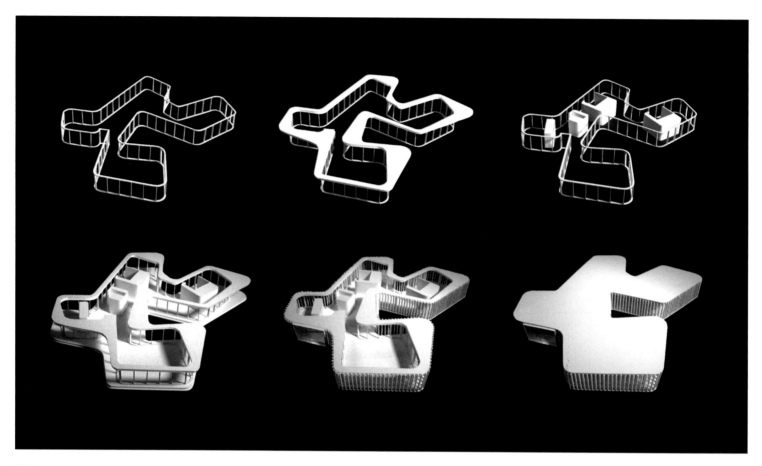

Scale model - Composition.

Scale model - Elevation.

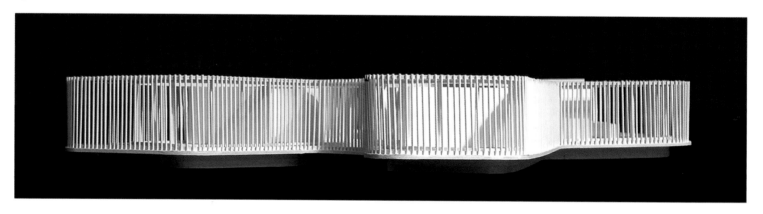

The inhabitable space becomes a clearing in the artificial for-est of cane. One shelters under a flat slab of concrete that rests over the perimeter of the two skins and outlines the space that 'one-needs-for-living-in'.

The slab is supported by laminated steel pillars that lie ap-proximately one and a half meters apart. The section of these pro-files is no more than 6 x10 cm and they are also used as the frames for the carpentry.

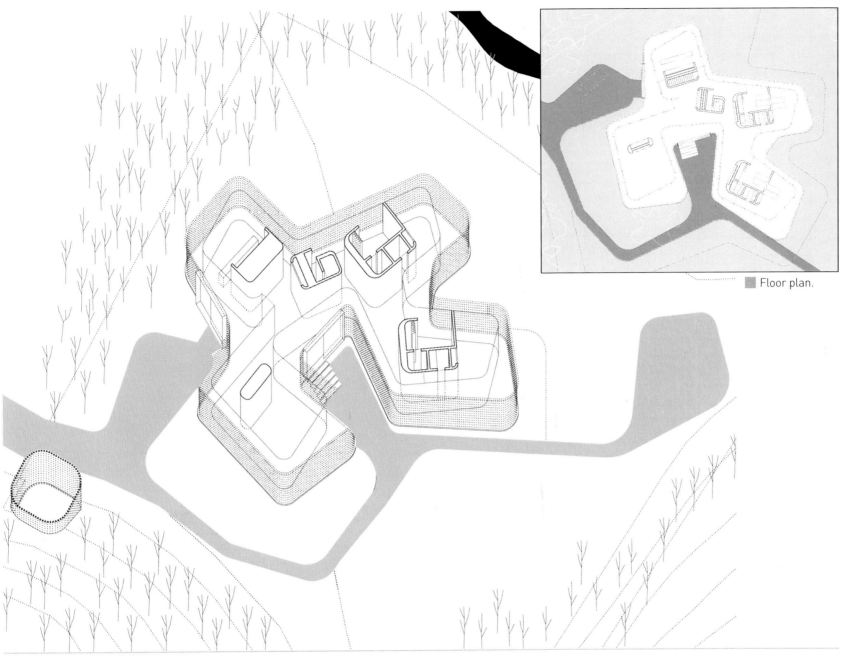

Floor plan.

Axonometric projection.

In this way, the vertical structure dematerializes and emphasizes the lineal continuity of the glazed part which in turn extends the interior into the landscape. The program allows for a versatile functioning of the residence making it suitable for different uses: it can be used by just one family or shared by different people. The communal living areas (kitchen and living room) are situated near the entrance and are typified by being completely uncluttered.

The other four areas, each with its own bathroom facilities, can be used as either bedrooms or small living rooms that extend outwards into the landscape.

Outside, a paved area near the entrance has been included to offer parking facilities.

The rest of the plot has been reserved for the garden in which there are gravel paths and places in which to relax or go for leisurely walks.

ilídio_pinho_
foundation
(competition)

TECHNICAL DATA
Location Oporto, Portugal.
Architects Emilio Tuñón, Luis M. Mansilla, Luis
Díaz-Mauriño and António Barbosa.
Client Fundación Ilídio Pinho.
Collaborators María Langarita, Catherine Cotting,
Teresa Cruz, Ainoa Prats and Andrés
Regueiro.
Date of the Project April 2004.

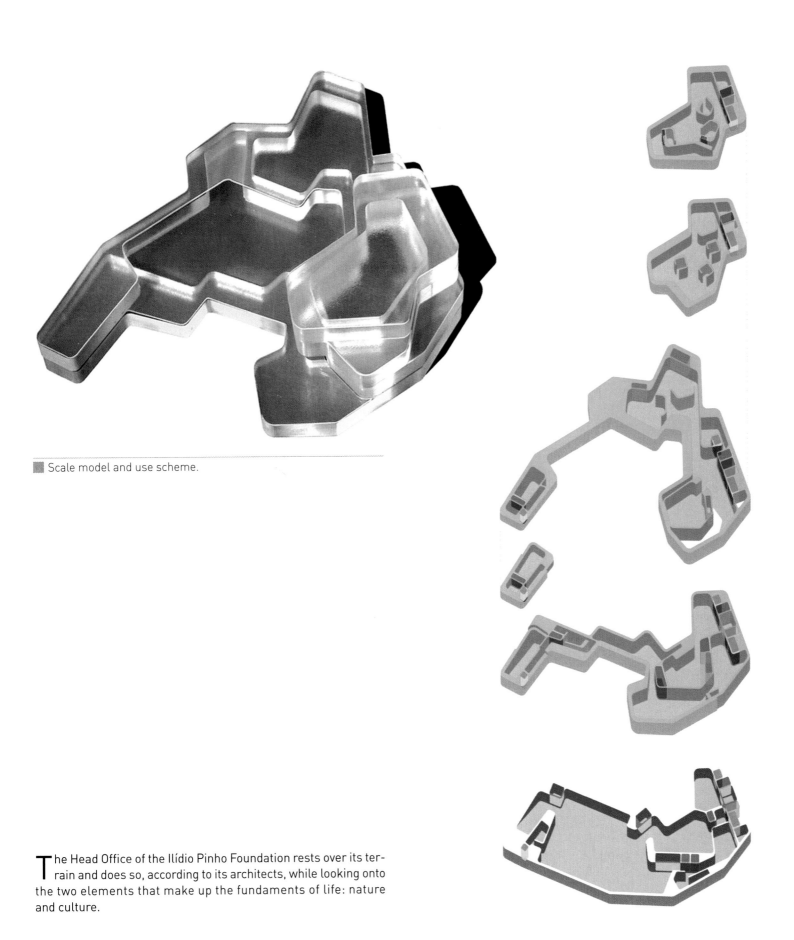

Scale model and use scheme.

The Head Office of the Ilídio Pinho Foundation rests over its terrain and does so, according to its architects, while looking onto the two elements that make up the fundaments of life: nature and culture.

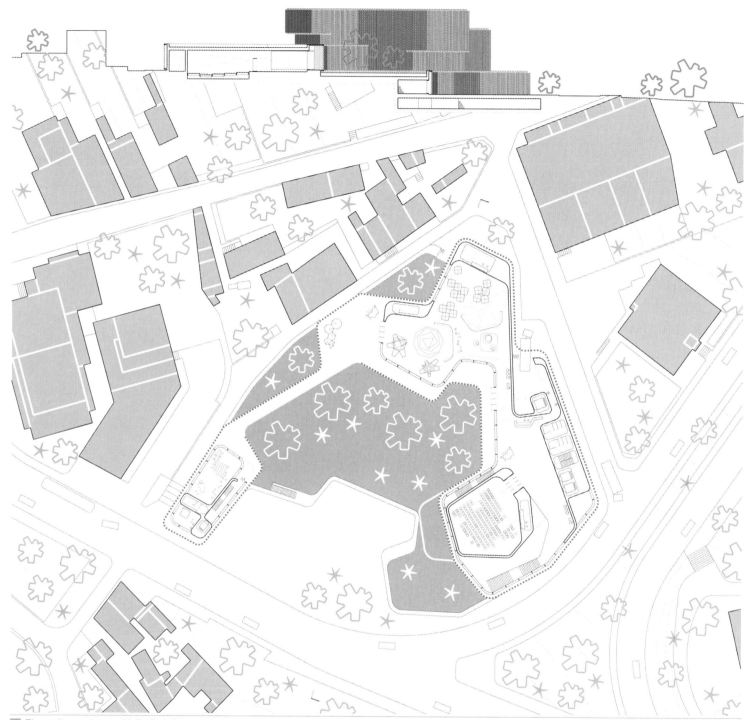

■ Floor dimensions +41,5 . Public space.

It identifies with the nature in which it sits in two senses of the word: that of being equal and at the same time, that of being different.

Man recognizes himself to be part of the world, however, at the same time, he feels himself to be unique and he converts frontiers into links of a relative nature.

Location. Entrance floor

And he settles into that culture understood as that specifically human and free which begins where nature finishes and permits one to think and modify the world.

The pencils with which man outlines his proposals are equality and diversity on one hand, and creative liberty on the other.

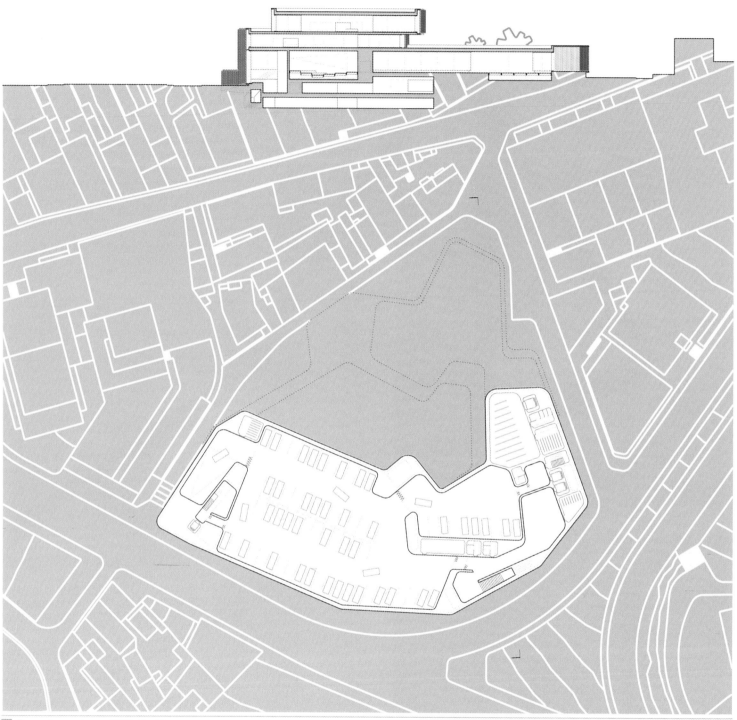

Floor dimensions +33,0. Parking.

The foundation leans out over the street to create a space for reception and refuge which provides an inviting entrance and enables it to share its space with the city and its inhabitants.

Culture is spread; it is made known in the surrounding areas. The different floors and the activities carried out on them extend and relate to their surroundings while the higher floors step back

before the presence of nature and open up their views of the sea. The façade is seen as a continual surface made up of glass cylinders that are illuminated by means of fiber optics or leds in different colors which offer a changing and luminous image that echoes an old lighthouse. A building made of light and life that can be seen to change in appearance, in hues, in intensity and that becomes a work of art in itself and a new reference for artistic, economic and cultural life in Oporto.

MEYE®
ARCHITECTS

Philippe F. Meyer is the leader of this firm of architects which has its head office in Switzerland. He graduated as an architect from the DPLG of Marseille in 1985.
Member of the Ordre des Architectes Français since 1986.
Collaborator with the firm Jourdà & Perraudin in Lyon in 1986.
He started his professional activity in Berne as a collaborator in the offices of the architects Reinhard & Partner from 1987 to 1992.

on_off

360_shadow

Collaborator with the Institute of Architecture of the University of Geneva from 1995 to1996 along with the professors Kurt Allen and Fernando Ramos. He wrote a catalog of architecture to commemorate the 700 years of the Confederation. Author of the Swiss architectural magazine "Face".

For eleven years, he shared the title of associate founder with Pierre Bouvier in the firm Meyer & Bouvier that opened its central office in Berne in 1992.

Establishment of the new architecture studio Meyer & Bouvier in the city of Geneva in 1995.

Prizewinner along with P.Bouvier for the project for the Faculty of Psychology and Educational Sciences of the University of Geneva.

In the year 2003, he set up his present studio, Meyer Architects.

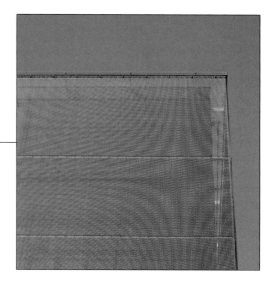

on_off

TECHNICAL DATA

Location	University of Geneva.
	42, bld du Pont-d'Arve 1205, Geneva.
Architects	Philippe F. Meyer & Pierre Bouvier.
Client	University of Geneva.
Collaborators	Didier Leclerc.
	Civil engineering: Guscetti & Tournier.
	Alain Dubuis.
	Engineering: Optitherm. Scherler.
Consultant companies	*Geometry:* Morand et Bovier.
	Façades: Ipan - Bovard.
	Enclosures: GKD.
Construction manag.	REGTEC S.A.
Project date	Competition 1997, winning project
	Definitive project 1999.
Completion date	2001- 2003.
Built area	3558 m².
Construction company	REGTEC, S.A.

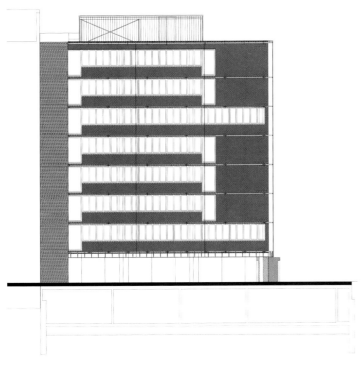

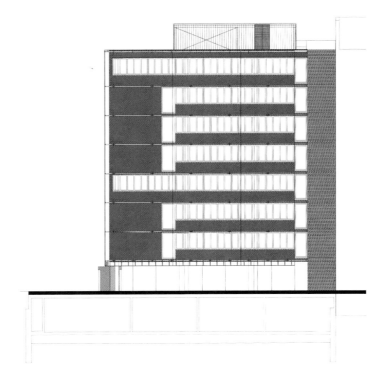

Exterior longitudinal side section.

Side cross section building entrance.

Longitudinal side section interior of the enclosure

Cross section. Vertical communication nucleus.

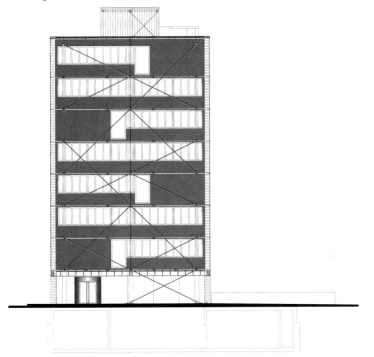

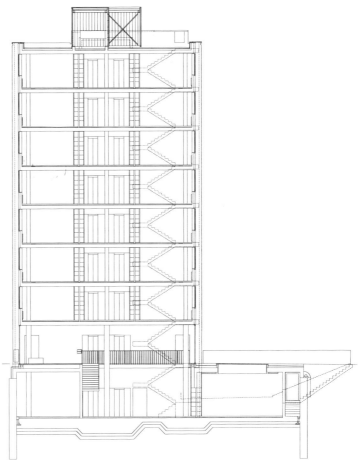

Meyer Architects' design for the new Faculty of Psychology and Educational Science for the University of Geneva won first prize in the competition in 1997.

ON / OFF is a seven-story building situated on the university campus of the University of Geneva to accommodate the new Faculty of Psychology and Educational Science.

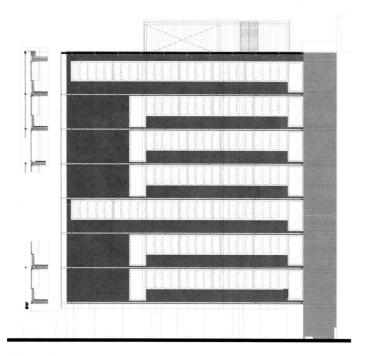

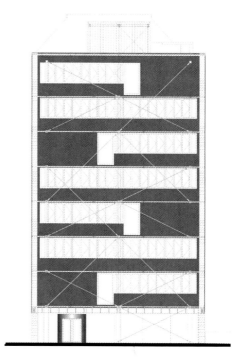

■ The different levels rest on the solid container prism of the service and communication elements.

■ Transversal side façade. The prism rises over a well-defined entrance.

■ The structural latticework of tensioners forms part of the composition.

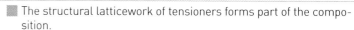

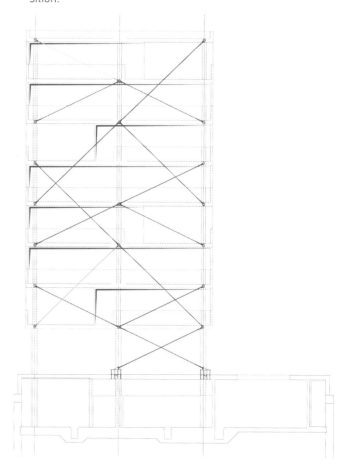

The building is situated in the patio of the university in such a way that it functions as a lobby to the campus. Over the fluid entrance floor, a volume seven floors in height rises.

In its implantation, the building was dug into the terrain and the space in which the seminar rooms have been installed occupies the area that was emptied. Skylights built into the structure of the entrance area illuminate the zone.

The new building comes up against, in the rear part over the wall, a building which was already in existence. This support has been used as a containing space in which all of the service and vertical distribution elements, which are repeated on all of the floors, are confined. The monolithic supporting wall in anthracite concrete creates a break from the existing while at the same time presenting a solution of continuity.

The different floors, freed from elements related to services and vertical communication due to the constructive system adopted, have been subdivided into three packets of modular offices that have been distributed in an alternative and independent way on each level. The situation of a fixed structural network allows for the variation in the modules of the offices that leads to flexibility of the spaces for interior circulation.

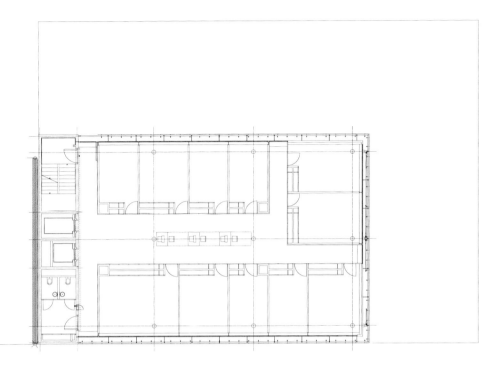

■ Standard floor plan (1st level). The offices are laid out in three independent blocks.

■ Standard floor plan (2nd level). The services container is arranged in the same way on each floor.

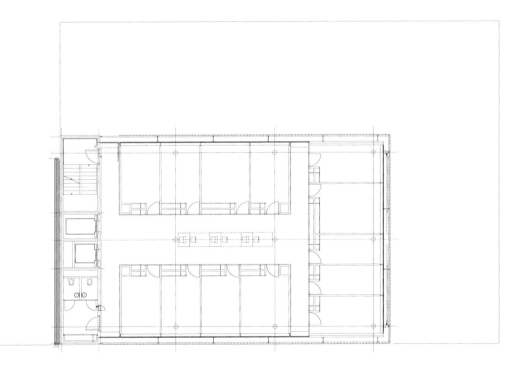

With this variability, it has been managed to create levels which each have an aspect of their own and which each make a distinctive use of the natural exterior light according to their particular necessities. A varying perception of the interior towards the exterior is achieved on each of the floors as a result of the change in distribution of the office modules and the hollows in the façade.

The cladding of the neutral office modules, plastered in white, contrasts with the wooden paneling in the communal communication areas.

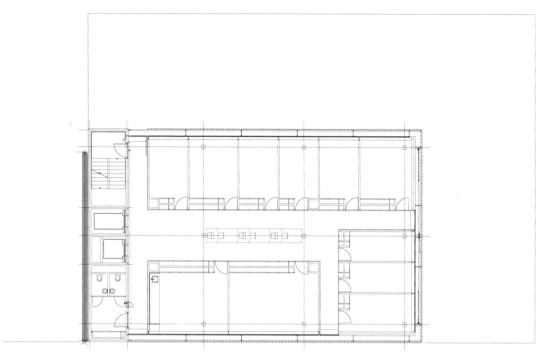

■ Standard floor plan (3rd level). This arrangement of the modules allows for different forms of circulation.

■ Ground floor. A both visually and structurally uncluttered reception area.

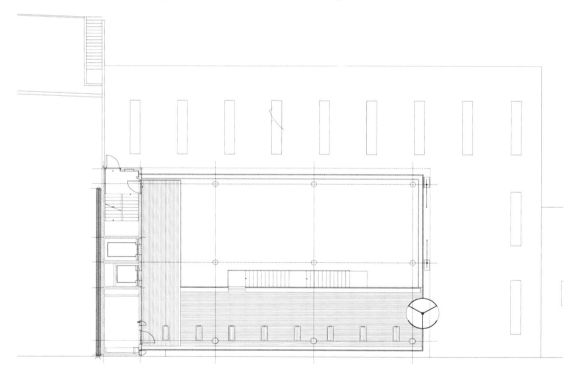

In the basement, a perimeter room gives access, from one part, to the container that groups the vertical communication nucleus and the services and, from the other part, to the main staircase that leads to the lobby.

The intermediate space functions as a foyer from which the seminar rooms are accessed. The rooms are distributed around the perimeter established by the plaza above and from which similar proportions marked by the imposing structure have been adopted.

Openings in the paving of the entrance plaza provide illumination for these rooms. These skylights have been fitted into the transit area to perfection.

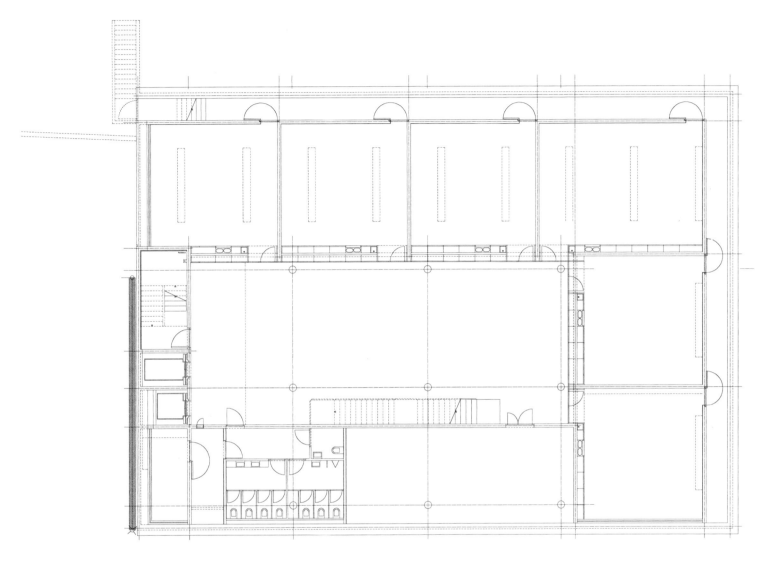

■ The double space forms the foyer which organizes the seminar rooms.

■ The prism rises defying gravity over a transparent lower floor.

The volume that makes up the different floors, each one of the materials used, the spatial combinations, the structural and constructive elements form an incomplete whole in terms of its exterior perception that should unify it with a new cladding.

With the intention of creating uniformity within the building, the resulting façades have been covered with a layer of black insulation over the solid elements and thermo lacquered black aluminum in the openings.

The stability of the different planes has been made evident in the façade by means of a formal abstraction that is free and unified and made up of a network of stainless steel braces that cross at different levels.

The visual interruption of the entrance communicates the interior of the campus with the city.

The protecting veil unifies the overlay of the façades.

As a superficial covering, a uniform metallic fabric, supported by the network of braces, bars and tensioners, forms a protective veil that shelters the façade from environmental aggressions. At night, the transparency of this wrapping makes the building stand out and it becomes an illuminated landmark, a reference in the university enclosure.

The wrapping presents the particularity of a changing perception according to the time of day, the angle at which the sun hits it, the brightness, the humidity in the air, the temperature, the color of the sky, the interior illumination, the group of vestibules and the unity of the city. This provokes a variation in the perception of the planes as opaque elements, matt, transparent... with differing textures: velvety, with the waviness of a prism that rises weightlessly over another prism floating and transparent like a landmark and symbol.

360_shadow

TECHNICAL DATA
Architects Philippe F. Meyer, Antoinette Schaer,
Christian Sheidegger.
Collaborators Civil engineering: Guscetti & Tournier.
Métallover, S.A.
Decisión, S. A.
Project date 2004.

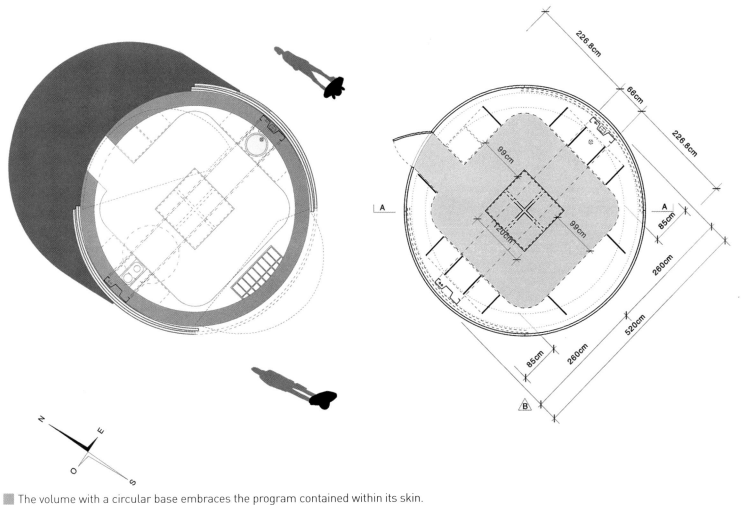

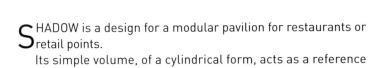
The volume with a circular base embraces the program contained within its skin.

The exterior cladding accommodates the mechanisms of articulation and accessibility.

S HADOW is a design for a modular pavilion for restaurants or retail points.

Its simple volume, of a cylindrical form, acts as a reference that is easily perceived in an unspecified natural environment.

The pure geometry of the element allows it to be quickly localized and resolves particular programs. It is a mass-produced product which an endless number of combinations that makes it adaptable to any requirements.

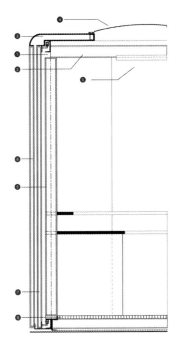

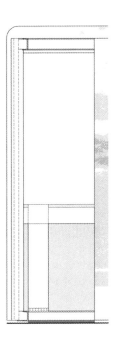

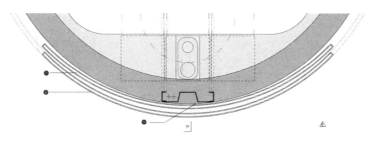

■ The treatment of the interior lining suggests creativity and versatility.

The cladding of the pavilion, designed exteriorly with great simplicity, embraces a simple homogeneous volume. This skin contains the mechanisms that modify its compactness and which allows it to unfold over itself in order to achieve permeability and offer access to the volume.

This makes it easily adaptable to the necessities of its uses in supposed situations and facilitates relocation.

The volume stands out in its environments and becomes a landmark of a pure neutral form in any undetermined landscape.

Its intended temporary use has lead to a simple distribution that adapts perfectly to the form of its volume which, as the nucleus that it is, radiates from the center an attraction that allows for the grouping that typifies the program.

The neutrality of the exterior cladding contrasts with the interior design of the enclosure. Its circular format offers a panoramic reading that adapts in a chameleonic like way to its use which leads to a subtle and suggestive perception of the space available.

museum_of_almería

PAREDES PEDROSA
ARQUITECTOS

Ignacio G. Pedrosa (Madrid, 1957) graduated in 1983 in the Higher Technical School of Architecture of Madrid, where he has been teaching since 1995.

Ángela García de Paredes (Madrid, 1958) graduated in the Higher Technical School of Architecture of Madrid in 1982 and is professor of projects in the ESARQ UIC in Barcelona.

PAREDES PEDROSA has been carrying on since 1990 a professional activity directed to competitions, projects and works of public and cultural buildings, together with urban projects in a number of towns.

They have been invited professors at national courses and seminars: Universities of Madrid, Pamplona, Valencia, Coruña,

palace_of_congresses in_peñíscola

olimpia_theater

Granada, and international ones: Rome, Mexico, Universities of Oslo, Munster, Santo Domingo, FADU Buenos Aires, City University of New York.

The following constructed works have received awards. Consistorial House in Valdemaqueda:

1999: (Finalist FAD, V Biennial of Spanish Architecture, Mention COAM, Honorable Mention Architécti, ar+d award); 2000. II Bienal Iberoamericana de Arquitectura, Comunidad de Madrid Prize for Architecture; Antonio Palacios Exhibition: 2001. Mention Ayuntamiento de Madrid, 2002. Mention FAD; Congress Center in Murcia: 2002. Mention ar+d, Mention FAD, 2003, Mention Arquitectura de Murcia; 101 Officially Protected Dwellings in Madrid: 2003. VII Biennial of Spanish Architecture, Prize COAM, Mention Ayuntamiento de Madrid; Palace of Congresses in Peñíscola:

Frst	prize in the following competitions:
1991	EUROPAN 2.
1993	Consistorial House in Valdemaqueda.
1995	University campus Murcia.
1996	EUROPAN 4 and Borghetto Flaminio (Rome).
1997	Olimpia Theater in Madrid.
1999	Archeological Museum in Almería.
2000	Palace of Congresses in Peñíscola.
2002	146 VPO EMV Madrid.
2004	Archelological Area in La Olmeda Palencia.

2004. Finalist FAD, ASCER Architecture prize; Museum of Almería: 2004. ARCO Prize and Finalist PAD.

museum_of_almería

TECHNICAL DATA

Location Almería.

Architects Ignacio García Pedrosa and Ángela García de Paredes.

Collaborators Silvia Colmenares. Manuel G. de Paredes. Eva M Neila. Danko Linder.

Coordinating architect Enrique López Burló.

Quantity surveyor Luis Calvo.

Works supervisor Patricia Largo.

Client Ministry of Culture.

Date of competition 1998.

Date of project 1999.

Building area 6.284 m².

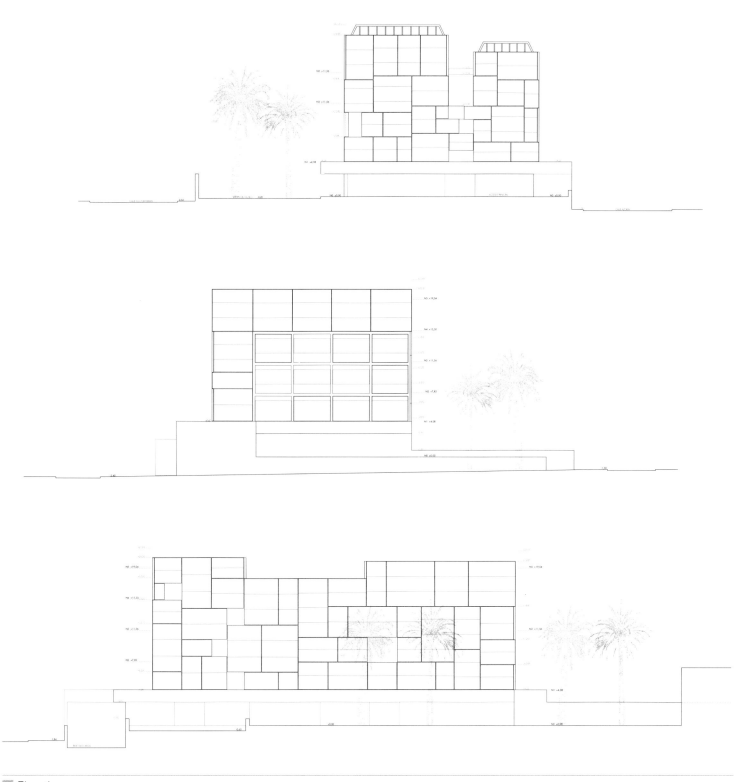

Elevations.

The museum, designed to contain the archeological heritage from various sites in Almería, stands in an environment with high-rise buildings and a road with heavy traffic. Standing on a corner site, it frees up space to a slightly elevated square which is planted with palm trees and opens up to the town; this serves as an approach to the museum.

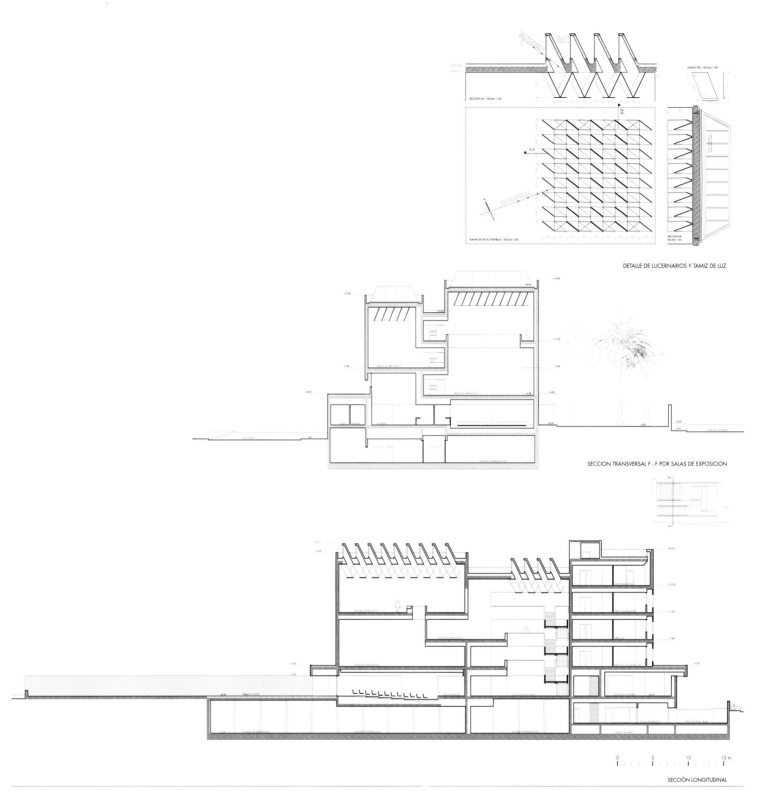

DETALLE DE LUCERNARIOS Y TAMIZ DE LUZ

SECCION TRANSVERSAL F - F POR SALAS DE EXPOSICION

SECCIÓN LONGITUDINAL

Sections of the building.

The building is designed as a hermetic, compact volume, built with large pieces of natural stone, and standing on a plinth of concrete which houses the reception area.

The rooms planned for the permanent collection are superimposed in three levels, vertebrated in section by an empty space which links and relates them, helping to orientate the visitor.

PLANTA DE CUBIERTAS
ROOF PLAN

PLANTA TERCERA. SALAS. CONSERVADORES
LEVEL 3. EXHIBITION ROOMS. CURATORS

PLANTA QUINTA. LUCERNARIOS
LEVEL 5. SKYLIGHTS

PLANTA SEGUNDA. SALAS. DIRECCIÓN
LEVEL 2. EXHIBITION ROOMS. OFFICES

N

PLANTA CUARTA. LABORATORIO DE RESTAURACIÓN
LEVEL 4. RESTORATION WORKSHOP

PLANTA PRIMERA. SALAS. BIBLIOTECA
LEVEL 1. EXHIBITION ROOMS. LIBRARY

N

Levels of the museum.

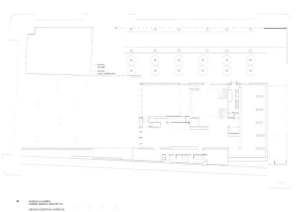

MUSEUM IN ALMERÍA
PAREDES PEDROSA ARQUITECTOS
GROUND FLOOR PLAN. ENTRANCE

On the other hand the technical premises of the museum, store-rooms, administration, library and conservation laboratory, are placed on five levels abutting on the public exhibition area.

 Top-lit inner space of three-story height.

Façade towards the square.

The top-lighting of the central three-story space, and that of the upper rooms, is filtered through modules of wood which constitute a coffering of light.

The hermetic volume of the museum and the raised square.

Façade enclosing the technical premises of the museum.

The lighting of the rest of the exhibition rooms is manifested in the façade in the form of hollows set here and there, embrasures through which the outside filters in.

palace_of_congresses in_peñíscola

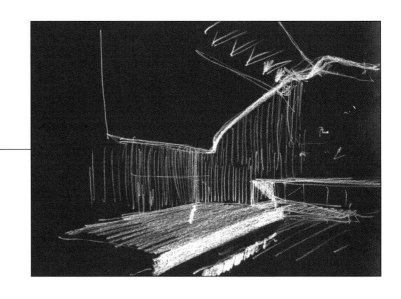

TECHNICAL DATA
Location Peñíscola, Castellón de la Plana.
Architects Ignacio García Pedrosa and Ángela García de Paredes.
Collaborators Eva M. Neila. Silvia Colmenares. Javier Arpa.
collaborating-work Jaime Prior. Ramón Monfort, architects.
Quantity Surveyors Luis Calvo. José Carratalá.
Client Proyecto Cultural de Castellón, S.A.
Date of competition 2000.
Date of project 2001.
Building area 6175 m².

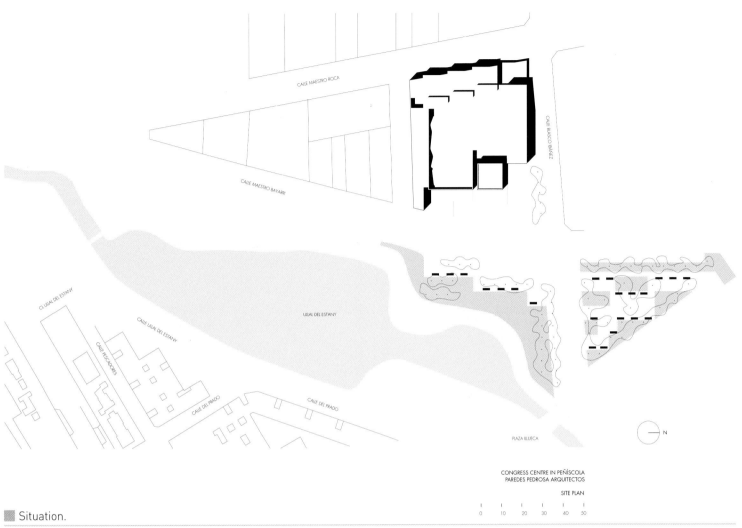

CONGRESS CENTRE IN PEÑÍSCOLA
PAREDES PEDROSA ARQUITECTOS

SITE PLAN

0   10   20   30   40   50

▨ Situation.

▨ Ante-room and lobby of the museum.

The Palace of Congresses stands at the foot of Peñíscola Castle, facing a garden and with the sea as a background.

With the aim of linking the interiors with the surroundings, the building appears as a continuous volume, closed to the adjoining streets, but fragmented and open on the entrance front, thus free-

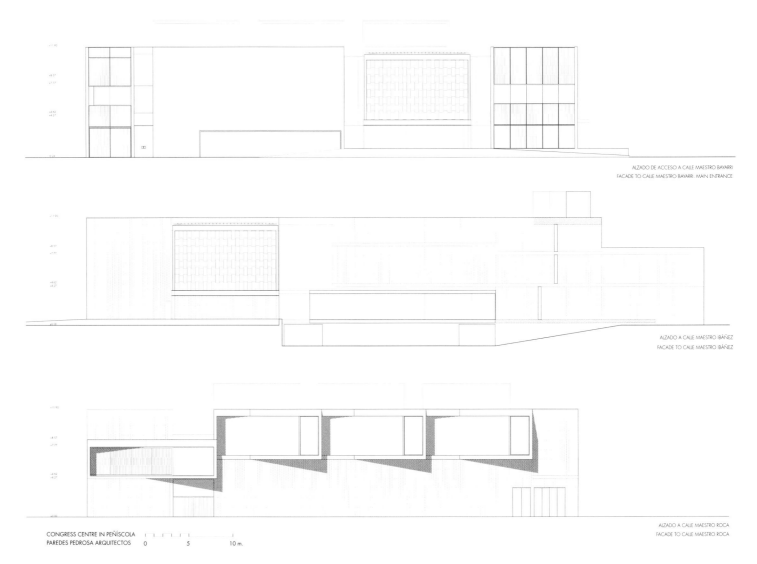

ALZADO DE ACCESO A CALLE MAESTRO BAYARRI
FACADE TO CALLE MAESTRO BAYARRI. MAIN ENTRANCE

ALZADO A CALLE MAESTRO IBÁÑEZ
FACADE TO CALLE MAESTRO IBÁÑEZ

CONGRESS CENTRE IN PEÑÍSCOLA
PAREDES PEDROSA ARQUITECTOS   0   5   10 m.

ALZADO A CALLE MAESTRO ROCA
FACADE TO CALLE MAESTRO ROCA

■ Elevations.

■ Transition between interior and exterior.

ing a large square and allowing for the future park to stretch right up to the doors of the building.

The transition between exterior and interior is formed by a feature which, resembling a pergola, slides between the volumes of white concrete and serves as an ante-chamber to the museum.

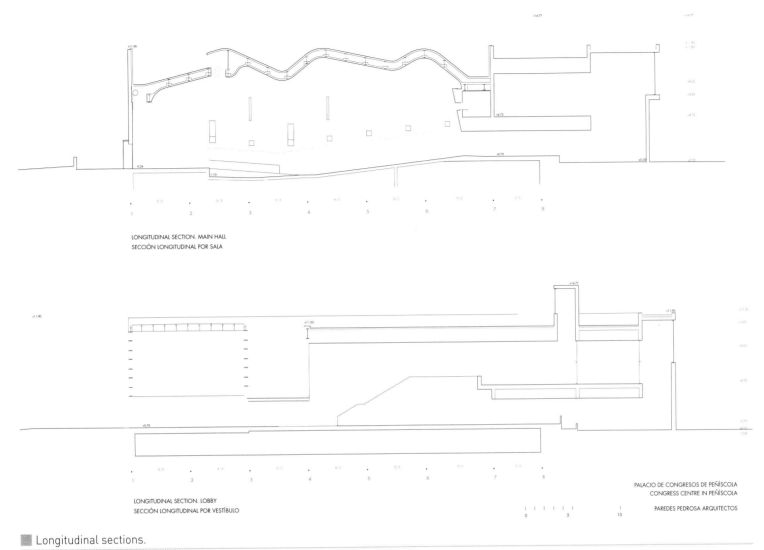

LONGITUDINAL SECTION. MAIN HALL
SECCIÓN LONGITUDINAL POR SALA

LONGITUDINAL SECTION. LOBBY
SECCIÓN LONGITUDINAL POR VESTÍBULO

PALACIO DE CONGRESOS DE PEÑÍSCOLA
CONGRESS CENTRE IN PEÑÍSCOLA

PAREDES PEDROSA ARQUITECTOS

▓ Longitudinal sections.

▓ Access to conference rooms.

Formed by a lattice-work of ceramic tiles, it creates a three-dimensional texture permeable to the air, but protected from the rain.

The entrance-hall functions as a lobby organizing around itself the different rooms of the plan: on the ground floor the main hall,

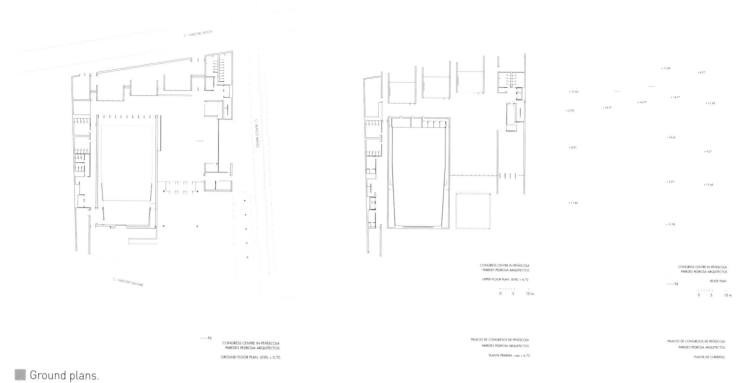

CONGRESS CENTRE IN PEÑÍSCOLA
PAREDES PEDROSA ARQUITECTOS

GROUND FLOOR PLAN. LEVEL + 0,70

PALACIO DE CONGRESOS DE PEÑÍSCOLA
PAREDES PEDROSA ARQUITECTOS

PLANTA PRIMERA. cota + 4,72

CONGRESS CENTRE IN PEÑÍSCOLA
PAREDES PEDROSA ARQUITECTOS

UPPER FLOOR PLAN. LEVEL + 4,72

PALACIO DE CONGRESOS DE PEÑÍSCOLA
PAREDES PEDROSA ARQUITECTOS

PLANTA DE CUBIERTAS

CONGRESS CENTRE IN PEÑÍSCOLA
PAREDES PEDROSA ARQUITECTOS

ROOF PLAN

▓ Ground plans.

▓ View of the pergola.

▓ Axonometric view of the different levels.

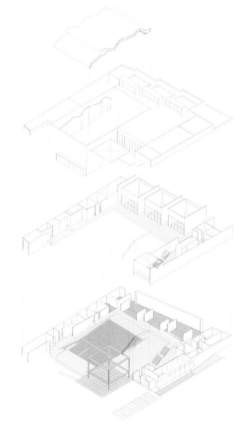

the administration area and the exhibition hall, and on the first floor the congress halls, press room and cafeteria, which open visually to the park looking towards the sea. The main hall, with a

Interior of the main hall.

The entrance hall serves as a central lobby.

capacity of 700 places, is planned as a single continuous floor with a shallow slope. The walls are clad in a wooden lathing, creating a counterpoint with the undulating ceiling of bare concrete, conditioning by its own structure the acoustic quality. These undulations are expressed externally in a zinc envelope which constitutes the fourth façade as seen from the Castle.

olimpia_theater

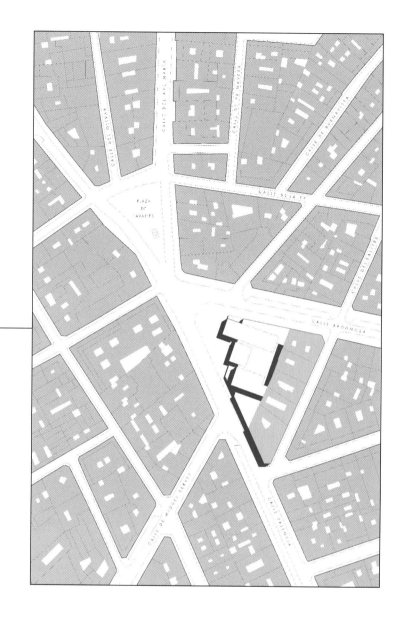

TECHNICAL DATA

Location Madrid.

Architects Ignacio García Pedrosa and Ángela García de Paredes.

Collaborators Silvia Colmenares, Eva M. Neila.

Quantity Surveyor Luis Calvo.

Client Madrid City Government. Premises of the Centro Dramático Nacional IN-AEM.

Date of competition 1996.

Date of project 2000.

Closing date of work 2005.

Building area 5180 m².

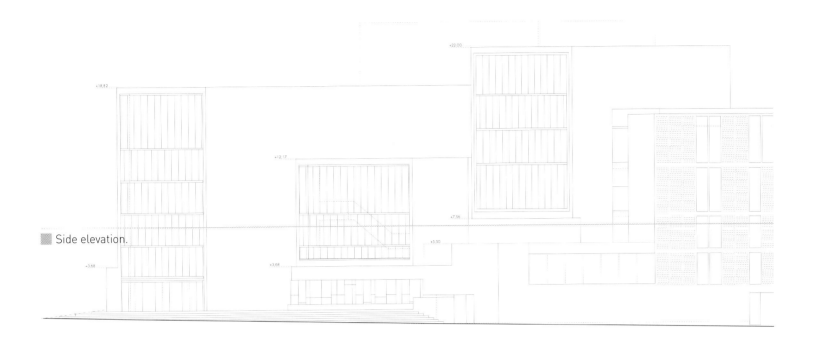

Side elevation.

Front elevation.

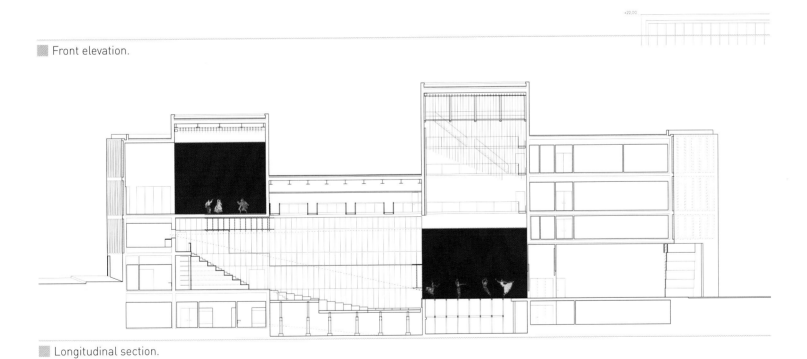

Longitudinal section.

The theater, occupying the site of the old Olimpia hall, stands on a triangular plot in front of the square of Lavapiés. The building breaks up into three parallel prisms shaped according to the geometry of the site, and abutting on the walls of the existing buildings so as to align themselves in height and thus reconstruct the volume of the block.

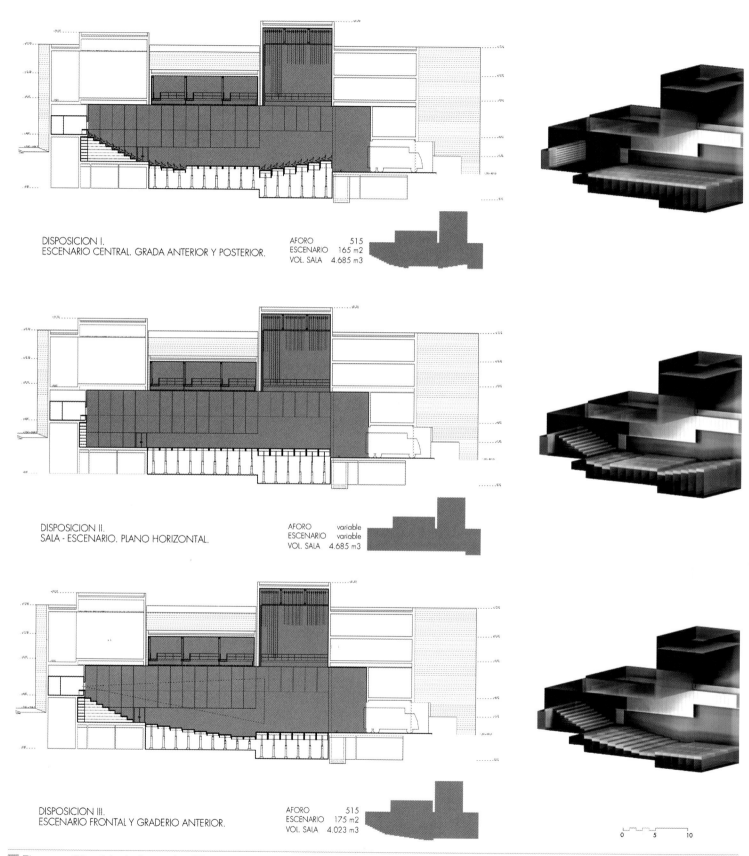

DISPOSICION I.
ESCENARIO CENTRAL. GRADA ANTERIOR Y POSTERIOR.

AFORO   515
ESCENARIO   165 m2
VOL. SALA   4.685 m3

DISPOSICION II.
SALA - ESCENARIO. PLANO HORIZONTAL.

AFORO   variable
ESCENARIO   variable
VOL. SALA   4.685 m3

DISPOSICION III.
ESCENARIO FRONTAL Y GRADERIO ANTERIOR.

AFORO   515
ESCENARIO   175 m2
VOL. SALA   4.023 m3

0   5   10

The versatility of the hall permits different types of scenic presentations.

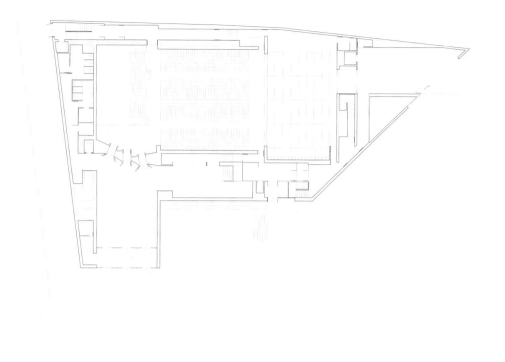

Level 0 - access.

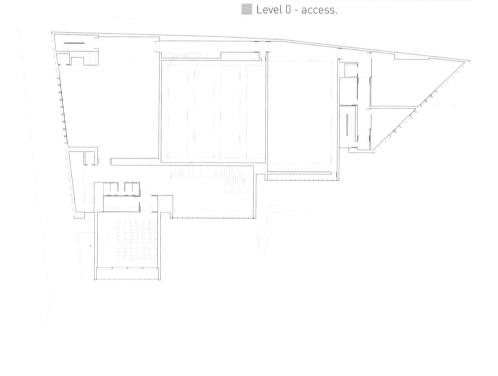

Level 1.

These concrete boxes have one façade opening towards the square. Through a partition composed by a curtain wall it is possible to glimpse the movement of the public inside.

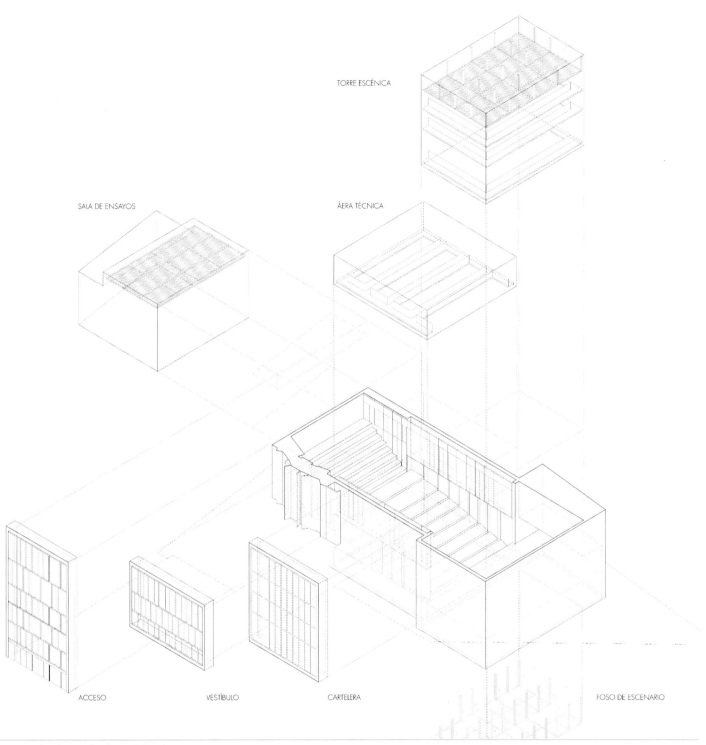

TORRE ESCÉNICA

SALA DE ENSAYOS

ÁERA TÉCNICA

ACCESO   VESTÍBULO   CARTELERA   FOSO DE ESCENARIO

Fragmented volumetric view of the theater.

The building contains a center for avant-garde theater comprising the main hall, a room for dramatized readings, a rehearsal room and spaces for theatrical and public use.

The main hall of 17 x 36 m is treated as a neutral and versatile space with a capacity of 500 seats, of which 130 are on a retractable tribune. A series of mobile platforms allow the floor of the hall to be leveled with the stage or its slope to be varied. Thus a versatile container is attained, in which any type of scenic presentation can be arranged.

The rehearsal room, equal in size to the stage, is above the amphitheater, and allows for the preparation of plays independently of the use of the main hall.

RIEGLER RIEWE

ARCHITEKTEN

Roger Riewe and Florian Riegler are the founder members of this architectural studio created in 1987 in Graz (Austria) and that since 1997 also develops its activity in Cologne, Germany.

Florian Riegler is a graduate in architecture from the Technical University of Graz. Roger Riewe is following architectural studies at the RWTH of Aachen (Germany). They both possess ample curriculums as lecturers in a number of architecture and design areas of European universities such as Amsterdam, Aachen, Prague, Barcelona, Basle, Zurich, Augsburg and Venice.

Riegler Riewe's past has been characterized by their efforts in the materialization of their own theories about architecture in the projects they have developed. They strongly bear in mind the nature of the materials they use and discriminate against those that have predetermined significances that provoke the observer's perception being subjected to interpretation. As far as possible,

housing_wallhof

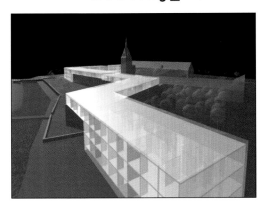

main_station_innsbruck

they use materials that lack meanings. These are denominated by the authors as being 'open' materials and give a neutral significance to surfaces. The constructive details are to have a subordinate role within the whole. It is a question of proposing spatial concepts which are empty of pre-established ideological content in such a way that the buildings adapt to their context and give a priority to their functionality over any other pretext.

The architecture of Riegler Riewe is considered a representative example of an aesthetic tendency which has considerable echo in Austria, Germany, the Netherlands and Switzerland. The designs are reduced to the purely essential, the minimal and without the addition of any formal or symbolic extras. The architecture proposed defines a reorientation in which the form creates a second plane and the function is the starting point, the result of the container of flows and activities. In a practical sense, the team has come up with architectural solutions that resolve programs of enormous complexity and volume thanks to those

Prizes	Award winning projects
2003	Trade Fair Graz.
2000	Franz-Nabl-Institute / House of Literature, Graz.
1999	Austrian clients.
1999	ÖBB Travel Center.
1999	Innsbruck Central Station.
1999	Austrian Cementindustry.
1999	6th. Mies Van der Rohe.
1998	Bruck/Mur Station.
1996	Geriatric hospital in Vienna.
1995	Offices and apartments "Entenplatz" in Graz.

that they have consolidated over the last few years. From Austria, they have extended their field of action to Germany, Switzerland and even Italy.

housing_wallhof

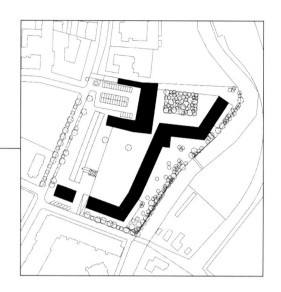

TECHNICAL DATA

Location Schwechat - Rannersdorf, Austria.

Architects Florian Riegler & Roger Riewe.

Client Magistrat Graz, Hochbauamt, Graz, Austria.

Collaborators Dragos Ciorobatca, Pert Balthes, Antón Hüttmayr, Markus Probst.

Project date 2003.

Built area 12.200 m².

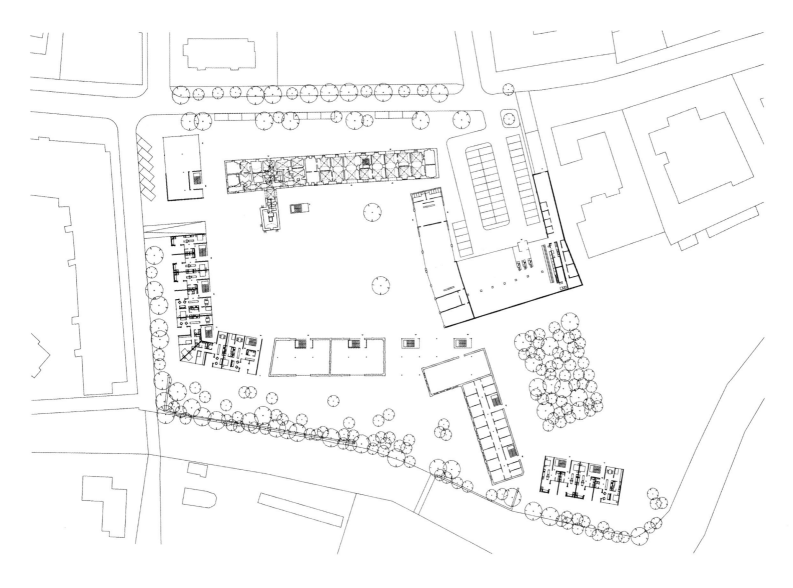

■ The residential group generates subspaces in the relationship between the preexisting and new volumes.

■ The typologies of residence organize the services in a central strip.

The residential complex is situated in the geometric center of the town of Rannersdorf which had preexisting defined although incomplete urbanized areas.

An arrangement based on an irregular line has been achieved that is even broken at ground-floor level and that responds to a reading of the perimeters of the emplacement. Above all, a desire to create the maximum amount of free space possible has been imposed.

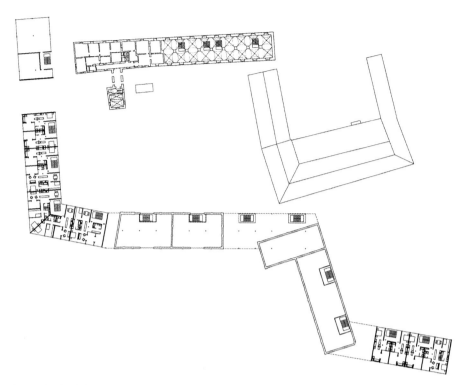

■ The central square that relates the buildings to one another accommodates a large underground parking lot.

■ The ravine like form of the building at its base generates subspaces.

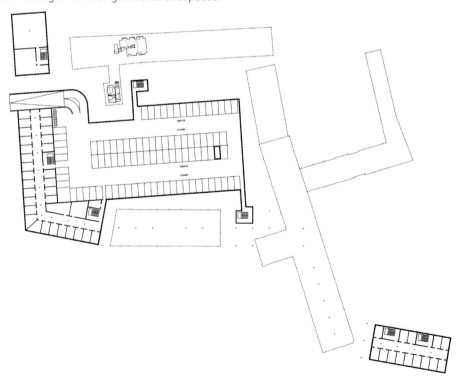

The new volume is situated closest to the street so as to emphasize the sensation of amplitude within the square. A plaza or a large semi enclosed patio that provides numerous views and that allows the continuity of the exterior space to be perceived. The preexisting transit routes also an influence the guidelines when it came to laying out the complex. The symbolic element of

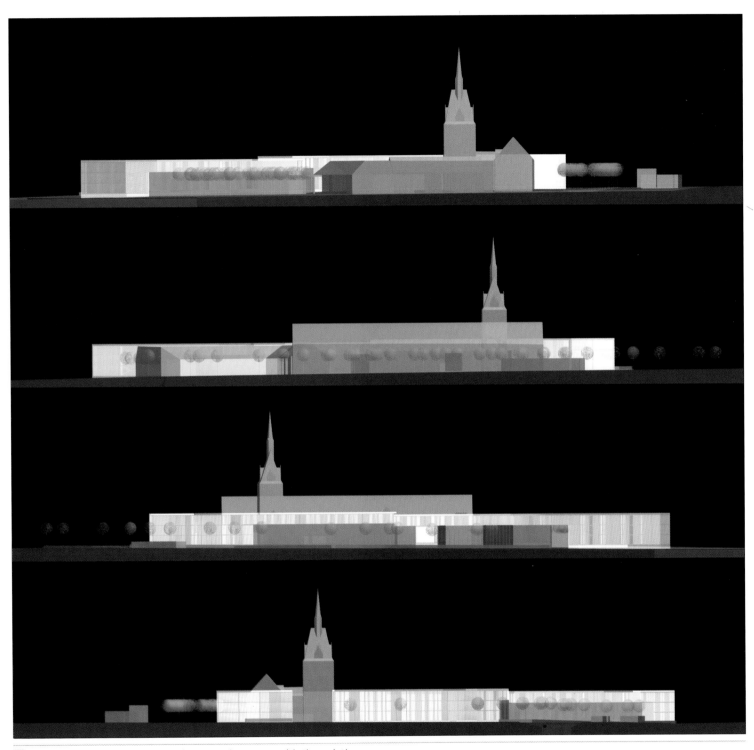

The new volumes are arranged so as to integrate with the existing.

the area continues to be the tower, the only landmark and against which no competition has been created. The new volumes discretely extend among the existing forms and in similar proportions. They are neutral as they fill the space in a zigzag manner following the contours of the land. They are respectful of the park that marks a less defined limit of the city. What is important is

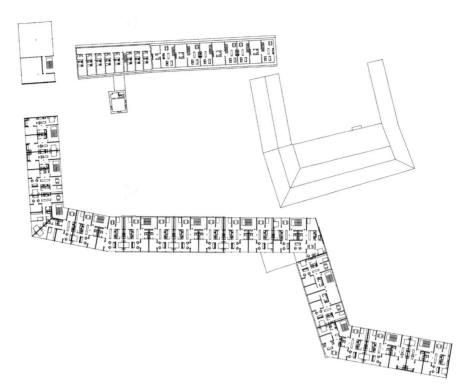

First floor. The buildings are joined together and three mixed patios and a view of the park are obtained.

Second floor. The preexistent volume maintains its proportions.

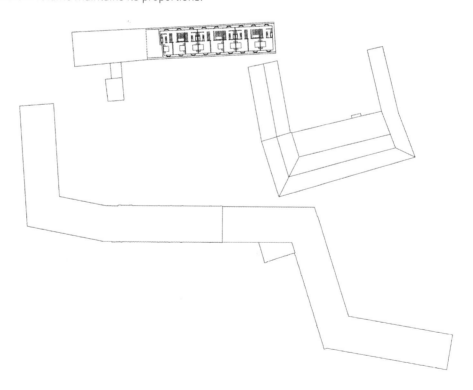

the flow and the creation of new exterior spaces that are semi open and with a more perceivable human scale. The views inter-cross, the spaces become dynamic, the park encloses the inter-

vention of which it forms part. Three semi open patios with abstract perimeters that are communicated one with the other and which all have clearly differentiated personalities of their own

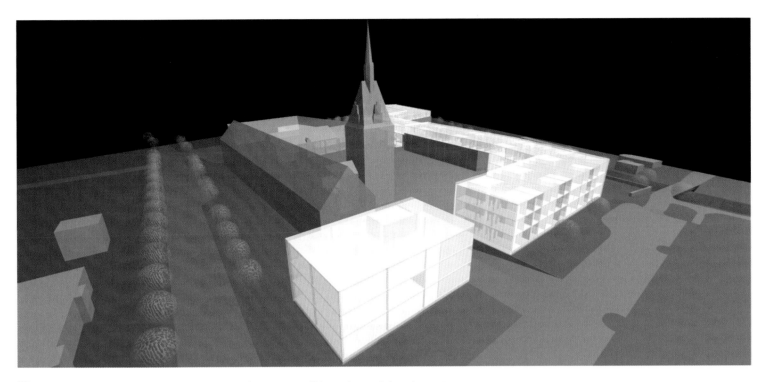

▧ The volumes are lined up and situated as close as possible to the peripheral streets.

▧ The integration of the park among the volumes brings great value to the complex.

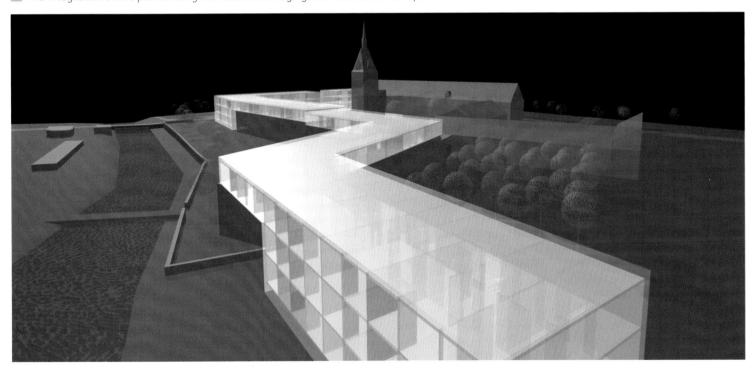

have been created. The buildings finally become no more than the stage set that delimit the perimeters of the patios, the park and which outline a succession of sequences, views, circulations... life flows through the spaces.

The formalization of the building, its finishes and its details are an anecdote which are unnecessary when it comes to understanding the true function which is the relationship established among the spaces.

main_station
innsbruck, Tyrol

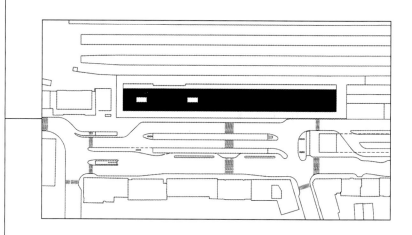

TECHNICAL DATA

Location Südtiroler Platz 2, 6020 Innsbruck, Austria.

Architects Florian Riegler & Roger Riewe.

Client ÖBB (Federal Railways of Austria), Vienna, Austria.

Collaborators Werner Maiacher, Friedrich Mob-hammer, Elemer Ploder, Eva Roiko, Maria Soledad Vidal Martínez, Johanna Digruber, Steffen Schössler.

Consultant companies Civil engineering: Gmeiner Haferl Tragwerksplanung KEG.

Building physics DI Karl Höfler.

Mechanical eng. ZPLAN Haustechnik GmbH.

Light planning Werning Tropp und Partner.

Project date 1999-2000.

Completion date 2004.

Built area 11.500 m².

Construction company Arge Abbruch Bf. Innsbruck / Alpine - Mayreder Bau GmbH / Alu Stahlbau Kreidl GmbH / SFL GesmbH / Trockenbau München / Hribernig Dachdeckungs GmbH / ISOLIT Isolier GmbH / Thyssen Aufzüge GmbH / Klik Bühnensysteme.

Longitudinal section of the building. Transit areas.

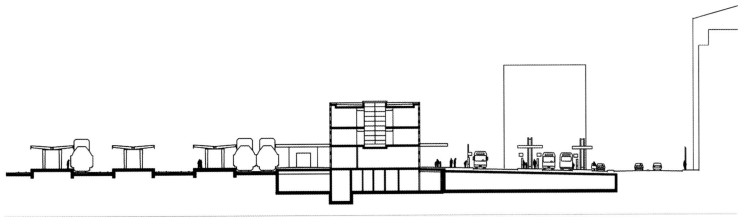

Cross section. The station as an element that relates to the city.

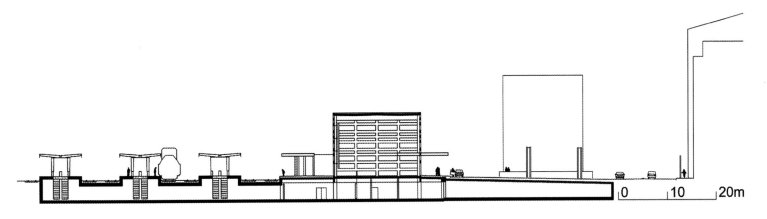

0 10 20m

Cross section. The platforms can be accessed directly from the interior or the exterior.

The main railway station in Innsbruck is a completely new construction located in the vicinities of the old station and has been a unique opportunity to improve the city's image. The station, from where the city is perceptible, fully integrates into the urban center of which it becomes part. The proportions of the building are imposing. It is a tumbler of nothing less than 180 m in length,

18 m wide and 12.5 m high that solely responds to its functional requirements. The station itself is situated on the ground floor while the basement accommodates an underground parking lot which also communicates with the platforms so as to facilitate transit. The formalization of the building responds to an autonomous space within an urban context that is independent from

View of the platforms and vestibules. The functionality is almost infinite.

Ground floor. The program of the station extends over one unique level.

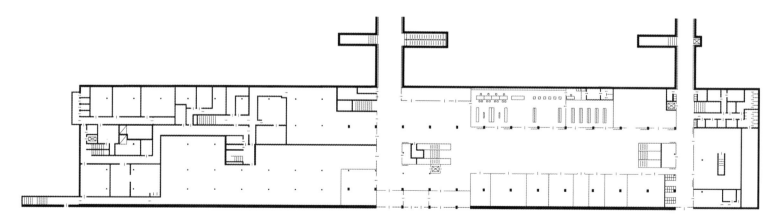

any preexisting or symbolic restraints and in which all of the necessary spaces are interconnected. What is again fundamental is the transit; the importance will be given to the users. The architecture is by no means primordial and should not stand out under any pretext or do any more than fulfill its function. The areas of railway traffic are found on the ground floor and can be accessed directly from the floor of underground parking with which they are connected by means of communication tunnels. The station can

The interior offices are characterized by their views over the city.

First floor. The building is subdivided into modules for private use.

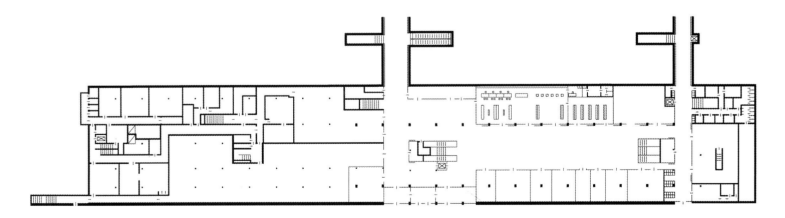

be accessed from the ground floor as well as from the parking lot. Both the station offices and those of private use are located on the upper floors. There is no room for interpretations of symbolic concepts in anyway whatsoever. The spaces are absolutely free of any details. They are austere and only characterized by the complete views over the city that they offer. The openings that give the façade the appearance of being a neutral and repetitive grid remind us of the view we may obtain by looking out of the window

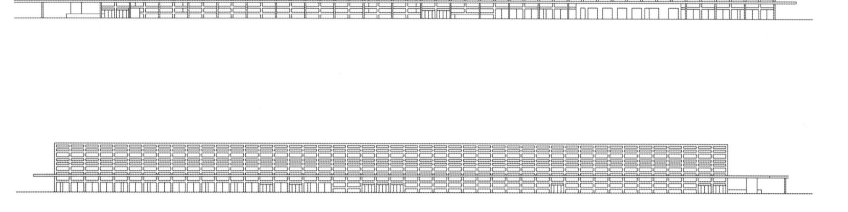

The façades of the building are a neutral and repetitive framework.

The architecture is a backdrop to the activity of the city.

while traveling on a train which in this case breaks its lines so as to extend equally and with no particular criteria until the structure has been completed.

The façades were conceived as simple geometric decoration, a repetitive network, neutral... It is not possible to make out any particularly characteristic element; once again, function dictates form. A façade that imposes due to its dimensions and which could clearly have been resolved by a quick and easy modular assembly construction. Nevertheless, once again, the Riegler Riewe team, basing themselves on their theoretic concepts, decide to break away from any preconceived meanings. There is no intention of achieving a well-resolved modular finish, the material should break down and reconstruct itself...

The chosen solution is clearly unexpected for a building of such huge proportions. The façade of the station has been constructed in situ in concrete using a special technique called "self-compacting concrete" and, for the first time in such a large extension as this station façade, a pigment has been incorporated.

The hollows are repeated in such a way that it seems that they would continue into infinity if they were not limited by function. The façade is simply a background to the life of the city and should therefore take on a timeless immaterial role far away from any limited context.

NO.MAD
ARQUITECTOS

Eduardo Arroyo founded in Amsterdam in 1998 this architectural studio, which now operates from Madrid. He qualified as an architect in the Escuela Técnica Superior de Arquitectura of Madrid and specializes in Town Planning and Building; besides his professional work with NO.MAD Arquitectos, he has been teaching since 1996 as associate professor of Architectural Projects in the Escuela Técnica Superior de Arquitectura de Madrid (E.T.S.A.M.). This is an architecture which approaches projects from a traditional perspective, with a philosophy of professional correctness in each of the parameters that may affect the space to be built. The different languages which affect the program are elaborated to decipher the needs of each project.

new_euskotrén headquarters

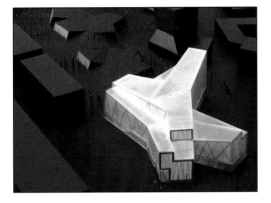

plaza_del_desierto

The landscape setting is important to achieve an integration within them, and thence is generated the geometry of the ground-plan, which in its turn will permit a correct volumetric creation of space.

The will to create spaces that adapt to those already existing and create new flows of movement and relation within the overall space they are to be integrated in, without these ceasing to be spontaneous. The dynamic language is worked so as to determine the type of communication that is to be made, and thus the task of control over space is facilitated. The final forms have to be adapted to the program proposed; extensive and rigorous proposals respond to all needs.

The study of architectural complexities is one of NO.MAD's interests, analysing them in every project with great rigor. The final conceptual justification is approached from a less material, more abstract angle, in an effort to endow with content the result of very strict parameters.

Prominent among his most emblematic projects are the Lasesarre Stadium (2004); the Plaza del Desierto Park (2002); the Cordoba project (2002); the Azken Portu Sports Complex, in Iran (2001); the Marijin Dvor University Center, Sarajevo (2000); the multi-use Municipal Center of Bolzano, in Italy (1999); the Palace of Congresses of Navarre, in Pamplona (1998), and the Leisure Center in the old Valkenberg mines, in Holland.

new_euskotrén
headquarters

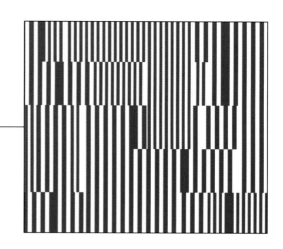

FICHA TÉCNICA
Location Durango, Vizcaya.
Architect Eduardo Arroyo.
Collaborators Francesco Monaco, Javier Tamer Els-
hiekh, Cristina Hidalgo, Enrique
Moya-Angeler. Architects.
Consulting firms Structural design: Joaquín Antuña.
Date of project 2004.

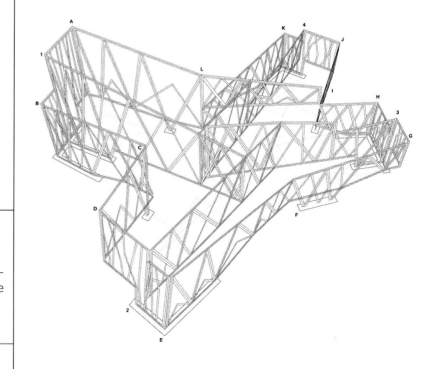

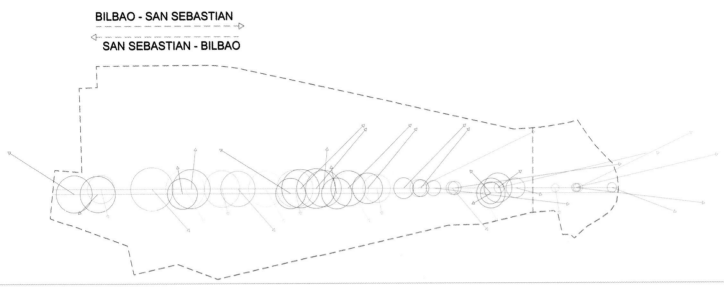

BILBAO - SAN SEBASTIAN

SAN SEBASTIAN - BILBAO

Construction of the new space-time from the train.

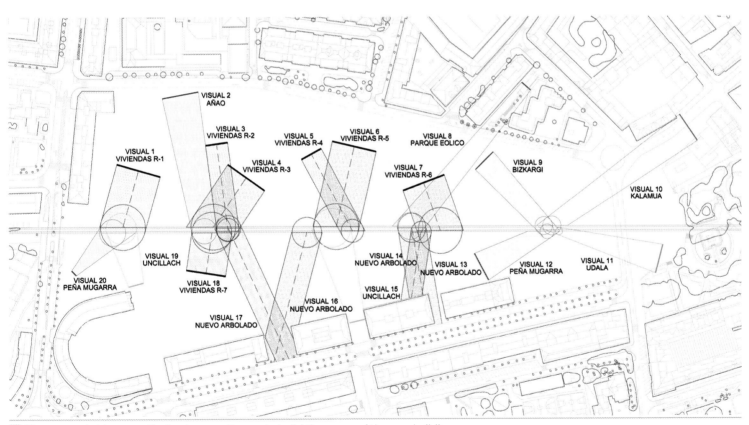

VISUAL 2
AÑAO

VISUAL 3
VIVIENDAS R-2

VISUAL 5
VIVIENDAS R-4

VISUAL 6
VIVIENDAS R-5

VISUAL 8
PARQUE EOLICO

VISUAL 1
VIVIENDAS R-1

VISUAL 4
VIVIENDAS R-3

VISUAL 7
VIVIENDAS R-6

VISUAL 9
BIZKARGI

VISUAL 10
KALAMUA

VISUAL 19
UNCILLACH

VISUAL 14
NUEVO ARBOLADO

VISUAL 13
NUEVO ARBOLADO

VISUAL 12
PEÑA MUGARRA

VISUAL 11
UDALA

VISUAL 20
PEÑA MUGARRA

VISUAL 18
VIVIENDAS R-7

VISUAL 15
UNCILLACH

VISUAL 16
NUEVO ARBOLADO

VISUAL 17
NUEVO ARBOLADO

The cones of vision over the landscape allow us to build the cones of the new building.

The project formalizes a complex program which addresses the location of the new headquarters of Euskotrén as it passes through the municipality of Durango, in Vizcaya. The town-planning of the exterior space, the integration of the station and shops in relation to the new buildings, are articulated by means of a thread of argument centered on the perceptions conveyed by the place in its visual approach from the train's axis of travel. The pro-

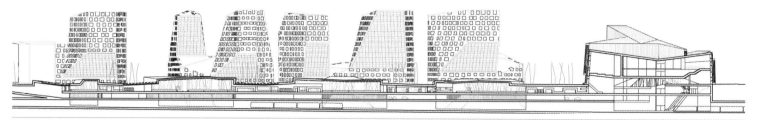

Views from the shopping center over the landscape and the new buildings.

Sections transverse to the train's axis and study of the cones of sight.

jeet is the result of an exhaustive, almost mathematical analysis of the landscape in movement, a space-time relationship.

The definitive volumetrics are defined a posteriori from the analysis of the visuals obtained from the train and the opening of its cones of sight. The new buildings are situated in the existing visual vacuums, creating new cones of sight from the underground passage of the train to be united with the existing ones, in an interesting sequence of photograms of approach to the station.

The geometry is first defined in plan, by the intersection between the cones of sight which will define the perimeter of the new volumes.

The layout of the station is organized bringing the public areas close to the park and the Etzuri square, creating a volume which changes shape as it rises to open the way to the station accesses, the exhibition rooms and the Euskotrén company headquarters, as well as the necessary light openings of the station lobby.

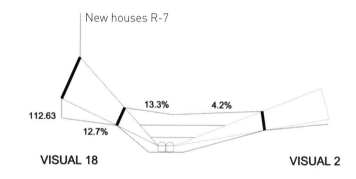

New houses R-7

112.63   12.7%   13.3%   4.2%

VISUAL 18   VISUAL 2

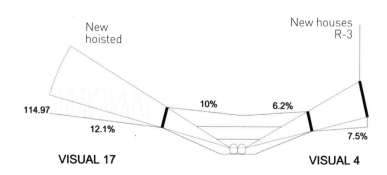

New hoisted   New houses R-3

114.97   12.1%   10%   6.2%   7.5%

VISUAL 17   VISUAL 4

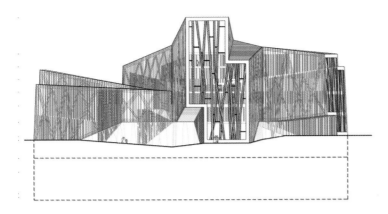

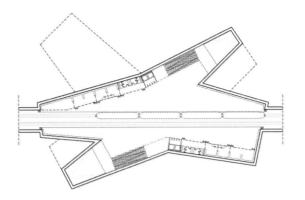

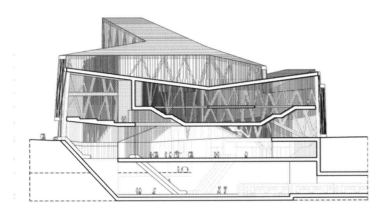

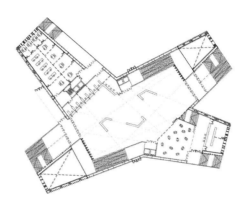

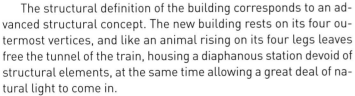

Building for the new Euskotrén headquarters.

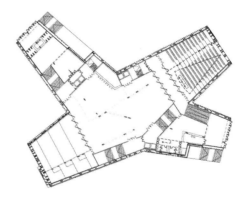

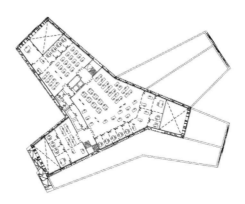

The structural definition of the building corresponds to an advanced structural concept. The new building rests on its four outermost vertices, and like an animal rising on its four legs leaves free the tunnel of the train, housing a diaphanous station devoid of structural elements, at the same time allowing a great deal of natural light to come in.

The façades, treated with a juxtaposition of translucent polycarbonate pieces and transparent glass, respond to the requirements of the layout and the orientation. The outer wall is made of translucent elements where it fronts the more private premises, and uses transparent glass in more public or commercial areas, opening completely to the landscape at the four ends, in the manner of large eyes looking onto the landscape, generating public spaces and working spaces of the highest quality.

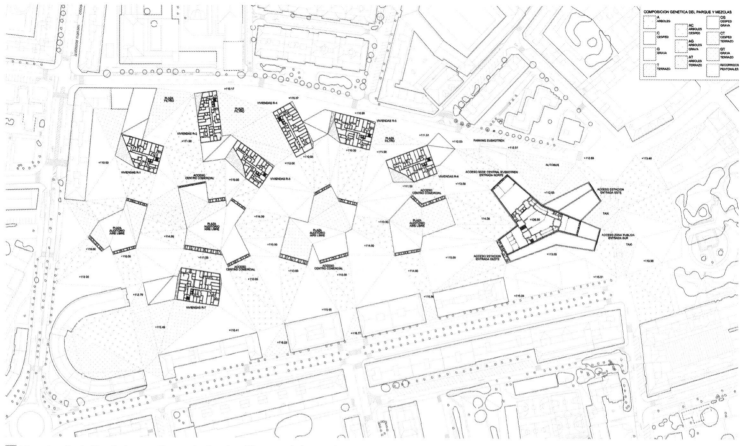

Visuals of relation between the park, the dwellings and the station.

On the outside, the new building masses contrast with the park, in a relation of blocks and spaces, with an irregular prism shape identical to that of the station building. A rotula building between the existing town and the planning of the new area.

The layout of the park is generated by absorbing the flows of circulation coming from the town and the new shopping center, turning it into a living piece. Through its irregular genesis, the space is dynamized in a network of varying textures, trees and lawn of intermingled use.

The residential buildings form part of the staging, marking the gradation between the different public spaces from the town to the park.

After dark, the corporate building and the new station of Euskotrén shine out in the night as a visual icon of the new urban complex.

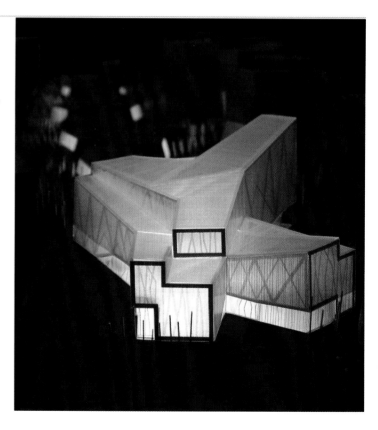

seat_of_the_desert

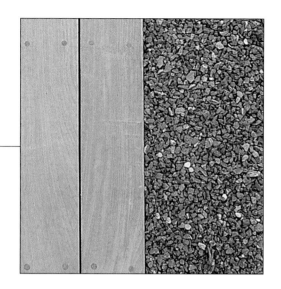

TECHNICAL DATA
Location	Urban area of Baracaldo.
Architect	Eduardo Arroyo.
Client	Bilbao Ría 2000.
Collaborators	Sergio L. Piñeiro, architect.
	John Garcés, student.
	AIE Galindo 96, Architects.
Consulting companies	Structure: Fernando Subinas.
Supervision of work	Eduardo Arroyo, architect
	NOMAD Arquitectos.
	Nerea Calvillo González.
	AIE Galindo 96, architects.
Quantity Surveyor	José Luís Villanueva and Javier Inclán, technical architects.
Date of the project	1999.
Completion of work	2002.
Building area	1,2 Ha.
Building firm	NECSO.

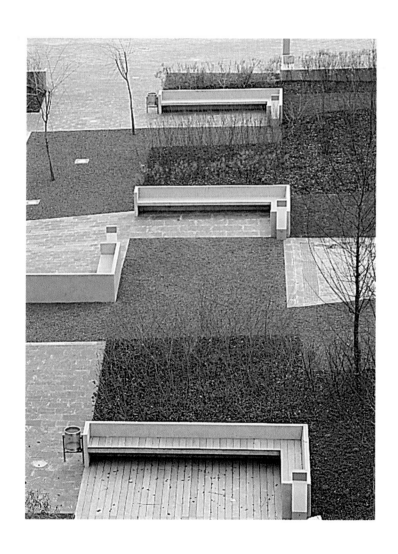

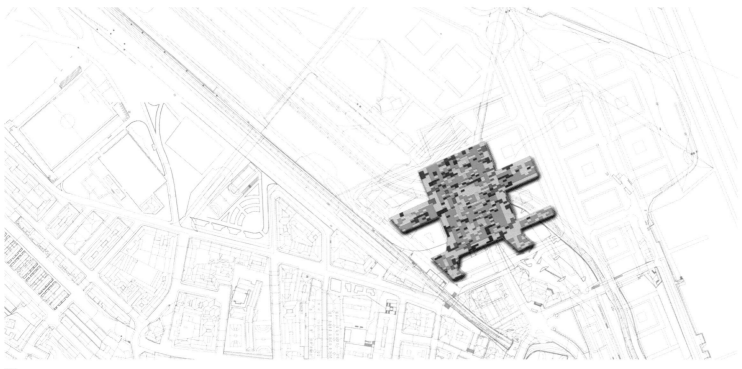

⬛ Setting of the park in the urban context.

⬛ Zoning and proportion of materials used in the design.

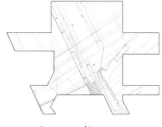

Territorio / Territory

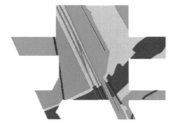

Materiales / Materials

Paisaje / Lanscape

Distribución del material / Distribution of the material

agua / water	2142 m2	13.7%
piedra / stone	3170 m2	20.3%
asfalto / asphalt	0252 m2	01.8%
arena / sand	1378 m2	08.8%
verde / green	4938 m2	31.7%
bosque / forest	2796 m2	17.9%
acero / steel	0268 m2	01.8%
madera / wood	0631 m2	04.0%

The project starts from a defined setting, an urban empty space within the consolidated town network. A site of irregular shape which stretches to the edges of the existing built-up area. The proposal begins with an exhaustive, almost academic analysis of the particular conditions of the place, so the proposal for use of different materials in varied proportion for the design of the new park will be integrated into the existing circulation, landscape, visuals and materials.

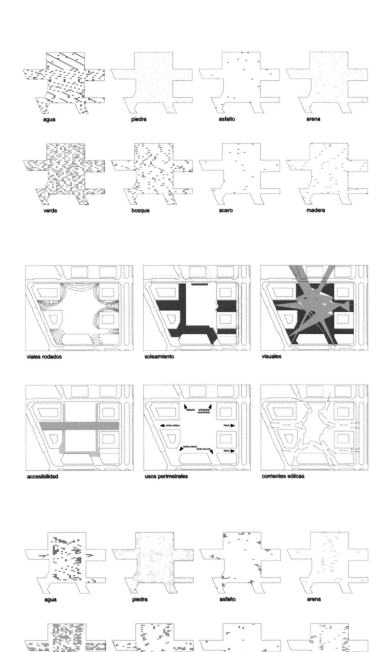

agua | piedra | asfalto | arena
verde | bosque | acero | madera

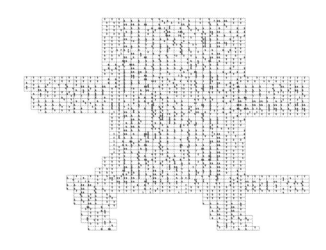

viales rodados | soleamiento | visuales
accesibilidad | usos perimetrales | corrientes eólicas

agua | piedra | asfalto | arena
verde | bosque | acero | madera

Materials proposal and analytic process of the characteristics of the site.

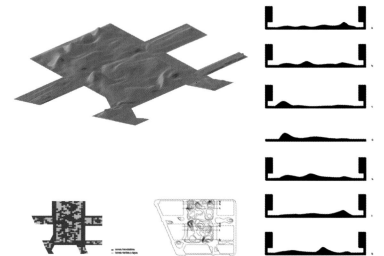

Profiles of the topography of the park.

Superimposed pixelated network.

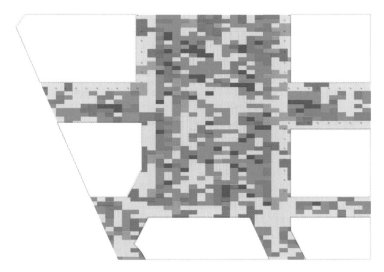

The process initiates the subdivision of the site, which is a large one, into small rectangular modules, a subdivision of small plots of manageable size on which a decision will be made on the particular material to be used, building up a variegated tapestry that creates a dynamic visual space.

The decision on the type of material for each plot will be taken with a view to the optimum, after analysing the traffic, the degree of sunlight, the visuals, the accessibility, the perimetral uses and

The public space is handled as an interesting tapestry of textures of different kinds.

The basic modules are repeated adopting different textures.

the currents of air affecting them. An evaluation is also made of the proportion of such allocations for each of the small plots.

Finally, each plot will opt for a material with a different hardness and texture of finish. The definitive great tapestry, a regular mesh of pixels which becomes a juxtaposition of areas of water, stone, asphalt, sand, lawn, trees, steel and wood. A strong relation of tension is generated between the materials and their proportion, which will define the tracing of the pedestrian ways, the permeable areas and the inaccessible areas. The park generates a public space which is lively and dynamic, achieving its function and creating with great personality a visual endowment of great spatial quality for the existing residential buildings.

KÖNIGS |
ARCHITEKTEN |

Ulrich Königs has directed this studio situated in Köln since 1994 along with Ilse Maria Königs with whom he shares identical studies (they are both graduates from the AA in London, the University of Innsbruck and the RWTH of Aachen).

These two architects exercise their profession from a very personal way of understanding the architectural process. In this, they mix their personal introspection and a critical analysis of traditional German architecture that, in general, they consider to be weak due to its lack of theoretic base and its sole concerned with the constructive aspect which makes if lose contact with reality. As a result, these two professionals seek an architecture that avoids formalisms and maintains an experimental autonomy.

ausstellungsgebäude einesshunfabrikanten

forum_cultural_westfalen

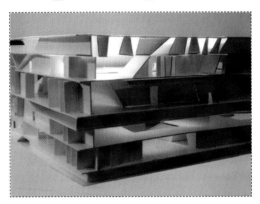

Königs Architekten design projects based on a strict methodology, a design strategy. In the first phase, they dedicate a lot of time to a respectful analysis in order to achieve their objective: a prototype that will be a stencil base for any proposal. The prototypes are quickly adapted to the context given that their method deals more with designing a process that defining a project.

Ulrich Königs' designs, in which the new technologies play a special role, do not transmit the delicate sensitivity of other designs of a human scale. This is because the first ones were worked in geometric forms based on rigor and homogeneity.

It is a question, therefore, of an architecture of practical values in which naturalness and simplicity are encouraged. The spaces are created in function to their uses without complex languages being sought.

The office became popular as a result of its formalization of the competition for the sports stadium Chemnitz, in 1997, in which it collaborated with the architect Peter Kulka and the engineer Cecil Balmond. Other prizewinning projects that have come out of this office have been: Saint Peter's Cathedral, in Regensburg (2004, first prize); the Cultural Center of Westfalen in Münster (2004, first prize); the Congress Palace Neue Terrasse in Dresden (1999, third prize) and San Francisco Parish Center in Regensburg (1999, first prize).

san_francisco parish_center

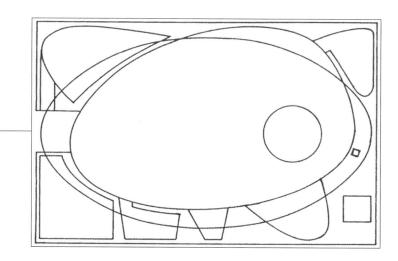

TECHNICAL DATA

Location Regensburg - Burgweinting Kirchfeldallee 3, Germany.

Architects Ulrich Königs & Ilse Maria Königs.

Client The Catholic Congregation of Regensburg-Burgweinting.

Collaborators Claudia Pannhausen, Thomas Roskothen, Volver Mencke, ILSA Abmann, Cristoph Schalaich, André Rethmeier, Bernd Jäger, Sabine Bruckmann.

Consultant companies *Engineering:* Bauleitung Ing., Arup Ltd, Dusseldorf.
Acoustics: Graner und Partner, Bergisch Gladbach
Illumination: Lichtplanung A. Hartung, Köln
Technology: Ingenieurbüro Martin, Regensburg.

Project date Competition 1999. Initiation date 2001.

Completion 2004.

Built area 1.386 m².

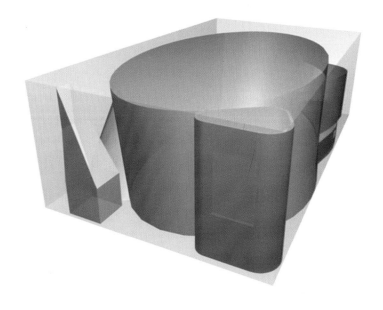

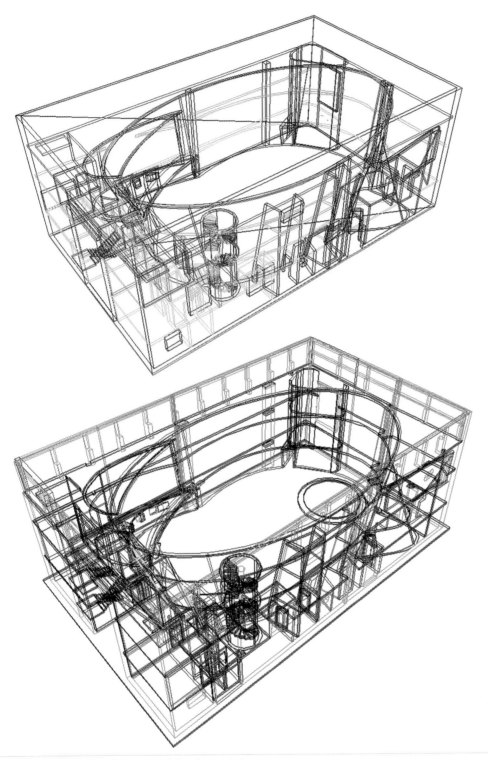

Study for the three-dimensional virtual framework for the prototype.

The new parish church of San Francisco in Regensburg was the prizewinning project for the extension of the parish complex.

The design makes references to traditional religious architecture, but incorporates simple geometric designs on a monumental scale. In this way, Königs presents a criticism of traditional architecture and opposes its pure rigorous forms.

The volume of the building is a parallelepiped form, a box that exteriorly defines its simplicity and which in its inside houses a large oval volume with an elliptical floor plan.

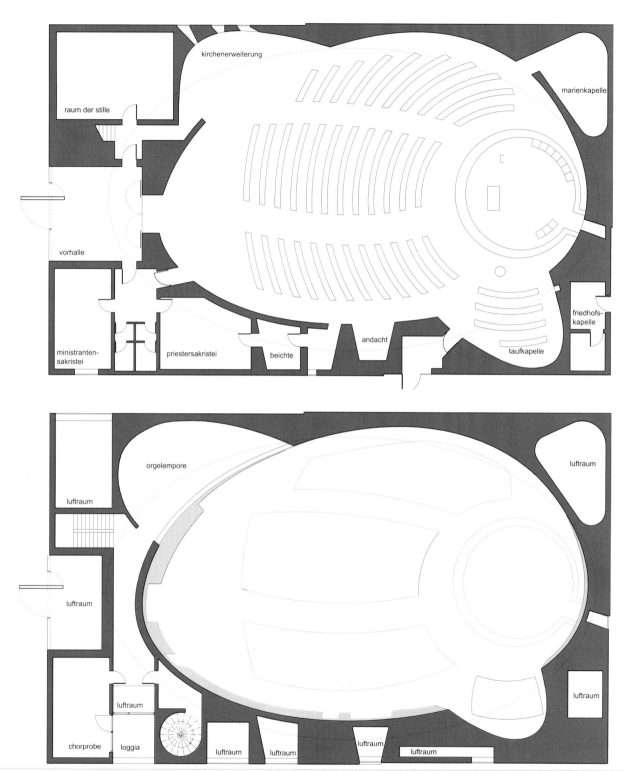

The labels in the upper plan:

- kirchenerweiterung
- marienkapelle
- raum der stille
- vorhalle
- ministranten-sakristei
- priestersakristei
- beichte
- andacht
- taufkapelle
- friedhofs-kapelle

The labels in the lower plan:

- orgelempore
- luftraum
- luftraum
- luftraum
- chorprobe
- loggia
- luftraum
- luftraum
- luftraum
- luftraum
- luftraum
- luftraum

The arrangement of the program is concentrated on a play of tangencies and intersections between the two geometries.

The mixing of the two elements, a static cube volume that envelops a dynamic curved space, creates spaces between which points of intersection are established and which lead to an interaction and a language that deals with space and time, walking and observing. Between the straight-lined geometry of the exterior and the curved lines of the liturgical interior space there is another space. This is a deep wall that accommodates small autonomous spaces for more private uses such as chapels, the

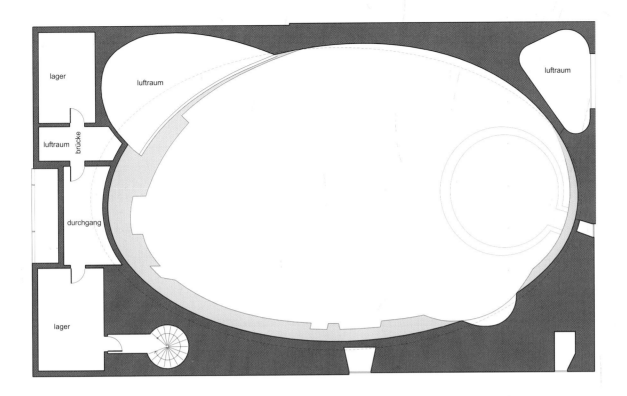

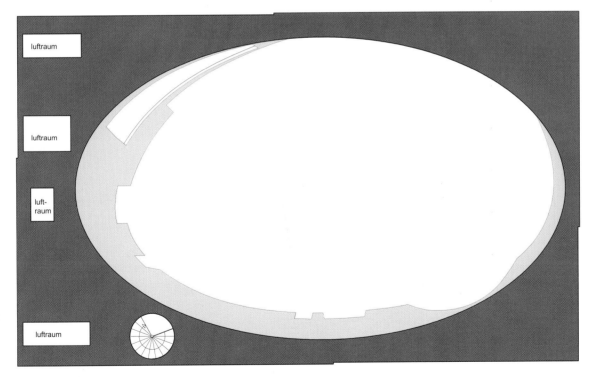

choir, the organ, the entrances... It is a clear reference to Baroque cathedrals in which the supporting walls are of a great magnitude due to the construction techniques used and into which the pro-gram was dug in the way of niches around the main center of the church. Each of the chapels has been resolved with a different form. This has been achieved by working twisting and winding

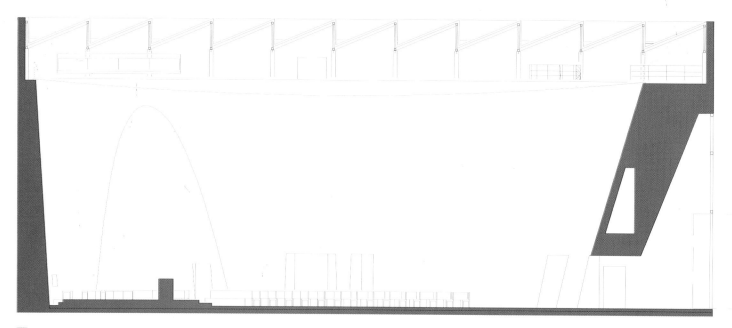

Longitudinal section.

Cross section through the area of the alter.

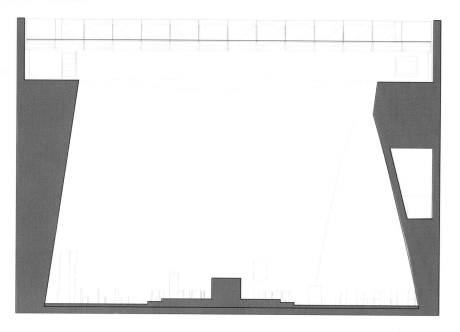

forms, small hollows in the wall, caves that enjoy their own light sources thanks to small skylights located in their ceilings. These beams of light produce warm spaces that offer refuge, favor meditation and communicate directly with the magnificent central liturgical space designated for congregation, where the community meets.

The form and the positioning of these openings come about as a result of the tangency or intersections of the two geome-

tries. The limits are broken in order to locate zones that participate in the magnitude of the central space of the curved inclined continuous walls that are of an extreme purity due to their white nudity bathed in the light of the large skylight in the ceiling.

The structure has been resolved with a system of triangular metal trusses of great luminousity and which free the interior space and are held up over periphery supports set equidistantly into the thick enclosing wall of the overall volume.

Night view of the southern elevation. Simplicity is expressed by openings that respond to the interior use.

Night view of the Northern elevation.

Due to its geometry, it not only manages to stabilize the roof, but it formalizes a number of lateral skylights of an industrial form that permit an enormous amount of natural light to be brought in through the light grid work of the structural bars.

Externally, the church is modest in appearance. It is of a static monolithic volume that generates a dialog with the other volumes existent in the parish center. The openings in the façade are discrete strips situated in an irregular way and without depth over the plane of the enclosure and constitute the illumination of a particular internal program that is not evident from the outside. This well-rounded volume is unified with the exterior by the material and by the real world while contrasting enormously with the interior oval space, of a particular geometry, hidden from the mundane in order to establish spiritual contact.

The light layer of finishing leads to interior spiritual perception.

Circular alter.

The central space of the church transmits an interior climate that favors religiousness given that it absorbs all of the tensions towards the center. The weightiness of the enclosures, the inclined brick walls painted white reinforce the idea of the earthly in opposition to the ceiling which incorporates lighting effects that could be classified as being "heavenly". A light continuous blanket of translucent teflon extends under the supporting trusses of the roof. The space is bathed by indirect light, a blurred sky is projected over the membrane which leads to a perception of the interior space that varies according to the climatic conditions and the inclination of the sun. All of this contributes to the creation of a mysterious atmosphere and interior meditation. The beams of light that come from the peripheral chapels emphasize this divine perception.

Chapels.

Access passage.

The community congregates on benches that mark two aisles that lead to the alter situated in the extreme opposite the entrance. The enclosing walls give good thermic insulation as a result of their magnitude. In addition, their inclination creates an interior space with good acoustics. The possible reverberations in the circular space are compensated for by the absorption produced by the concavities of the small cubicles. The situation of the organ has been resolved by a hollow in the wall that presents a perfect acoustic shell.

The shape of the church symbolizes the passing from the mundane to the heavenly, of the earthly to the spiritual through a conscious succession of spaces. The door, the vestibule, the passages, the interior spaces... establish a "procession" from darkness to light.

exhibition_space

"eines_schunfabrikanten"

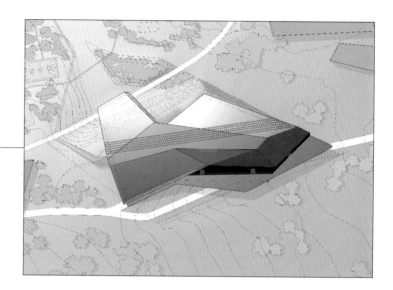

TECHNICAL DATA

Location Germany.

Architect Ulrich Königs.

Collaborators André Rethmeier, Thomas Roskothen, Jan Kallert, Oliver Ackerschewski.

Consultant companies André Rethmeier, Thomas Roskothen, Jan Kallert, Oliver Ackerschewski.
Structures: Arup, GmbH, Dusseldorf
Illumination: Lichtplanung A. Hartung, Köln
Construction and costs control: Haushoch Architekten, Nümberg
Construction physics: Graner + Partner, Bergisch-Gladbach
Technologies: Arup GMBH, Berlín

Project date 2004.

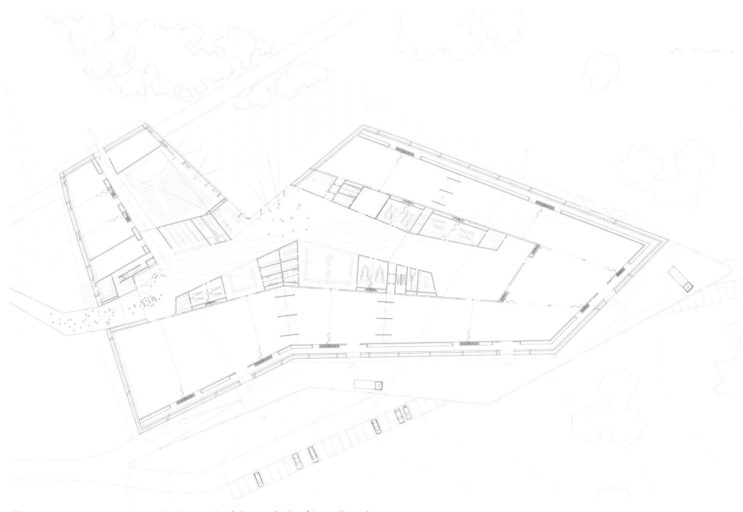

The creation of the volume is the result of the analysis of transit routes.

Exterior view of volume.

The project is a study, which has not been constructed, to create a prototype for a possible space for exhibitions and conferences.

The starting point for the initial analysis was a group of parameters that should be blended together. It deals with the program, the form, the materials, the construction and the function all

■ The building emerges dispersed in the surrounding vegetation.
■ The building of irregular forms adapts to the lie of the land.

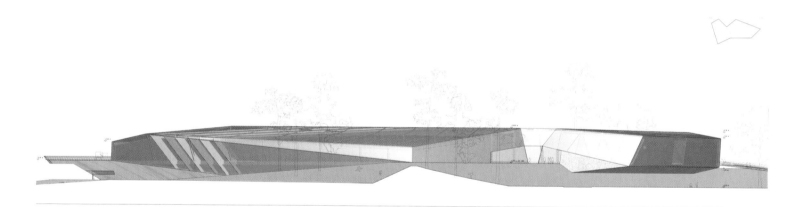

mixed together and defined for a particular environment. An environment in which man has not intervened and which is far away from any urban context and surrounded by vegetation and hilly relief.

The strategy of the design stems from a clear methodology that identifies certain transit routes, some possible flows.

The building settles on a small outcrop situated between two transit routes, two lines among the vegetation that direct the traffic.

The building embraces the totality of the area over the transit routes and it "sews together" the flows and separates pedestrian areas, which are concentrated around a separate access porch,

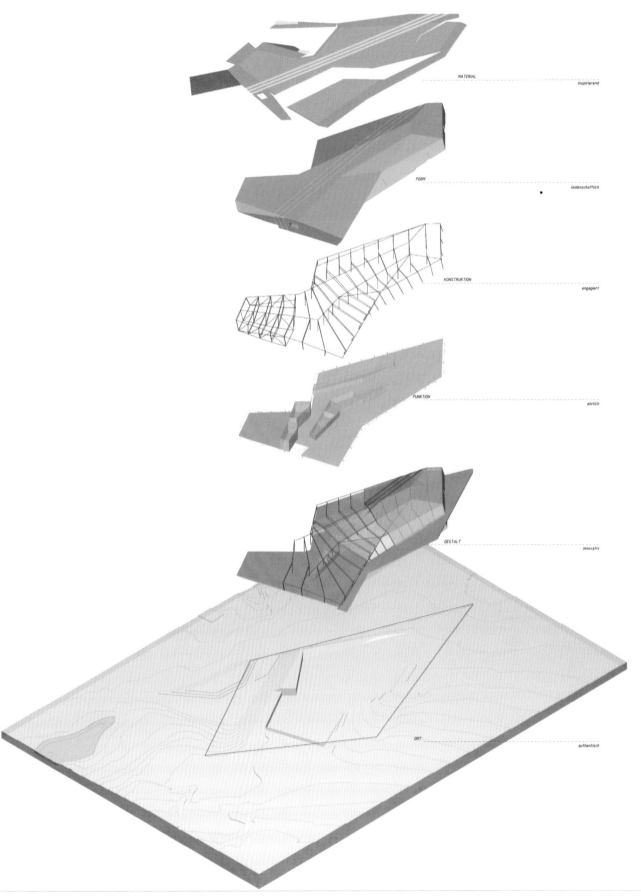

MATERIAL — *inspirierend*

FORM — *leidenschaftlich*

KONSTRUKTION — *engagiert*

FUNKTION — *ehrlich*

GESTALT — *innovativ*

ORT — *authentisch*

The virtual prototype includes location, the functional program, the structure, transit routes and the enclosures.

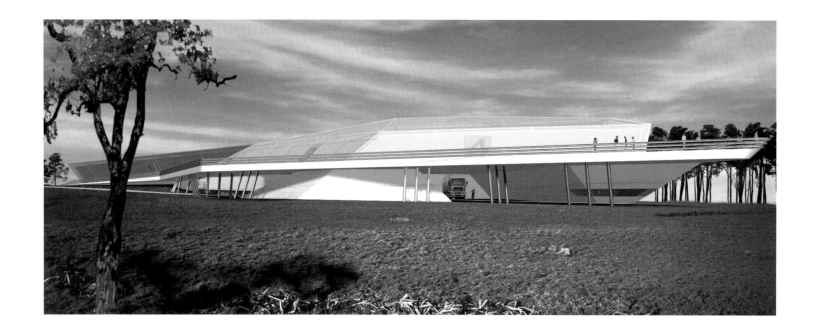

Lateral elevation of the access porch that creates lookout points in its higher areas.

The volumes mold into the topography of the landscape.

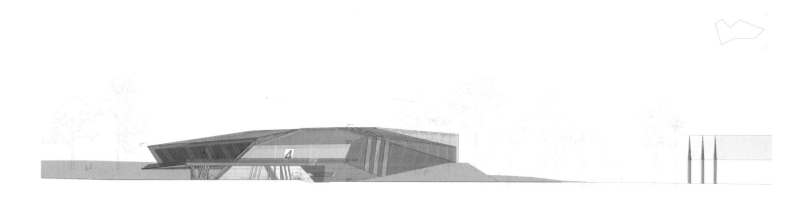

from the circulation of vehicles and from the parking areas situated in front of the other façade. In this way, possible interference and incidents in flows disappear.

The prototype, which is completely molded to the terrain, is analyzed in an almost scientific way. The virtual programs help develop the pieces that make up the internal machinery with which the parts are adapted to the complex. From this the result is an emerging innovative form that resolves its function and which adapts to the context in which it should act in an honest way. The flows define the spaces that are free from transit, those for the exhibitions and the auditorium. The services are closed strips that extend longitudinally and separate the exhibition spaces, but bring

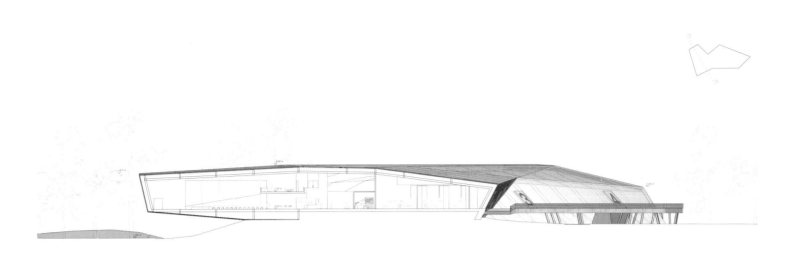

▨ Section through the auditorium .
▨ Cross section. The building molds itself to the terrain.

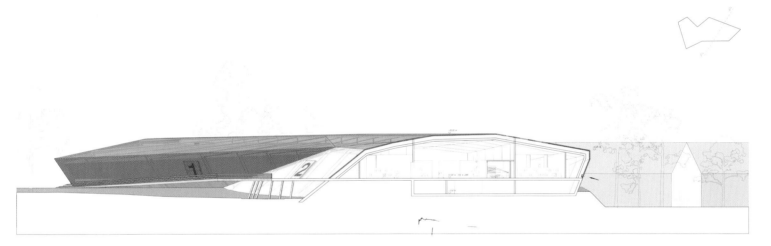

everything together within the structure that encloses the complete program. The irregular forms of the building depend, in the first place, on the terrain. They fix the program over the ground into which the service areas, the storage areas and the supporting walls are to be sunk. The irregular volumes that come about due to the natural surroundings define a light skeleton structure that extends in the way of an arcade along the principal route. Finally, the building is enclosed with a continuous skin that adapts to its form and which is integrated into the winding lines of the surroundings. The edifice forms part of the hill thanks to its folding volume, a three dimensional network that is fully integrated into the landscape.

forum_cultural
westfalen

TECHNICAL DATA

Location Münsters.

Architects Ulrich Königs & Jörg Rekittke.

Client Münsters City Council.

Collaborators André Rethmeier, Jan Kallert, Oliver Ackerschewski, Marc Wiwnecke.

Consultant companies *Acoustics:* Graner + Partner, Bergisch-Gladbach.
Structure: Arup GMBH, Berlin.
Illumination: Lichtplanung A. Hartung, Köln.

Project date 2003.

Built area 24.000 m² (area of implantation).

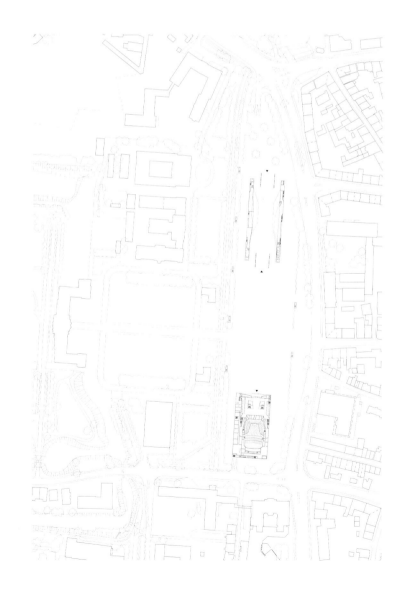

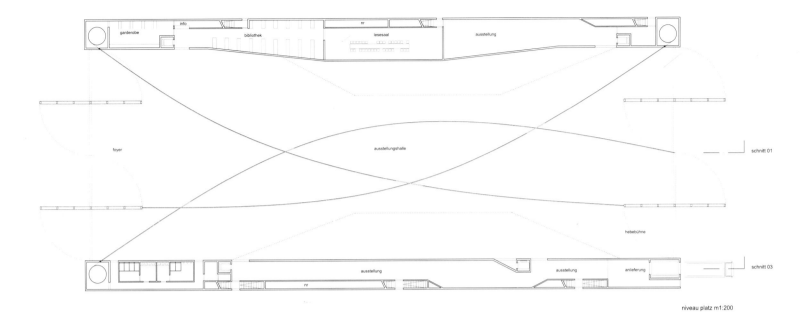

▨ Ground floor of the art gallery.

▨ First floor of the art gallery.

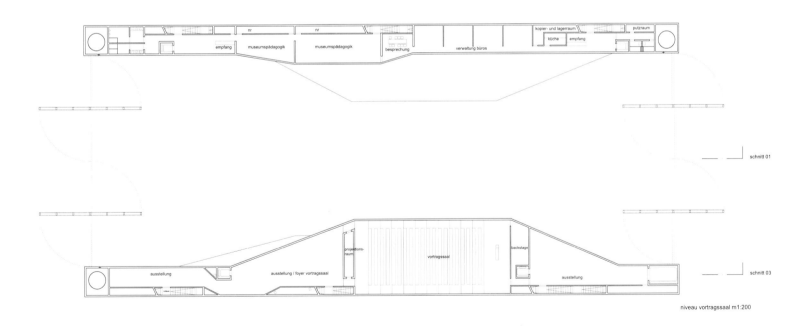

The definition of the project responds to the implantation of two new buildings, two volumes which are to be situated as key pieces on one of the most emblematic plots in Hindenburg. The design is based on the siting of two tumblers, two complementary pieces with their access façades facing one another from each extreme of the square. The work liberates the maximum space possible so that the square does not lose its magnitude and leaves as scenery the profile of the old market, Kalkmarktes, to emphasis its presence and so constitute a historical reference to the setting. A constant dialog between the two forms from con-

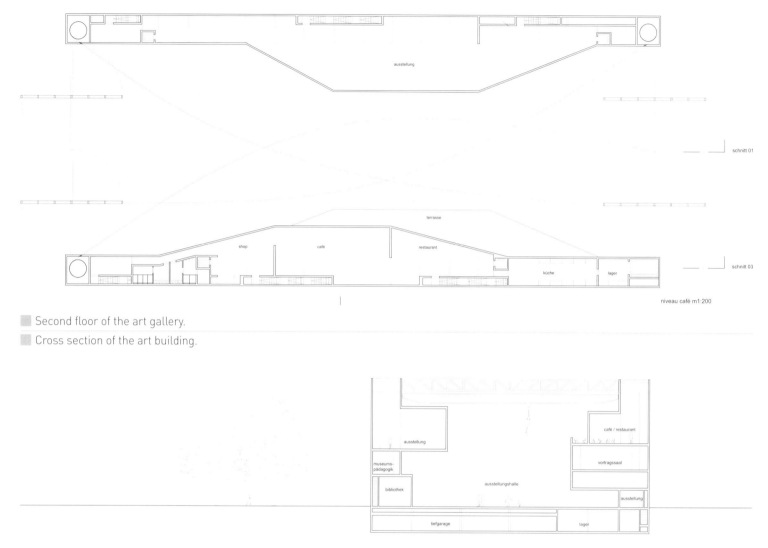

ausstellung

schnitt 01

terrasse

shop   café   restaurant

küche   lager

schnitt 03

niveau café m1:200

- Second floor of the art gallery.
- Cross section of the art building.

café / restaurant

ausstellung

vortragssaal

museums-
pädagogik

bibliothek

ausstellungshalle

ausstellung

tiefgarage

lager

schnitt 02 m1:200

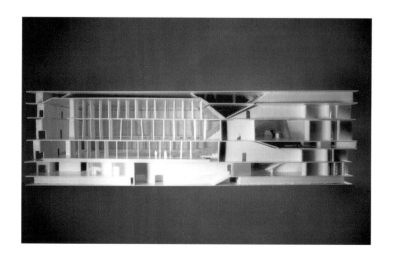

ceptual and formal perspectives is established given that we are dealing with two complementary buildings in terms of use and concept. The art gallery is situated in the extreme north of the square. It is a building that wishes to participate in Hindenburg Square and exhibit its program beyond its enclosures. Its visual aspects extend to the building that houses the concert hall. In

Volumetric scale model of the exterior of the concert hall.

Interior structure stripped of its enclosing skin.

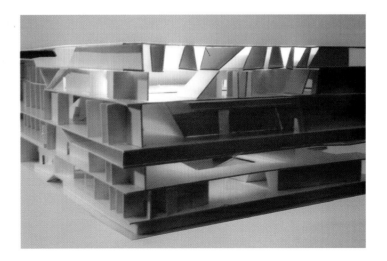

this way, a tumbler that is permeable, participative, open and fluid is achieved that allows for an exchange of experiences given that it provides a space for observation and from which to observe. The program in its most specific and private terms is situated along the narrow longitudinal strips that free the interior central space. As a counterpart, the concert hall is situated in the south of

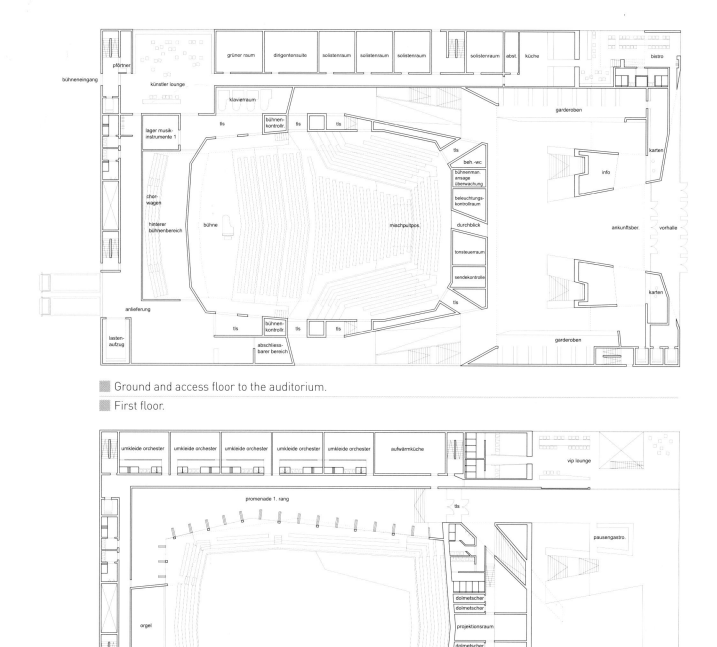

Ground and access floor to the auditorium.

First floor.

the square as a landmark to the intervention and in dialog with the consolidated urban area. It is a closed compact building that isolates its program in its interior and that does not allow more permeability than that which is strictly necessary. It is a static introverted space and a work to be observed that offers a spectacular and curious enclosure to the city.

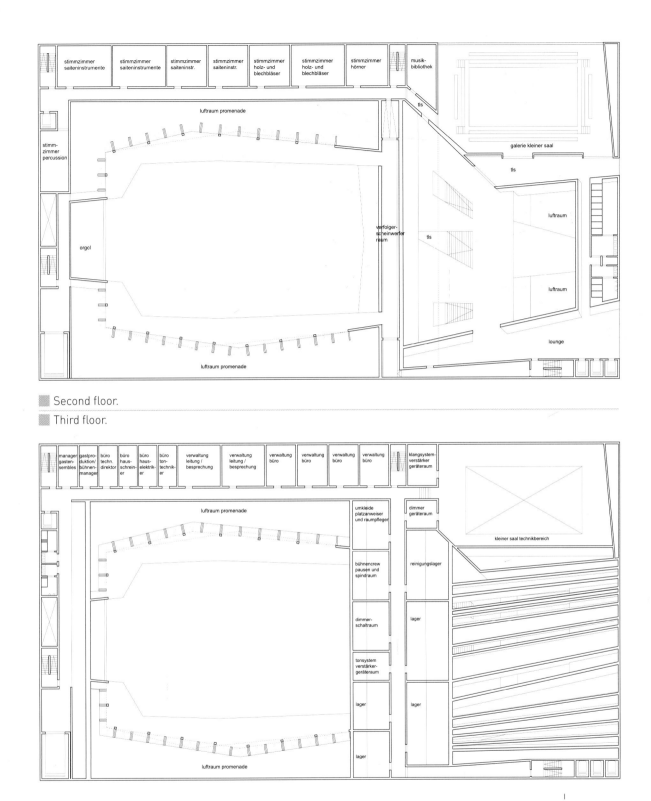

Second floor.

Third floor.

The concert hall is technically prepared to accommodate a large number of spectators and become scenery to great concerts given that it has a precise constructive resolution that assures excellent acoustics and optimum functionality. The hall of the auditorium is located in the center. This leads to an almost symmetrical distribution of the accesses and of the complementary uses.

■ The large "foyer" of the art gallery frames the façade of the auditorium as if it were a masterpiece of the exhibition.

■ Skin of the auditorium's enclosure.

Between the entrance and the hall, a great foyer connects the upper part of the access to the stalls and the higher balconies that completely surround the hall. In the intervals, this foyer leads the users to the rest areas, the services and the cafeteria which are directly accessible from the different areas by secondary staircases.

The two volumes are set face to face and give way to an interaction of opposing and complementary tensions. The auditorium, which assumes an introverted and intimate program destined to deep sensory perception contrasts with its "opponent", the art

 The building seems to disappear at night.
The volumes of the auditorium (floor by floor).

gallery, which responds to a program of creative liberty which is open to transmission and the exchange of experiences.

Esthetically, the subjective perception of the area, the light and the material used, have an enormous significance. The building seems to blend into its surroundings while small points of light scratch the enclosure of the solid opaque volume. Timidly, through small cracks, the passionate internal program of the auditorium is transmitted. Like a flock of birds that takes to flight, the building seems to disappear into the night and attract the passer-by poetically towards it.

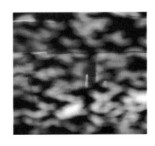